W9-BTM-285

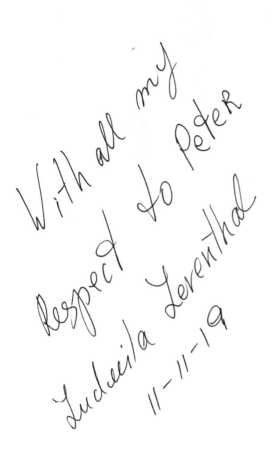

With all my
Respect to Peter

Ludicila Lerenthal

11-11-19

STAR OF DAVID
PRESS

Many people wanted to tell this story, but they were not able to do it for various reasons. Ludmila achieved the mission she was entrusted with. She has written this book not just for herself and our family, but for all those who wanted to speak but were unable to do so. These things should not be forgotten. Memory has enormous power.

Alexander Leventhal
Boston, 2005

Ludmila Leventhal

STAR OF DAVID

LAST SONG OF SHOFAR

Boston

Ludmila Leventhal

Star of David or Last Song of Shafar

A Memoir Novel

Copyright © 2006, Ludmila Leventhal
Copyright © 2006, Star of David Press

All right reserved. No part of this book may be reproduced or
utilized in any form or by any means, electronic or mecanical,
including photocopying, recording, or by any information storage
and retrieval system, without the written permission of the Author.

Editor-in-Chief: Danielle Potvin Curran
English Translation: Elena Fairchild
Cover Design: Larisa Taldykina
Illustrations: Vitaly Dudarenko
Photos: Vladimir Pushak and Mikhail Kisler
Book Design and Layout: M-Graphics, mgraphics@comcast.net

Library of Congress Control Number 2006920067

ISBN-13 978-0-9777214-1-2
ISBN-10 0-9777214-1-8

Printed in the United States of America

To my Dad
Alexander Leventhal

...My heart is racing. Oh, it is so hot. Water, water... Give me just a sip of water... Where am I? There are barred windows. Ah, I'm in prison. I'm being transferred to solitary. What do they want from me? I won't sign anything. I need to bear it until the end. Who is calling me, "Dad, dad..."? It is my children. I love them so. God, why do they torture my family. There's a voice again, "Dad, dad..." Where am I?

"Dad, daddy, you're home. You're dreaming..." It was just a dream. A bad dream. So many years had passed. Twenty-six years in America already, but Alexander still suffers from this nightmare. Years spent in Soviet prisons and concentration camps had left their mark. But they did not break him. He endured them. Survived. And remained human. Human with a capital H.

INTRODUCTION

Since my early childhood I have listened to my father's stories. I looked at him wide-eyed and hung on his every word. He showed me the places where the events he described had taken place, and I immediately pictured each scene. My father's words will remain in my memory forever:

— Look how beautiful nature is here my dear. God created this beauty, but why did He create such vicious people and settle them in this area?

As a child I was unable to fully comprehend what my father was talking about, but when I grew up I began to understand. Nobody in our town wanted to remember the past. Nobody wanted to recall the recent history, pretending it didn't exist.

My father's stories sank deep into my mind. I dreamed of telling the whole world what I learned from my father. But most importantly, I wanted my children and my grandchildren to remember their roots and their history, to remember where they came from.

My father, Alexander Grigoryevich Leventhal, and I dedicate this book to the memory of the living and the dead who experienced unimaginable inhuman ordeals during World War II and the post-war years. We would like this book to become a memorial to all those who perished at the hand of executioners and a tribute to remind the younger generation about their ancestors' lives and deaths. And to all, a reminder of the courage and endurance the human spirit is capable of in the darkest moments in life.

I'd like to express my enormous gratitude to all the people who helped me with this book, but most of all to my father, Alexander

*Alexander Grigorievich Leventhal and his daughter, Ludmila
Boston, November, 2004.*

Grigoryevich Leventhal. Whenever I had an unbearably tough situation in my life, I would remember my father; I would remember what he had gone through. I thought if he had been able to endure such ordeals, I would be able to handle my problems, too. My father's example has always helped me in my life.

I'd also like to thank my family for their support: my daughters Svetlana, Olga and Yelena, and my husband Vladimir. Thank you, my darlings!

Ludmila Leventhal
Boston, 2005

CONTENTS

PART THREE
At the Front and in the Rear

A modern map of locations described in the book.

PROLOGUE
DOBROMIL

There were about fifteen hundred Jewish families living in Dobromil in the early 1930s. It was a clean and cozy European
town with lots of trees, and well developed garment, timber
and dairy industries.

In the middle of Dobromil there was a big city hall in which
all the municipal authorities were located. There was a large paved
square adjacent to the city hall and next to it a park with a memorial
to a Polish writer, Adam Mitskevich, which was put up at the place
of his burial.

The city hall was surrounded by two-story stone houses with bal-
conies and big windows. There were various workshops and stores situ-
ated on the first floors of the houses.

At the intersection of the two main streets there was a large synagogue. The most pious Hasids attended it.

Not far from the synagogue — no farther than about six hundred
feet away — there stood a Catholic church with a big bell tower. The
tower was built a few feet from the church, and a big cast bell showed on
the top of it. Stone steps led to the bell and to the little loft, where the
bell ringer sometimes sat. They said that the bell tower had been built
first, and construction of the church followed a hundred years later.

The outside of the church was surrounded by a strong stone wall
built back in the Middle Ages by crusaders. It was extremely beautiful
and grand inside. Large iron gates on one side and a small gate on the
other side were always open.

I

Polish church in Dobromil, 2004

Behind the church was a convent. Its main attraction was a huge orchard which was taken care of by the nuns. The cells in the nunnery were tiny and dark.

On the other side of the synagogue, approximately 1,500 feet away from it, there was a Ukrainian Orthodox Church with beautiful bell towers and a large yard paved with stones. It was surrounded by an exquisite enclosure made of stone and metal. The church gates were open just on Sundays, whereas the small gate was always open. There were grand, centuries old trees towering on both sides of the church with crow's nests all over their crowns.

Jews prayed in the synagogue, Ukrainians in the Orthodox Church, and Poles in the Catholic Church. And everybody honored each other's religions and customs. They all celebrated the New Year holiday together. They put up a big Christmas tree in the square beside the city hall, decorated it and threw public festivities. Residents of Dobromil led quiet and happy lives.

Ukrainian church in Dobromil, 2004

PART I
THE LEVENTHALS FROM KVASENINA

t the bottom of the Carpathian Mountains, half way between the two frontier cities Dobromil and Peremyshl, there used to be a large village with the unusual name of Kvasenina. The village was, as is customary to say now, multicultural: Side by side, there lived Poles, Ukrainians and Jews, working, raising their children, harvesting their crops, and celebrating weddings. And there was neither hostility nor hatred among them.

One of the Jewish families living in Kvasenina was the Leventhals. Like the majority of villagers there, they raised cattle and farmed. The family lived in a large house, half of which was occupied by an eatery kept by Leon Leventhal.

The eatery was known in the neighborhood for its ingeniously cooked dishes, smoked sausage, and home-made plum and cherry liqueurs; but what patrons loved most was when the owner played the violin for them. The sound of music captivated them, making them forget their daily hardships and troubles for a while.

Leon's brother Gersh and his family lived in the other half of the house. Gersh earned his living buying cattle in surrounding villages and selling them at the Dobromil market. With the money he made he bought clothes and treats for his children. With his wife Mindlya, he was raising three children — daughter Rosa and sons Shmul and Moisha.

Leon's and Gersh's mother, Hanna, also lived in the house. She had raised twelve sons and a daughter. Many of her children had left home

5

to seek their fortune in foreign lands — they went to America, Argentina and Palestine, while their elderly mother remained in Kvasenina with two of her sons.

LEON

Since childhood Leon was in love with Matilda, the girl next door. All the neighbors were touched by the young couple, especially when Leon danced with Matilda while playing his violin for his sweetheart. The violin sang of his love, happiness, joy — about everything that filled the young man's heart.

While growing up, they would often run deep into the forest surrounding Kvasenina, sit by a brook and Leon would play anything his intended requested. He would kiss her soft fingers and a shiver would run over his body when he touched her hair or her lips. He would breathe in the scent of her body like a balm, and when their lips touched, he would be overcome by bliss.

— I will go to your father and ask him for your hand in marriage. I want you to be my wife, — Leon blurted out once.

Matilda blushed in reply and began caressing his shoulder. They were happy like no one ever before them. Life seemed exceptionally beautiful to them. Spruce and pine trees were bowing their tops over the lovers and birds were singing jolly songs to them. Hand in hand they ran down the hill, the wind playing with the black locks of the girl's hair. Approaching the village they slowed to avoid the disapproving glances of the villagers. Matilda went home glowing with happiness.

Upon entering the house Leon announced to his mother from the door,

— Mom, I want to get married. I want to marry Matilda.

Hanna nodded in approval. — Well, she is a nice girl. I'll talk to her father tomorrow. — Tomorrow? What's wrong with today? — You must be crazy, Leon. It's not the way it is done. We should observe the customs.

Leon slowly lowered himself into a chair. His mother was disturbed by her talk with her son. She was pacing the room, restless.

That night lasted forever for Leon. He was dreaming about embracing and kissing his Matilda, enjoying the scent of her skin, and his

heart felt faint in anticipation of imminent happiness when she would be all his.

It seemed morning would never come. When dawn finally came, Leon jumped off the bed, hastily dressed and rushed outside. Fresh wind blew in his face. What a pleasure to get up early and admire the mountains covered with forests! Fog was rising, leaving sparkling dew-drops on the grass. Rays of sun were working their way through the trees. Oh, how wonderful! How beautiful that land was!

He went back inside and grabbed his violin, but his mother stopped him.

— Leon, I am going to milk the cow, and you want to play the violin! What will people think?

He hugged his mother and ruefully put back the violin. Dropping by the cow stall which accommodated two cows and a calf, he gave them some grass and patted the cow. He looked at his mother who was sitting on a little stool by the cow.

— Mom, when are you going to see Matilda's parents?

— Today. I will first talk to her mother. After all, a woman will better understand another woman than a man would. I don't believe there will be any problem there. You are a good son, and you will be a good husband. We'll build a house on our land, and you'll be living there.

Leon gave a skip for joy. Yes, he would love Matilda, and he would be a good husband.

The day was running its appointed course. Hanna intended to talk to Matilda's mother at 1 pm, so as not to disrupt the work day for her and the neighbors. She put on a new skirt and blouse, fastened her hair and headed for her neighbors' house. Matilda was throwing wheat on the ground feeding the chicken; her mother was cleaning in the kitchen after dinner, and Haim, the girl's father, went to the stable to visit the horse. Hanna greeted Matilda's mother and started a friendly conversation about their lives and children.

At the sound of Hanna's voice Haim came out of the stable.

— How are you Hanna? How are the children?

— Very well, thank you. I have come regarding a matter of great importance.

— What's the matter, Hanna?

— As you know, Haim, I have a son Leon. He is in love with your daughter.

Haim was silent. — Why aren't you saying anything? — Hanna grew suspicious. Haim hesitated. — Yes, Hanna, I know... — Haim, Leon is asking for your daughter's hand in marriage. You know he is a good son. And he will be a good husband.

Haim was quiet. With his head down, he turned all red and droned in a low voice,

— All your son has got is his violin. What can you do with a violin? We are working so very hard, and look at how we live! Would I want the same kind of life for my daughter? Just think, Hanna, what can Leon give my Matilda?

— Come to your senses Haim! What are you saying? I'll give them a piece of land, we'll build a house, and they will live there. They are in love, Haim!

— Love is not everything. One has to have something to support himself with. I don't want my Matilda to live with chickens and cows. I've made a match for her to get married in Peremyshl. She is marrying a wealthy man. He keeps his own store. She'll be living in a city, not in a village. And love will pass. Everything passes and so will this. Leon will find himself another girl. Tell this to your son, Hanna. We love him, but we want a better life for our daughter.

Hanna understood very well. From the parents' point of view there was truth in the father's words — they wanted a better life for their daughter. But how was she supposed to explain it to Leon? He was so sensitive and vulnerable. How was she supposed to tell him that his fate was being decided for him, and that his loving mother Hanna was unable to change it?

Hanna came home with her head down.

Leon met her on the door steps.

— Why are you silent, mom? Tell me! — he grasped his mother by the arms.

— There isn't anything I can tell you, son, nothing at all. They want to have Matilda marry a wealthy man in Peremyshl. We are way too poor for them.

— This cannot be... I don't believe it. I can't believe it! I don't buy it! I don't! — shouted Leon rushing out of the house.

Gasping, he was racing to Matilda. His heart was breaking, and his thoughts were all jumbled together. Leon entered Haim's house and froze. Matilda was kneeling in tears by her father, her mother was embracing her shoulders, and Haim was listening to his daughter with a guilty look on his face.

— Matilda, darling, give me your hand, — whispered Leon. — Give me your hand. Dropping to his knees, he began to kiss her hands.

— Come with me. We will go to America or Argentina. I will be working. I love you. Come with me, my love. Let's go.

And then Haim came out of his daze:

— You are pushing my daughter to shame, Leon! If you love her, back off! Back off, Leon!

Leon crept out of Haim's house like a wounded animal. He couldn't breathe. Everything turned dark before his eyes. Birds stopped singing, the sun stopped shining, and everything became gloomy and cold.

Hanna looked in horror at her son getting instantly drained. Where could she find words to comfort him? Life had dealt him a cruel blow. How would he survive, who would he become after that? Hanna gently hugged her son and quietly picked up the violin.

— Play, Leon. Play, my son! It will be your cure. Play, my son, play!

Leon took the violin into his dead hands. He struck the bow across the strings. The violin wept. It was the voice of his tormented heart. The violin's wails were bursting out, getting louder and louder. No one among those listening to him dared to move, unwilling to scare away the sounds of that music. And the violin was singing and crying, as if telling everybody about Leon's broken heart.

MATILDA

Despite Matilda's pleas and tears, her father decided to marry his daughter off to a man she didn't love. If only she dared to run away with Leon to America! He had saved the required sum of money, and prepared everything for a long journey. But she was afraid. She especially dreaded the dishonor that would be brought upon her family. Her parents would curse her.

And so she became the wife of Itsik Gud, a childless widower who was twenty five years her senior. Gud was a highly respected man who was famous all over Poland due to his prosperous stores and sewing factory.

The wedding took place in Peremyshl. All the distinguished people of the city were invited. After the wedding Matilda was taken to a snow— white bedroom with large windows and an elegant balcony. The balcony's trellis was artfully decorated with laced metal flowers and trees, which intertwined creating a design of wondrous beauty. Wind, bursting into the room, was blowing the lacy curtains hanging on the window.

The maid, who was following Matilda to the bedroom, rushed to shut the windows, but Matilda stopped her.

— Please don't, — she said quietly. — I love the wind. It brings me news from home.

The maid looked at the young mistress in surprise.

— Dear mistress, I will help you take off your wedding dress. With these words she began to unbutton the dress.

Matilda's face was very sad and the maid tried to comfort her mistress.

— Dear mistress, Mr. Itsik is a very intelligent and good man... Mistress will be happy with him.

Tears were rolling down Matilda's cheeks. Was this the marriage she had dreamed about? Did she want riches? She was so happy with Leon! Could anyone replace him? Why would she need all that? These were strange unfamiliar people, whom she didn't know and who didn't know her. She needed only Leon. Oh, how she missed her precious beloved. And there was no one to exchange even a word with. She was like a bird in a golden cage.

The maid stared at Matilda, her eyes wide open with fear.

— Dear mistress, forgive me if I said something inappropriate, — she began to apologize.

— No, no, it's not you. It's me crying about my lost happiness, — Matilda replied quietly.

She was sitting in a luxurious lace negligee, looking at herself in the mirror. The maid was carefully combing her black curly hair which stood out in contrast with the pale lace.

There was a knock on the door. Matilda was startled. Jumping off the chair she ran to the open balcony doors.

The bedroom door opened, and Mr. Itsik stood in the doorway wearing a beautiful brocade robe. The maid bowed her head humbly and ran out of the room closing the door behind her.

As if turned to stone, Matilda stood by the balcony doors with her arms crossed on her chest. Mr. Itsik reached out with his hand to his young wife and took a step towards her, but immediately heard a quiet, anxious, but very steady voice.

— Please do not approach me or I will jump out of the window.

Mr. Itsik froze in surprise. He was afraid to move. A few minutes later he regained his senses and replied in a whisper.

— Matilda, don' do it. I will not touch you. I am leaving. Please don't do it. I will not touch you until you are ready. I want you to be my wife, not my slave. I am leaving.

With these words he began to back towards the door, trying to find the door knob by touch in order to open it.

He opened the door and discovered the maid standing there.

— What are you doing here, Zosya?

— Nothing, Mr. Itsik, nothing. I thought Mrs. Matilda might need something, that's why I stayed here, — babbled the frightened girl.

Mr. Itsik knew she was not telling the truth. Zosya was eavesdropping by the door. But it didn't matter to him. At that moment what to do with Matilda was important, as he had not expected such a rebuff from her.

— Zosya! — he said. — I want you to stay by Mrs. Matilda and do everything she asks you to, so that she is pleased with you. Do you hear me? I will reward you. But you must report to me all her thoughts. Tell me about all her dreams. Become her friend, a close friend... and one more thing, Zosya. If you don't mind, I'll visit you tonight. I've got a little present for you. What do you say to that?

Zosya was all smiles. Her pink cheeks turned even redder.

— Mr. Itsik, I am always glad to see you.

— All right then. Go to Matilda and remember what I have told you.

Beaming with joy Zosya entered the bedroom of her young mistress. Seeing the frightened young lady still standing by the balcony door with her arms crossed, she ran up to her and put her arms around her shoulders like a close friend, leading her back into the room.

— Mrs. Matilda, I am your devoted servant. Trust me, I will do anything to make you happy in this house, — she prattled in her mistress' ear.

Zosya's words helped Matilda calm down.

— Is that true, Zosya? — she brightened.

— Yes, dear mistress. I am here for you. I will do anything you tell me to do.

— That's great. Zosya, I'd like to see my... acquaintance, Leon. Will you take my letter to him?

— Sure, dear mistress. I will do anything you tell me to do.

— Zosya, you are my savior. I'll immediately sit down to write it, — she rejoiced.

She rushed to look for ink and paper, but couldn't find any in the room. Kind Zosya offered her services, and quickly brought everything she needed.

Excited, Matilda was writing very quickly. When the letter was ready, she blotted it, folded it into a triangle and gave it to Zosya.

— When are you going to Dobromil, Zosya? Tomorrow morning?

— Yes, dear mistress. When you wake up tomorrow, I'll already be back with the reply.

Suspecting nothing, Matilda handed the letter to the maid. She knew the girl did not read Hebrew, and therefore wasn't worried. She would deliver the letter to Leon. "What good luck having Zosya here!" — thought young Matilda naively.

Leaving the bedroom, Zosya went immediately to Mr. Itsik. He was sitting by the burning fireplace, drinking red wine. He took the letter, neatly unfolded it and began to read it. His face was expressionless. Zosya quietly stood by his side, awaiting further orders. After he finished reading, Mr. Itsik broke the silence.

— Well done, Zosya! I commend you. And now, go get ready and take the letter to Leon.

— Mr. Itsik, but you said...

— It'll wait, Zosya. You will come back. It's not far away. And do everything to make sure they meet. I need that.

Zosya made for the door with her head down, but Mr. Itsik stopped her.

— Zosya, here is something for you for your good work. There's twenty zloties here.

And he put the money into her hand.

She immediately pepped up and almost ran towards the door.

Leon got the letter from his beloved, and without saying a word to anyone rushed to Peremyshl. Zosya brought him in through the back—door entrance that was used by the help.

Leon was prepared to do anything to see his sweetheart.

Entering her bedroom and seeing Matilda sitting in a chair, he dropped to his knees, seized her alabaster hand and began kissing it. Matilda slipped off the chair down onto the floor. There they were, both kneeling, kissing each other. Soon it was impossible to stop the passion that burst out.

Choking from love, Leon caressed Matilda's tender body, and kissed her on the lips, forgetting for a moment where he was.

While the lovebirds were consumed with passion, Zosya was reporting everything that had happened to Mr. Itsik, who was sitting in front of the fireplace wrapped in his beautiful robe.

— Mr. Itsik, she is not faithful to you. Kick her out like a dog, — babbled Zosya non-stop. — She will disgrace you.

— Zosya, please don't tell anyone about it. And here are a hundred zloties for you. Keep doing what you do. Nothing else matters. It's important that nobody knows about it... And now, dear Zosya, I'd like to have some tasty red wine in your company, if you don't mind, of course.

Zosya was all smiles.

— Of course not, Mr. Itsik; I am always happy to keep your company. You do me a great honor and give me expensive presents.

Mr. Itsik laughed and pulled her to his bedroom.

The next morning Mr. Itsik asked Zosya to invite his young wife to breakfast.

Zosya knocked on the door, and waited for an answer. Matilda opened the door quietly. She looked pale and frightened.

— Mrs. Matilda, Mr. Itsik is inviting you to the table.

— Tell him that I do not feel well.

— No, dear, I will help you dress. You need to have breakfast.

Zosya saw how nervous Matilda was, and it pleased her. How stupid this lady was! If she knew how Mr. Itsik could love, she would have forgotten Leon a long time ago.

Coming down to the parlor, Matilda saw her husband. He got up promptly, ran to Matilda, kissed her hand and helped her get seated. The girl was very wary and still pale. She didn't know how to behave, and was very nervous.

After breakfast Mr. Itsik announced that he was leaving for France on business, and asked everybody to take care of his young wife whom he was leaving behind.

Matilda heaved a sigh of relief. Mr. Itsik didn't say how long he would stay in France, but his departure gave Matilda time to get used to the new house and routine.

Mr. Itsik kissed his wife's hand and left.

Without hesitation, Matilda called Zosya and gave her another letter for Leon, not suspecting that half an hour later it would fall into the hands of Mr. Itsik...

Assuming that Mr. Itsik had left Poland, Matilda met Leon every day. Leon was making big plans trying to get some money in order to run away with his beloved to America or Argentina. But it wasn't so easy.

A few weeks later Mr. Itsik came home, bringing expensive presents for his young wife. Zosya was the one who was happiest with his "arrival", as she got a significant sum of money as a reward for her efforts. During all that time she was carefully following Matilda's every step and reporting everything to Mr. Itsik, who had actually never left Peremyshl. He was playing a waiting game. Matilda, still unaware of any tricks, had no secrets from Zosya.

Mr. Itsik would politely talk with Matilda and respectfully kiss her hands.

One day Mr. Itsik gave a big reception, to which there came all the distinguished and respectable people of the town. They were noisily talking with each other, drinking wine and enjoying delicious refreshments. Only Matilda, quiet and pale, kept out of it. They began to serve hot dishes. Appetizing smells started to spread all over the reception room. The guests scurried at the sight of the elegantly laid table.

But what was this? Matilda lost more color, shook and covered her mouth with her hand in a lace glove.

Mr. Itsik had his eyes glued on her.

— My darling, are you not well?

— No, no. I am just tired. With your permission, I will retire.

— My darling Matilda, how will I be able to excuse your absence to our guests? Have a seat in the chair, and I will bring you some champagne.

— No, no need to, thank you. I'll sit here.

Mr. Itsik patted her on the hand and went to his friends.

Suddenly he saw Matilda stand up abruptly from her chair. After making a couple of steps, she fainted and fell to the floor.

There was a commotion. The guests rushed to help. Somebody was calling for a doctor. Mr. Itsik scooped Matilda into his arms and carried her to the bedroom. The doctor showed up, and all the outsiders left the bedroom.

Matilda opened her eyes and asked wonderingly,

— Where am I? What's happened to me?

Patting her on the hand, Mr. Itsik gave her an encouraging smile,

— My darling, you just fainted. You are tired and need some rest.

With that, he left the room too.

The doctor examined the patient and whispered quietly into her ear,

— Congratulations, dear, you are going to be a mother.

Matilda looked at the smiling doctor in horror, and could not say a word.

The door opened and Mr. Itsik came in.

— Congratulations, dear Mr. Itsik, your long-awaited dream has come true. You are going to be a father. I've always told you that you have the world before you.

Hearing that, Matilda fainted again. And the doctor began to revive her again.

Mr. Itsik went out to his guests and joyfully announced that everything was fine.

The doctor ordered bed rest for Matilda. Zosya never left her side.

Mr. Itsik brought a big bouquet of flowers to the bedroom and kissed a puzzled Matilda.

— My darling, I am so happy that we are going to have a baby. I am so happy.

Matilda opened her mouth to say something, but Mr. Itsik softly covered it with his hand.

— Don't talk. It is harmful for our baby. Tomorrow we are leaving for Italy. You need the sea and warm climate. And you shouldn't worry, that's important.

Matilda did not understand anything. Her thoughts were all jumbled together; it seemed like a dream. Why was Mr. Gud behaving so strangely? Where was Leon? Why didn't she hear anything from him?

She would be taken away the next day, and she would not be able to tell him anything. She had to send him a letter.

She quickly wrote a few lines.

— Zosya, Zosya, come here. Give this letter to Leon. Hurry up. Tomorrow I will be taken away, and I won't see Leon.

Zosya smiled at her mistress, took the letter and left the room.

Matilda calmed down. Leon was coming. He was sure to come.

At that moment Mr. Itsik had finished reading the letter intended for Leon, and threw it into the burning fireplace.

He quickly turned to the mail.

— Zosya, I have paid you well. There will be further rewards. Tell Leon that mistress Matilda doesn't want to see him again. Make up anything you want. We are leaving tomorrow, and nobody must know where we are going. No one must know about the baby, it should be kept in secret. And not a word to Leon.

CRUSHED DREAMS

Leon had been working day and night to save money to move to America or Argentina. Everything was finally together and ready. Leon went to see mother Hanna.

— Mom, I want to go to America or Argentina. I am sorry I have to leave you, but there is no other way out for me.

— My dear Leon, — Hanna said quietly. — My beloved son, I want only happiness for you. Don't think about me — I've lived my life to the fullest. I loved and was loved; I have raised you, my children, and I can say now that I have given you roots and wings. Where you fly and where you will put down your roots is entirely up to you. I bless you for life. And I'll be praying for you and hoping that you'll find a good woman there and start a family. Just write to me frequently to send news about yourself.

— Mom, I've got to tell you something... Just don't judge me, mom...

— Leon, I am your mother, and you are my life. Tell me. I'll understand or I'll try to understand.

— Mom, sit with me.

Leon sat down on the bench holding Hanna by her hand.

She sat down next to him.

— Mom, I love Matilda, and I will take her away with me...

Hanna turned white.

— What are you talking about, Leon... Such shame! She's got a husband. What will people say? Leon, come to your senses! Her parents are our neighbors.

— Mom, I can't live without her. I can't see any meaning in life.

— Then get yourself another girl. Look how many beauties there are around. You will get married, and it'll be over. You will have a family, children, and you will see meaning in life.

— I can't, I just can't, mom. I love Matilda. I can't look at other women, I don't want them.

— No, Leon, it's a big sin to take somebody else's wife. God will punish you.

— But I am already punished now, mom. I wanted to marry her, but her parents arranged it differently, they didn't give her to me.

Every word was painful for Leon to utter.

— Mom, I am sorry, but I am going to do it. I will not be able to live my life any other way.

With that said, he got up, kissed his mother's hand and left the house.

When he came to Peremyshl, Leon immediately went to Zosya.

He knocked on the door, but nobody answered. He knocked again, thinking he had not been heard. But to his great surprise, the door didn't open.

Leon went to the front door and pulled the door-bell string. There was a loud ringing, and the door opened. Yuzek, Mr. Itsik's old servant, was at the door.

— Excuse me, I am looking for Miss Zosya, — Leon addressed him.

— Miss Zosya has left for Krakow, old Yuzek said through coughing.

— Hmm... Then can I speak with Mrs. Matilda, if she agrees to see me, — he dared.

— Mrs. Matilda and Mr. Itsik have left for Italy.

Leon looked at Yuzek fearfully.

— How could she leave? How long will they stay in Italy?

— We are not expecting them before spring. But don't worry. Zosya has not left with them. She will be here in a week.

Leon's thoughts raced. Zosya? Why would I need Zosya? I need Matilda. Where should I look for her? Why has she left? Why didn't she warn me?

Leon left quickly, unaware of the fact that he had forgotten to say good-bye to old Yuzek, and that the latter remained standing at the door with his mouth open in surprise.

"What should I do? Where should I be looking for her?" — These questions were pounding in his head.

Taking no notice of the passers-by, Leon walked along the sidewalk. His every thought was about Matilda. He was overwhelmed. The news old Yuzek had given him ruined all his plans.

A week later, he met with Zosya, but she was not able to explain anything to him either. Nobody knew where Matilda was.

Leon went back to Kvasenina and took to bed. He stayed in bed for a week and Hanna nursed her son and gave him her potions. It seemed to Leon that he was dying. He often dreamt of Matilda kissing and comforting him. In his dream he was happy and he didn't want to wake up.

Leon never succeeded in finding Matilda, and he abandoned the idea of leaving for America. Why go anywhere? Life without Matilda had lost all its meaning.

In Italy, Matilda was put up in a luxurious villa at the seaside. She eventually delivered a handsome and healthy baby boy she named Aaron. She loved with all her heart. Mr. Itsik never asked her anything and always stopped her in mid sentence whenever she wanted to say something. Itsik's dream to have a child had come true and he spoiled his young son and wife any way he could

Matilda saw how much her husband loved her son, how he treated him with affection, and she began to love him for that. And Aaron loved his father very much. Zosya was the only one who knew their secret. But she would keep silent. Itsik was paying her well for her silence.

And so Itsik, Matilda and Aaron were living in Italy, sometimes going to France, and very seldom — only on grand occasions — coming to Poland.

Hanna often talked to her son about getting married, but he would firmly reply,

— I will never get married. My violin is my wife.

When his mother pestered too much, he would hug her tenderly and say,

— Mom, Matilda is my only love. I will not be able to love anyone like I love her.

HANNA

Leon remained in Kvasenina and eventually opened the eatery in his house. Mindlya and Gersh were making different kinds of herb teas and vegetable broths and Leon served these to his patrons.

Leon showed skill as a businessman and business was good. There were more and more guests in the eatery, and the family was no longer able to manage it alone. Hanna decided to hire a Ukrainian girl, Marichka, to help in the restaurant and assist around the house.

Business at the "roadhouse" was thriving. The number of guests was growing and the eatery was becoming a very profitable business. The whole family worked very hard. Marichka didn't turn out to be a very good helper. She worked at a snail's pace, but no one ever reproached her for that, thinking that efficiency and skills would be acquired with experience.

— It's OK, she will master it — and will be a better help, — Hanna would say.

Mindlya shouldered most of the work and made her daughter Rosa help Hanna.

Hanna's usual routine was to get up early, tie a scarf on her head, wash her hands with cold water from the bucket, and wake her daughter-in-law. Together they would go out to milk the cow. One morning, Hanna decided to go to the stall alone in order to let the chickens and geese out — they had quite a few — gather eggs, put out some more food for the calves, and only then call Mindlya. But, to her surprise, the doors of the stall were ajar.

She proceeded to the stall with a smile on her lips, expecting to see her favorite daughter-in-law there. During the entire time they lived together, Mindlya never once said a rude word to Hanna, nor did she ever contradict her. She was respectful, courteous and humble, but the main thing Hanna liked was that she was a good housewife. She loved and respected her husband and was raising their children in harmony with all the family and religious customs.

Thinking about that, Hanna approached the stall. But what was that? Somebody was moaning. Who could be there? Hanna opened the doors hurriedly.

— Who's here? — she asked harshly.

There was silence in reply. Hanna went inside and froze in shock: Marichka was sitting in the corner wearing a white night gown.

— What's going on, Marichka? — asked Hanna anxiously. — What are you doing here?

There was moaning in reply.

Hanna came closer and discovered with horror that Marichka's shirttail was all bloody. Hanna screamed flinging her arms up to her head in a gesture of shock, but seeing Marichka's eyes full of excruciating pain, she immediately rushed to her aid.

The old woman was not strong enough to lift Marichka, so she ran to the house to get Mindlya. Mindlya ran out with her hair down, followed by Gersh who was dressing as he ran.

They, too, stopped on the stall threshold as if frozen. Marichka, all bloody, was writhing on the dirt floor in agony. Nobody suspected that this young girl, so quiet and slow-moving, had come into their house pregnant. And at that moment they were trying to help Marichka without saying anything. Mindlya brought some water. Gersh started a fire in the stove to make it warm. Although Hanna was famous in the village for her skills as a healer, and had delivered a number of babies and seen many women in labor, this time her hands were shaking and she was very anxious.

— Gersh, — she said to her son, — go to Dobromil and get the doctor. Tackle up and hurry up. Tell the doctor we will pay him well. Please, hurry. Things don't look good.

Suffering merciless agony, Marichka took no notice of things around her. Her heartrending cries affected everybody. Neighbors came running to find out what was going on. Some were nodding their heads in sympathy with the woman in labor; some smiled malevolently and left. The baby was being born in hard labor.

Hanna ran out to the road peering into the distance, impatiently waiting for the doctor. The doctor finally came two and a half hours later, when Hanna was already holding the baby in her arms. Marichka

23

was bleeding to death. Mindlya was making a potion out of herbs, given to her by Hanna.

— Drink up, Marichka. It will help you, it should help, — she whispered tying the baby's umbilical cord.

Mindlya slapped the baby on the bottom, and it shrieked. Mindlya quickly took the baby, put it into the basin and started washing her, while Hanna and the doctor bent over Marichka trying to stop the bleeding. The placenta had difficulty separating from the uterus, blood ran in torrents, and everybody was in panic. Through her numbing lips Marichka was whispering something. Hanna bent closer to find out what she wanted.

— Bring the baby.

Hanna took the tiny pink creature and brought it to Marichka's face.

— It's a beautiful girl, every inch like you.

In response Marichka glanced at Hanna with empty eyes and whispered,

— Christen her Yarinka.

She was trying to kiss the baby, but was losing strength. — I want a priest. I need to make a confession. I have sinned... — No, you haven't! Mindlya, go get the priest, quick! Doctor, do something, she is slipping away!

The doctor just shrugged his shoulders. Hanna passed the baby to young Rosa and asked her to leave.

Marichka was fading away like melting wax. Hanna scurried about trying to ease her suffering, but there was nothing that could help the poor woman any more. Holding Hanna's hand, she was dying. Her blue eyes turned glassy, and her lips turned grey. The priest appeared at the entrance of the house, but Marichka was unable to say a word. Her eyes were fixed on Hanna's and her hand gripped Hanna's hand tightly. The priest approached and looked into Marichka's eyes.

— She is no longer with us.

— Yes, — echoed Hanna, — she is no longer with us.

She freed her hand from Marichka's grasp, gently touched her eyes to close them, and went to the corner. The doctor was gathering his instruments, with his head low.

— Hanna, we did all we could. It's his turn now, — and he pointed to the priest. — Let's go outside.

The curious crowded around the fence. Almost half the village came to watch. Hanna looked at the onlookers, wiped off her tears and went to the doctor's cart. He turned to her.

— Hanna, we did all we could, all that was in our power. Only God knows why it had to happen. What are you going to do with the baby, Hanna?

— I don't know. Our family is Jewish. And the baby should be raised as a Christian. The mother asked that her daughter be named Yarinka. I must carry out her wish.

Gersh held out money to the doctor for his services, but he flatly refused to take it. With that they parted.

The funeral was arranged in accordance with all Christian traditions and paid for by Hanna. Afterwards everybody interested went to the eatery for a cold-meat party set for sinful Marichka's soul.

After the funeral Hanna was racking her brains about what to do with the baby. Marichka had asked that the baby be christened, and that meant that she was to be raised in Christian spirit. Would a Jewish family be able to honor Marichka's request?

That night the whole family came together to meet in council. Leon came home and, as Hanna's oldest son, he was the first to speak, — Mom, I think the baby should be taken to church, and some Christian family will take her. Look how beautiful this baby is! Everybody sat quietly. Hanna had gotten attached to the girl during that week. She was feeding and changing her, and singing Jewish lullabies to her. It had been a long time since she buried her husband, and both her strength and youth were fading. But her love of life and everything living was still strong.

What was to be done? Mindlya and Gersh had three kids of their own. And they were all working day and night. They had to put together a dowry for Rosa, and to provide the boys with an education. It was decided that Hanna would take the baby to church on Sunday morning, and get the priest to baptize her, and maybe some Christian would take pity on her and agree to raise the orphan.

In the morning Hanna and Mindlya milked the cows, gave the baby a bath with flavored herbs, wrapped her in swaddling clothes brought by Leon from Peremyshl, put a lacy cap on her and set off for church.

They stopped after approaching the church fence. Hanna's heart was pounding. Mindlya took Hanna by the hand.

— Mom, we've got to do it. I am nervous too. But that was Marich-ka's request and we have to honor her last behest.

— I know, — Hanna responded quietly, — but I have never been here before... You know what I'm thinking? How will they take it? According to them, the baby is a bastard, an illegitimate child... What's illegitimate or legitimate? We are all equal before God. All right, let's go and see what happens.

Hanna entered the church. The old Jew calmly carried the baby and confidently headed for the altar, where the stunned priest stood looking at her. Dozens of astonished eyes were watching her every step. Hanna's daughter-in-law followed her. Hanna's voice sounded loud and echoed under the vaults of the Christian hermitage.

— Father! I have brought this baby to church at the request of her mother. Her mother, may she rest in peace (here everybody made the sign of the cross), asked me before her death to christen the baby and name her Yarinka.

A smile of relief appeared on the priest's face.

— Yes, Hanna, it's very noble of you to act on the deceased's be-hest.

And he loudly addressed the congregation,

— Parishioners! A young Christian soul has departed from us leaving behind a little creature for us to take care of. We need to christen this baby, and assume Christian guardianship of her. Who is willing to be the girl's godmother and godfather?

Dead silence reigned under the vaults of the church. The priest repeated his question. Again there was no answer. Hanna stared at the priest, and he felt uneasy under that look. After a moment she said,

— Father, go ahead and christen the baby!

— But you must be aware that according to the law a godmother and a godfather are required.

— Father, there is no mother and no father. God will forgive you your law. Christen her and name her Yarinka.

Once again the priest addressed his congregation: who wanted to be the baby's godfather and godmother? Again there was no answer. The number of parishioners visibly thinned. Then the Holy Father began to pour Holy Water on the baby's head, and rub her arms, legs and belly with consecrated oil, and say prayers, blessing the little being for life.

When the priest finally raised his head to look at his parishioners, he was surprised to find just a few old women remaining in the church, casting curious glances at the two Jews by the altar holding a baby.

Ashamed for his own kind, the priest said,

— Hanna, I apologize for them, but let's forgive them. For as the Lord said, "they know not what they do". I will take the baby to the convent in Peremyshl where she will be cared for. And thank you for everything you have done for Marichka and her baby.

Hanna and Mindlya stood in front of the apologetic priest. Hanna was cuddling the baby, and the warmth of Yarinka's little body spread all over her. She felt like a mother. And as though a miracle happened, her youth came back to her for a moment.

— No, Father. I will raise her myself. I cannot trust this baby to someone who has never had children. I will raise her as a Christian although I am a Jew, because all people are equal to me. Holy Father, you know I have helped many people in the village, and have treated lots of people with my herbs. The Lord will repay me in kind. I believe in God. God is one.

With these words the old white-haired Jew left the church, gently embracing the baby. Bow-backed, humped old women sitting on benches whispered and discussed what had just happened. Some of them, burning with curiosity, tried to approach Hanna wishing to see the baby. But Hanna covered Yarinka with the laced coverlet. She did not want anybody's spiteful look to disrupt the little one's sleep.

ROSA

Grandma Hanna loved all her grandchildren very much, but she loved Yarinka most. The little girl was growing up quickly and would always make Hanna laugh. Hanna dreamt of getting her into a good school. She registered her everywhere as Yarinka Leventhal, and did not let anyone treat her poorly.

Yarinka repaid mother Hanna with daughterly love and would only sleep next to her, tucking her nose into her armpit. Hanna would make a pacifier for her by wrapping a lump of sugar in a piece of cloth. The child would lick it and fall asleep. Hanna would then take the sugar out of the Yarinka's mouth and put it on a plate.

Blonde and blue-eyed, Yarinka differed dramatically from Hanna's other grandchildren. Curly-haired Rosa often asked Hanna,

— Grandma, why does Yarinka have blonde hair, and I have black?

And Hanna would reply, smiling, that Yarinka was of Slavic origin.

— And of what origin are we? — Rosa persisted.

— We are of Israeli origin. All our ancestors came out of Israel. And that is why our hair is black.

Hanna told the children about Israel, about King Solomon and King David. And the children kept inquiring. And the main question was how they had come to Kvasenina; and why they were not in Israel; and why Israel was called Palestine; and how it had all happened. Hanna did not know the answers to many of the questions. In order to satisfy the children's curiosity she would sometimes make up answers.

Rosa was old enough to pasture the goats. One spotted goat stood out due to its stubborn disposition. It would run away into the woods, drift to someone else's herd, or hide in the bushes.

One day a horse-drawn wagon with goats in it was traveling along the road and all the goats were bleating invitingly. The awful spotted goat chased after them. Rosa tried to catch the goat, but it ran fast and Rosa was not able to overtake it.

The man driving the wagon was enjoying the scene and urged the horses to go faster. Rosa ran as fast as she could, but soon got exhausted, stumbled and fell down. Realizing that she would not catch the goat, Rosa got very upset. Upon returning home she found the whole family worried — everybody was concerned by her long absence. But the loss of the goat was not the biggest misfortune: That night Rosa got a fever, and fell seriously ill.

Hanna made medicinal tea and gave it to Rosa, but the poor girl was fading by the hour. She got pale and so thin that it was painful to look at her. She had no energy to play with the kids; she had no strength to live. Gersh kept taking her to see doctors in Peremyshl, and paid them a lot of money for her treatment. He sent her to mountain resorts. Rosa's illness practically made the family broke, but nobody pinched pennies. They all tried to restore the girl's health. But the money went fast.

During his sister's illness, Shmul tried his best to help his father. He was still a child, but still managed to buy rabbit skins and sell them in the market in Dobromil. That was how he helped get bread for his family.

Once while Gersh was reading a newspaper he gleefully shouted to Mindlya.

— Some doctor wants to test his tuberculosis medicine.

She immediately jumped at the offer,

— I beg you, let's trust him, Gersh. Let's send him money and try the medicine.

Is there anything in the world parents could begrudge for their children?

A week later Mindlya was giving Rosa the new medication. And — what a miracle — Rosa began to get well by the hour. She got her appetite back and her cheeks regained color. When Rosa was taken to the doctor again, he didn't recognize her at all. He could not believe that it was the same girl he had seen a month before. There were no limits to the family's happiness.

Mindlya started to put together a dowry for Rosa. The girl was growing up and in these days it was very difficult to marry a daughter off without a dowry — especially when the entire neighborhood knew about Rosa's sickness. Who would be brave enough to marry her? But if there was an abundant dowry, it would be worth thinking about.

Mindlya expected that when the time came she would ask her father for a piece of land for Rosa. Mindlya's father, Aaron Gleikh, was a rich man. He had 23 hectares of land in the village of Pyatnitsa. He gave a big piece of land to each of his three daughters and he would help his granddaughter, too. But even her grandfather couldn't help Rosa's dream to get married and have a family of her own come true.

SHMUL

Shmul, was five years younger than his sister Rosa. Together they attended school in the synagogue where they were taught by the rabbi. Rosa was a model student. Shmul, on the other hand, had the reputation of being brainy but was too fidgety and that was why the rabbi wrote notes to Gersh almost every day. At first the father punished the boy, but later he talked to him explaining that he would not have a good life without going through school. Shmul would listen obediently to everything, but he kept right on behaving the same way.

Of all her children, Mindlya loved Shmul most. He became her main helper in everything. Like an early bird, Shmul got up at dawn. He helped Mindlya take care of the cattle and fed the geese and chickens. He did all the work about the house with great love. If he saw his mother carrying a bucket of water from the well, he would run to help her, grabbing the bucket from her hand.

There were times when Mindlya would brush Shmul off like a troublesome fly. He bothered her with all sorts of questions. Occasionally he asked her questions which his mother couldn't answer.

Shmul was a healthy and handsome boy and he was successful in everything he started. Sometimes Gersh said to Mindlya,

— Shmul has got a good head on his shoulders. Look — he succeeds in everything. Whatever he starts to do, everything goes smoothly. He is a smart guy. Do you think he takes after me?

And he looked into Mindlya's eyes with a cheerful smile.

Mindlya smiled in reply and softly kissed Gersh on the forehead.

Yes, she thought, Shmul would make a good businessman. He could easily count mentally, adding, subtracting, dividing and multiplying any numbers. Once shown how to do something, he knew what to do. Mindlya could not wish for a better son. She just wished she would live to see him marry a good girl and have children.

The boy wanted to be a businessman like Uncle Leon. He wanted to dress nicely like his uncle, and he wanted to have everything his uncle had. Sometimes he would sneak into his uncle's room and put on Leon's vest and hat and look into the mirror. He would take out the watch that was in the vest's pocket, look at it with an air of importance and put it back. The hat was too big and covered his eyes, but he managed to push it back in such a manner that it would stay on his head for a while. Looking respectable, Shmul would swagger back and forth in front of the mirror, and then put everything back in place and run out of the room.

He especially loved it when Uncle Leon was shaving. He watched his uncle lather his cheeks heavily, and then remove it with a straight razor. Shmul could not wait to start shaving himself. He often ran to Grandma Hanna and asked her if it was time for him to start shaving. Hanna would solemnly feel his cheeks and chin and then shake her head,

— No, Shmul, you need to come to me after your Bar Mitzvah, which is when you turn 13. According to Jewish law you will become a man after your Bar Mitzvah. Maybe then you will be able to shave.

31

Shmul would go away with his head down, but he wasn't dejected for long. He would run to help his mother or Grandma Hanna. He loved helping Grandma Hanna milk the cows. He would proudly hold the towel and the bucket with water. Grandma Hanna would pour water on her hands, wash the udder and dry it with the towel. Then she would put some oil on her hands so that they would slide smoothly along the teats. Milk would flow into the bucket and raise foam. Grandma Hanna would switch her hands from one teat to another as if playing them. Shmul loved it very much.

One day he decided to go and milk the cow called Minka all by himself. He prepared a towel, a bucket with water and some oil. When he entered the stall, Minka looked at him apprehensively, but Shmul put the bucket down with an air of importance and started to splash water on her teats.

Minka the Cow turned her head to him and mooed briefly, as if wanting to ask him something. Shmul petted the cow on her smooth back and began wiping her teats. Then he set the little stool Grandma Hanna usually sat on, sat down and began pulling Minka's teats, but for some reason milk didn't appear.

At a loss, Shmul got up, circled the cow making sure he was doing everything exactly like Grandma Hanna, sat back on the stool and began pulling the teats. At that point Minka could not take it any more and began flicking Shmul with her tail. The tail was switching from left to right and from right to left. Having gotten what he deserved, Shmul shot out of the stall like a bullet.

MOISHA

Rosa and Shmul's youngest brother, Moisha, had a talent for music that amazed and pleased everybody. Their father bought Moisha an accordion and he learned to play it. He also loved to dance with the girl next door while Uncle Leon played the violin. And Leon liked to play and watch them dance. It reminded him of the good times he shared with Matilda in his childhood.

Moisha liked to play with all the neighborhood kids, but he was especially close to his friend Peter. He would spend all day with him. They were the same age and understood each other perfectly. When the rabbi gave Moisha assignments, Peter and Moisha studied them together. And it was hardly possible for anyone to tell who learned their lesson best.

Peter was an orphan being raised by his grandparents. His mother had died during delivery and his father had found himself another woman in Dobromil and married her. Soon his father started a family with his new wife and forgot all about Peter.

His grandpa was very old and his grandma was feeble. They survived by begging. Peter often spent the night at the Leventhals, where he was treated with kindness and attention. Hanna would seat him at the table every time he showed up in their house. The hungry boy felt more at home there than in his own house.

Grandma Hanna was getting packages from her eldest sons in America. The moment each new package appeared in the house Hanna would open it right in the middle of the room and start to divide the presents among them all. Young Peter would get something, too.

One day the boys were playing outside, frolicking and running about. Something drove Moisha to squeeze through a hole in a fence woven out of willow. His head went through the hole all right, but his shoulders got stuck. He tried to back out, but failed: the willow wouldn't let him. He pulled and pulled, hurting his ears, but he couldn't move. At that moment Moisha started screaming at the top of his lungs. Peter got scared and rushed to the Leventhals' house for help.

— Rescue! Help! Rescue! — Peter was screaming through his gasping.

Mindlya heard the screams, ran outside, saw the boy tearing along like the wind, and realized that there was trouble.

— Help! Save me! — Peter was shrieking.

— What has happened?

— Moisha has squeezed his head through a hole, and he can't get out of it.

— What hole? Where?

— In old man Vasily's wicker fence.

Stumbling, Mindlya ran to old man Vasily's place. Some neighbors gathered by the fence including old man Vasily who was trying to help Moisha get his head out. He tried to do it carefully without inflicting unnecessary pain on the boy. He stood in front of Moisha's head and was taking the fence apart twig by twig. Moisha wiggled his head, and it pressed into the old man's pants which smelled of tobacco. Finally, the old man liberated the sufferer, and everyone heaved a sigh of relief. Moisha's head was intact, and so were his ears. Mindlya did not know how to thank the old man for saving her mischievous son. Soon the crowd went away; only the old man stayed to mend the hole in the fence to prevent any more heads from going through there.

GERBURT'S CASTLE

Unlike his older siblings, Moisha was not into studying much. But he loved to go on field trips to Gerburt's castle. He always looked forward to this event: Once a year in the spring teachers took students to the castle that stood high on a mountain. If you climbed the castle's wall, you could see all the woods, mountains, valleys and villages in the vicinity.

The castle was built in the Middle Ages by the knight Gerburt to defend against warlike nomads — Tartars and Turks. Even in those days you could see the ruined walls and embrasures on that site. By its shape the castle looked like a circle. There was a yard in the middle, and in the center of the yard a deep well had been dug. There were multiple underground tunnels beneath the castle, one of which led to Peremyshl.

In ancient times it was practically impossible to reach the castle by land: There were just two narrow paths leading through the wild forest to the gates which were protected by guards. When Tartars or Turks attacked the neighborhood villages, local residents ran to escape under the protection of the powerful walls. Many people had been saved from death and slavery under its roof.

But the castle was eventually seized and destroyed by Tartars. Treachery and betrayal helped them conquer the previously impenetrable castle.

There were many legends going around about this castle. Teachers told students about knight Gerburt's young wife, who had jumped into the deep well clutching her baby boy, escaping from the conquerors and preferring death to slavery and rape.

Children always loved these legends and field trips to the castle. Teachers made a fire and baked potatoes. Kids frolicked, jumped over the fire and sang songs.

Ruins of the Gerburt Castle, 2004

During one of the field trips to Gerburt's castle, while the rest of the children were having fun and playing, Moisha and three friends decided to check out the tunnel which supposedly led all the way to Peremyshl. And although the teachers had strictly forbidden the children to climb in dangerous places, Moisha did not pay much attention to bans — he always climbed wherever he liked. That day he decided to become an adventurer.

He found the place where there was an entrance to the largest tunnel and began to clear it of the trees and branches which had fallen over it. His friends were helping him enthusiastically, and soon the entrance to the tunnel was free.

Tying one end of a rope to a bush, Moisha took a torch prepared in advance, lighted it, and was the first to proceed into the depth of the tunnel. Peter, with the other two boys, followed him.

Moisha and Peter walked bravely, looking inquisitively at everything along the way, but the other two boys were afraid to go too far from the entrance. One of them stopped Moisha, touching him on the shoulder and said,

— Moisha, we shouldn't go so far. It is very dangerous. There may be a collapse.

But the young adventurer was not stopped by that warning. Moisha said with a sneer,

— You are just afraid, that's all there is to it. If you are scared, go back.

Holding the rope the two boys began to make their way back from the tunnel.

When they came out to the surface, they walked right into a teacher standing in front of the tunnel. He looked seriously worried. Seeing the boys, he rushed to them and gave them a hug. But when he heard that there were two more boys remaining down there, he was shocked. He did not dare go into the tunnel. What could he do? Leaning over the entrance to the catacombs, he began to call to Moisha and Peter begging them to come back.

Although Moisha heard the teacher's pleas to come back before something bad happened, he kept stubbornly moving forward. But soon he was out of the rope. The boys stopped. After looking around they decided to come back another time with a longer rope and con-

tinue exploring the tunnel. After drawing a big sign on the wall with chalk, they started back.

By the time the teacher saw Moisha's head appear in the opening, he had almost lost his voice from yelling. Dragging the madcap out by his ears, the teacher began to spank him on the bottom. Anticipating that he would get his fair share, Peter sat quietly in the tunnel, hesitant to go outside. But soon it was his turn to receive the thrashing.

As cross as a bear, the teacher took a thick nut-tree stick and was strenuously beating the taste for dangerous adventures out of the boys.

Moisha and Peter were very downcast on the way home, knowing that the punishment that awaited them would probably be much graver than the teacher's stick.

KOSHER SALT PORK

All the children — Jews and Christians, Ukranians and Poles — played together. The kids especially loved to play hide-and-seek. Moisha and Peter knew every bush and tree in the neighborhood. They often ran into the woods to find new places to hide, and the others would look for them. The inseparable friends always won in that game — it was impossible to find them. No one could imagine that their secret hiding places in the woods would one day save their lives.

All the little cowherds would bring food to the pasture. When the kids got hungry they sat down and ate together. Everything seemed so tasty — black rye bread, milk, potatoes, cucumbers, boiled eggs and onions — a sumptuous feast!

One day Peter brought a piece of salt pork. All the Ukrainian children began to eat it with great enthusiasm, but Shmul didn't even touch it. The kids were amazed.

— Shmul, don't you want to eat it? — Peter asked in disbelief.

— I do, but I can't.

— Why can't you? — Peter wouldn't quit.

— I just can't, that's it. It's not customary for us to eat pork.

— Who's "us"? — the kids didn't get it.

— The Jews, — explained Shmul.

The kids dropped their mouths so wide a crow could have easily flown in there.

— Why are you looking at me like that? Grandma Hanna said that the Jewish God has forbidden the Jews to eat pork because it's not kosher.

Everyone kept staring at Shmul.

— Why isn't it kosher? — asked Peter in bewilderment.

— I don't know, I just don't know, — Shmul shook his head. — All I know is that it shouldn't be eaten.

— Look, Shmul, I don't know whether this salt pork is kosher or not, but it is extremely tasty. In fact, my granny says that there is nothing tastier in the world than Ukrainian salt pork.

Shmul set to thinking. He wanted so much to taste salt pork. Besides, he was really hungry. And everybody was eating it with such gusto. Shmul looked at his friends. There they were, eating salt pork, and nothing bad had happened to them, so why couldn't he do it — taste it just this once? Could it be that Grandma Hanna had made a mistake? Could it be that God was talking about ordinary pork, and not about Ukrainian salt pork? Oh, he wanted to taste it so much! In addition, as if on purpose, Peter was urging him.

— Shmul, we are not going to tell on you to anyone. Go ahead and eat with us!

— Well, all right, I'll taste it. But only once, — Shmul finally gave in.

And he fell to the salt pork. He licked it, bit into it, smacking his lips with delight, and thought that there had been a mistake made. There was no way God could have denied the Jews a pleasure such as Ukrainian salt pork.

From that day on Shmul never refused to eat salt pork, and when somebody offered it to him, he would eat it with great pleasure.

One beautiful fall day the adults were digging potatoes, the children were frolicking on the forest grass, and the cattle were pasturing nearby.

They made a fire, threw potatoes in to bake them, and began to eat. Peter brought a slice of salt pork again and shared it with Shmul. Closing his eyes Shmul was chewing it with delight when a hysterical scream sounded. Everybody jumped. What was that?

It was Moisha screaming, peeping from behind the bushes.

No one except Shmul was able to understand anything. Moisha was yelling in Hebrew that he was going to tell, that he saw everything and that Grandma Hanna, mother and father — everybody — would punish Shmul for eating sowbelly.

Shmul was stupefied. What should he do? He knew that Moisha would for sure do what he threatened to do. Then it struck him. He stooped to Peter, whispered something quietly into his ear, and got up from the ground.

Peter ran up to Moisha and grabbed him by the arm. Moisha just kept on yelling. Shmul grabbed his screaming brother by the other arm.

— Look, Moisha, I haven't done anything bad, I've just tasted some salt pork.

At the very moment Moisha opened up wide in order to begin screaming again, Shmul quickly put a piece of salt pork into his mouth.

Moisha was stunned, and Shmul said to him,

— See, Moisha, everybody is watching you tasting the salt pork too. If you tell about me, I'll tell the same about you.

The children let Moisha's arms go. Moisha did not know what to do. The salt pork was still absurdly sticking out of his mouth. The boys were dying of laughter. But Moisha suddenly began to cry with hurt.

Shmul rushed to his brother right away, took the salt pork from his mouth and started stroking him on the head and hugging him.

— Moisha, I was just kidding... Say, don't you understand jokes? It was a joke, please stop crying.

He took Moisha by the arm and brought him to the fire. He found a big potato in the fire, brushed off the ashes and gave it to his brother. Wiping his tears with his dirty hands, Moisha succeeded in smearing dirt all over his face.

That night Moisha snitched on Shmul to Grandma Hanna. Shmul was punished. Grandma blamed Gersh for not paying attention to his son's religious upbringing. She said that Shmul was supposed to stand next to Gersh in synagogue praying instead of counting crows in the window. And if grandpa Aaron had got up from his grave, he would prefer to die again after he had found out what Shmul had done.

Shmul was silently standing in the corner with red ears and his head down, but Moisha really regretted that he had reported his brother. From now on he, too, would have to stand next to his father in synagogue and pray aloud. And that meant that he would have to learn all those long prayers by heart.

NOVICE BUSINESSMAN

One of the richest people in Dobromil was Mr. Lihtman, the owner of two sawmills. One of the sawmills was located very close to the railroad which allowed Mr. Lihtman to easily ship board lumber all over Poland and France. When he got a large contract it directly affected the town's economy, since many people were able to get temporary jobs. Mr. Lihtman was a good employer and paid his workers generously. Residents of nearby villages dreamed of getting a job with him.

Mindyla's brother, Gersh Gleikh, was an engineer at one of Mr. Lihtman's sawmills. He was an educated, well-mannered and kind man. He was impressed by Shmul's smarts and savvy and helped him get a logging job at the sawmill. Uncle Gersh had good instincts. Shmul became very valuable at the sawmill because he could determine how much lumber would result from a tree just by looking at it.

Shmul had a similar talent for estimating the weight of a cow which he developed while trading cattle. Shmul's father had taught him that trade and said that it was even more important not to cheat the owner. "You must deliver what you have promised". If you cheated once, the next time nobody would trust you and they would never want to deal with you again. You would not be respected, and being respected was essential for a businessman.

One day Shmul needed to go to Peremyshl to sell a bull-calf. The calf had never been taken out of its stall before. When they opened the gates and the calf was finally able to run, there was no limit to his joy. He was jumping and frolicking while circling Shmul, who could barely restrain the slap-happy calf.

Realizing that he would not be able to handle the calf alone, Shmul asked his friend, who was always willing to make an extra zloty, to help him. According to all the business laws, they were supposed to make fifty zloties and share it evenly. The trip to Peremyshl was a long one — 20 miles, and the calf got completely out of control; he dragged Shmul and his friend from one side of the road to the other. The calf seemed to be in charge, leading them to the market, and not the opposite.

Exhausted and frustrated the young businessmen did not know how to get a handle on the frisky animal. Before they got to the market the calf suddenly lay down on the road and wouldn't budge.

Shmul tried to win him over; he tempted him with green grass and just about chewed the grass himself in order to show the cow how tasty it was. But the calf looked at him with his big beautiful eyes and shook his head. It was obvious that he was exhausted and was not going to move, not for anything.

Shmul was at a loss. What could be done? He had a sudden inspiration. What if he brought the buyers to the calf? He sent his friend to get them and, for the moment, sat down next to the bull to wait for the buyers. Everybody passing along the road looked at the weird couple curiously.

The business deal was closed, although it turned out not to be as profitable as expected. The young businessmen, tired and disappointed, came home. Gersh was getting worried waiting for his son, and he sighed with relief when he showed up at the door.

— I was really worried, Shmul!

His son stood there with his head down and explained what had happened.

— Cheer up, son. You are young, you will learn everything. Any trade needs mastering, and business is not an easy thing.

YARINKA'S WEDDING

That night Shmul slept like a baby.

Mindlya woke him up in the morning.

— Well, young businessman, get up! We've got news. Yarinka is getting married.

Shmul had known Michael Batz since childhood. He was a good guy. But the news came as such a surprise.

— When did that happen? — he responded.

Earlier in the day, Michael came over and saw Yarinka sitting on the steps. There was an expression of concern and apprehension showing on her face.

— What has happened, Yarinka? — Michael asked her, touching her shoulder.

He loved Yarinka with all his heart and tried to please and protect her from anything bad.

— Oh, Michael. I'm pregnant, — a worried Yarinka replied.

— It will be okay, Yarinka. Don't worry. You'll see.

Overjoyed, Michael rushed home. He was so happy. He was going to be a father! He had dreamt of starting a family. But the most important thing was that he would be with Yarinka day and night. When he fell deeply in love with beautiful Yarinka, he stopped noticing anything or anyone else around him. Yarinka's blue eyes seemed like a sea in which he was drowning. He could spend hours admiring her face, her soft sloping shoulders and her long fingers. The slender blue-eyed blonde was the goddess Aphrodite to him. Now, he would always be next to her, always with her and nothing but death would ever be able to separate them.

When he got home, Michael ran into the house, took off his shirt and glanced at his mother. She was busy by the stove, paying no attention to him.

— Mom! — he addressed her. — Mother!

The woman turned her head to look at him: a slim, tall young man, her only son. Boy, did she love him! They had waited so long for him. Their first two children were girls, and only then was he born, a precious son. The birth of an heir was the summit of happiness.

— Mom, I want to get married!

Those words sounded like a bolt from the sky to his mother. She stood stunned, with a jug of milk in her hands.

— Mom, aren't you happy? I want to marry Yarinka Leventhal.

His mother dropped the jug and milk spilled all over the floor. She sank to the bench. Michael froze in surprise.

— What's wrong with you? — he asked, bewildered.

His mother could not say a word. A few moments later she recovered, but her hands were still shaking. She wiped the sweat off her face.

— What's wrong with you, mom?

And then there was a scream.

— Are you out of your mind, Michael? Do you really want to bring a bastard into my house? And what's more, raised by these Yids? No! No! No! I'd rather die before she sets foot over my threshold.

Michael was struck dumb. He was so shocked that he was not able to say a word. And his mother's ferocious words kept hammering on his head. He couldn't believe that everything he was hearing at that moment was said by his mother. Blood rushed to his head. He would not let anyone, not even his own mother, insult Yarinka.

— Mom, stop! What are you saying? Remember, you told me yourself that Yarinka was baptized in a church. And she goes to church every Sunday. I've heard you talking with neighbors and praising her for being hard working. So what's going on with you?

— I know, — his mother said. — But she is not good enough for you. I'll find a wealthy fiancée for you. Why do you want this poor bastard? Do you think these Yids will give her any dowry? She even speaks like them.

— Mom, what's wrong with that? What's wrong with Yarinka's ability to speak Hebrew? She went to our school. She is a fine girl and I love her. Why are you talking about her like this?

— I will not give you my blessing, Michael. I didn't raise you to marry a sheeny bastard.

The last statement was the straw that broke the camel's back. Grabbing his shirt, Michael stormed out of the house. His heart was pounding and he was turning red with rage.

He got to Yarinka's house in a hurry, leaned on the porch railings and froze. At that moment Mindlya was coming out of the house holding a ladle in her hands. Her puzzled look came to rest on Michael's shirt which was fisted in his hand.

— Mrs. Mindlya, I'd like to talk to Yarinka.

— She is inside, come on in!

Michael stepped inside. His eyes became sad and seemed to be impatiently searching for Yarinka. When she saw him, Yarinka froze from sudden fear and flattened herself against the wall. Unaware of anybody else in the room, Michael ran to his beloved, took her hand and placed it on his chest.

— Yarinka, do you hear my heart beat?

She was shaking all over with fear and wanted to pull away, but Michael didn't let go.

— Yarinka, I want you to be my wife.

And then Michael heard Hanna's voice.

— Michael, don't you know how you are supposed to ask for a girl's hand in marriage? Shame on you! Where are the marriage brokers? I know that your father passed away a while ago, but you have a mother, and she is the one who should match you. After all, Yarinka has got her own family and that needs to be honored, too.

— Mrs. Hanna, — Michael cried out, — my mother is against this marriage. But I love Yarinka, and we are going to have a baby.

At this point Yarinka fainted and slipped off a bench. She regained consciousness only after some cold water was splashed on her face. Michael was holding Yarinka tightly in his arms and was tenderly cuddling her. Then Hanna seated the lovebirds at the table, took an embroidered Ukrainian towel and joined their hands. That meant that they were engaged now.

The whole world seemed to be against the young couple, except for old Hanna and her family. Since the young couple didn't have a place to live, Grandma Hanna and the family decided they would give Yarinka a piece of land as her dowry and would help her build a house.

The wedding ceremony took place in the Kvasenina church. The reception was held in the eatery. Neighbors and fellow villagers came to celebrate. Leon played the violin, Moisha played the accordion, and everybody was having a good time. Guests drank vodka and liqueur, yelled to the couple to "Kiss!", did the traditional gopak dance and sang Ukrainian folk songs. It was a wonderful event.

A rumor quickly circulated throughout the village about the dowry that the old Jew, Hanna, was giving to the man who married her adopted daughter. Everybody was oohing and aahing over the news. What a deal! What a fortune for a bastard! Who would have thought? If they did that for Yarinka, what kind of dowry would be given for the biological granddaughter, Rosa? The suitors began to ponder. The Guds, who lived in a neighboring village, decided to send matchmakers to the Leventhals for Rosa.

BRICK'S SUIT

It needs to be said that the Gud's son was quite well off. He owned a sawmill in the village of Yurkovo. The Leventhals were happy to have the matchmakers. But Rosa, turning red up to her ears, looked at her parents pleadingly.

— Mom, Dad, please don't marry me off to Gud!

Her parents were stunned and stood silently by the table. They wanted so much for Rosa to get married. And also, here was such a good suitor. She must have gone crazy, that girl.

— Don't have me marry Gud, — Rosa kept saying, — I don't love him.

— Come to your senses, Rosa! Gud is handsome and rich. What else do you need? As to whether you love him or not... you'll love him some day!

— No, I won't, I won't love him ever. I am in love with somebody else. I love Brick Zusman.

— What's this I am hearing? How can you love him? Let me see him now! — roared Gersh. — What is going on here?

At this point a frightened Brick came out from behind the doors.

— Mr. Leventhal! I wanted to send matchmakers, but they beat me to it, — Zusman explained gasping. — I have been in love with Rosa since childhood. Please, Mr. Leventhal, don't destroy our love!

Brick crumpled his hat so hard that it would never again be fit to be put on a head.

A deadly silence fell. Everybody looked at young Zusman.

— And what will your parents say? — Leon was the first to wake from a stupor.

— I am the only son of my parents. And they want me to be happy. And my happiness is with Rosa, — Brick blurted out hastily.

Rosa blushed like a rose. She stood there looking down, and twitching her apron out of emotion.

Gersh did not know what to say. It all happened as fast as lightning and so out of the blue that everybody was at a loss. Oppressive silence hung in the house.

And then a quiet coughing was heard — it was Hanna. She was the first to break the tense silence.

Gersh got up from his chair, slapped his sides, shrugged his shoulders and said,

— Gentlemen, no offence to anyone, but we are not able to resolve this issue today. Give us some time to think, and we will give the answer in a week.

Everybody got up, said their good-byes politely and left the house, but Brick and Rosa stayed.

Red with emotion, Brick approached the girl.

Rosa Leventhal, 1939.
Photo from the archive of A. G. Leventhal

— Rosa, I want to marry you.

Embarrassed, Rosa lowered her head.

— Why don't you say something? — insisted Brick.

And then he heard a quiet coughing. Hanna, who was sitting on the bench, reminding them she was still there.

Brick grew even redder.

At that moment Gersh and Mindlya came back after seeing the matchmakers off.

— Well, what should we do with you, Brick? — Gersh was the first to speak.

— I want to marry Rosa, — he repeated stubbornly.

Mindlya came up to her daughter.

— How about you, Rosa? What do you say?

Despite her excitement Rosa answered firmly.

— Mom, I love Brick and he is the only one I want to marry.

With that she approached her father, took him by the hand, looked into his eyes and asked him,

— Dad, do you want me to be happy?

— I do, — Gersh answered quietly.

— Then let me marry Brick.

Gersh lowered his head and said,

— Go ahead, Brick, send the matchmakers. Everything must be done by the rules.

Giving a skip for joy, the guy went out the door like a bullet.

Gersh turned to his wife,

— Well, Mindlya, let's hope we have made the right decision. Brick is a good guy, a hard worker, and our Rosa is not an idler. Everything should work out fine for them.

Mindlya nodded her head in agreement.

Gasping, Brick flew into his parents' house.

— Mom, get ready, he yelled, catching his breath.

His mother turned her head towards him.

— Get ready for what?

— Mom, I am getting married, — he was barely able to gasp.

His mother opened her mouth, unable to say a word. His father, who was sitting on the chair, was bug-eyed.

— What's wrong with you? — the son wondered.

His parents didn't answer, but kept staring at him in silence.

Finally, Brick took a deep breath in and then out; catching his breath he said once again,

— Mom and Dad, get ready. Let's go to propose to Rosa Leventhal for her hand in marriage. I am getting married.

His mother kept standing by the stove, and his father dropped the hammer he was holding.

— I don't get it! — cried Brick. — Can't you hear me? I am getting married! Married!!!

Abram, Brick's father, lowered the boot he was mending to the table, took off his glasses and was still not fully clear what was going on.

— What is it that you have come up with, my son? Where do we need to go?

— What do you mean — where? To the Leventhals! I am marrying Rosa Leventhal.

— What makes you think she will want you?

— Because I am in love with her, and she loves me back, — his son explained patiently.

His father got up and approached him.

— Brick, marriage is a serious matter, and you can't make such a decision hastily.

— It requires a very quick decision. The Guds from Yurkovo are already seeking her in marriage. However, I managed to drop in and ask them not to give her to Gud, but to me.

The parents were bewildered again. What was going on here? Each piece of news was more astonishing than the other.

His mother was the first to come to her senses. Turning to old Zusman she said,

— Abram, Rosa is a nice girl, but she was seriously ill. Who knows if this illness comes back?

Her husband nodded in agreement.

— Son, let's carefully think it through. After all, you are our only son, — his mother implored. — There are so many wealthy and healthy girls around, but you had to choose Rosa.

Brick didn't expect such a response.

— Mom, I'll marry Rosa. I love her, and if you wish happiness for me, your only son, then go and seek Rosa Leventhal in marriage, otherwise I am going to get married without a broker — I can't even imagine somebody else marrying her.

Brick had been extremely stubborn since childhood. That could be because he was the only child, and therefore spoiled. But he was a hard-working handsome guy and Rosa was a good match for him. Besides, the Leventhals had a solid reputation in the village.

Abram patted his son on the shoulder and said,

— Yes, son, if you are in love — get married.

Then he turned to his wife,

— Well, mother, we are going to have a helper. Get ready! Let's go to the Leventhals to talk.

The marriage brokerage was proceeding quickly and quietly. There was nothing much to discuss, as Brick was the sole heir. The Zusmans had enough land; they also had quite a big piece of forest land — a wide band of the forest they owned extended through the mountains to the end of the village. And grandpa Gleikh, Mindlya's father, gave Rosa twelve acres of land in Pyatnitsa village as her dowry. It was decided to have the wedding late in the fall after the harvest.

ON THE EVE OF WAR

Life was running its appointed course. Everybody was happy.

Yarinka had given birth to a handsome baby boy — Ivan. Hanna delivered her baby with the doctor — the same doctor who had once tried to help her mother. Yarinka, in turn, did not forget about Hanna — she would come and help her and Mindlya. Rosa helped the Zusmans with their household, and Brick brought fire wood and helped Gersh. Everybody was looking forward to Rosa's wedding and getting ready for it.

Hanna had taught her granddaughter how to gather and dry herbs and Rosa loved it. She knew when and at what time different herbs were supposed to be gathered and how to dry them. She knew how to brew potions and what herbs to use for what illness. Brick always accompanied Rosa to the woods and they brought back a lot of herbs between the two of them.

Rosa was very shy and polite, whereas Brick was dynamic, full of energy and inquisitive. He seemed to be interested in the whole world, in everything that was going on. He wanted to know everything and be able to do anything. Sure enough, he failed in some things, but he enjoyed trying.

Time flew. Everybody worked like ants helping each other. The old helped the young, the young helped the elderly and the kids went to school and played.

After a while the Batz had another child, a daughter Marichka. Their family lived happily with love and harmony. But the times were troubled.

Shmul was drafted into the Polish People's Army. He passed the military commission and got a certificate of fitness for military service in category "A". It was the highest category which meant that the guy was strong and healthy.

His parents were very upset that Shmul was drafted. Gersh was getting old, plus his asthma was acting up, and fall was coming. They had to harvest and get ready for the winter. Their son's help would be very important.

Gersh decided to apply for a deferment for Shmul as the sole helper of his elderly parents and the family provider and he succeeded. Shmul was given a deferment for a year, until the next fall.

Everybody was very happy about it. Gersh was especially pleased — his beloved son was going to stay with them as before.

But the troubled times continued. There were articles in the newspapers daily about the fascist atrocities in Germany. Everybody listened to the radio broadcasts in fear.

All the Leventhals spoke German well, which allowed them to easily read German newspapers and listen to Hitler's speeches over the radio. After reading the latest newspaper, Gersh would keep silent for a long time, Mindlya would cry, and Hanna would pray.

All of them recalled the time when Pilsudskiy ruled Poland. There had been no anti-Semitism whatsoever.

One time a bishop came to Kvasenina from Warsaw. The local rabbi with his ten young confidants took the Torah and went to meet the important guest. Stopping by the church fence, they waited for him. Upon learning that they were waiting, the bishop came out of the church, approached the rabbi holding the Torah, made the sign of the cross and kissed it. The bishop and the rabbi had an amiable talk, and then they all went to have dinner at Leon Leventhal's eatery. Mindlya treated them to a kosher meal, while the crowd of villagers curiously peeped into the windows. It was 1931.

In 1933 Pilsudskiy died, and the regime changed in a flash....

Michael was sitting on the steps with Yarinka after listening to one broadcast. He asked her what she thought about the events in the news.

— This is what I think... — Yarinka answered. — I've read in the papers that the Germans are killing Jews. There will be a war, Michael. It is scary. I fear for the children and for us.

— There may not be a war. — Michael tried to set her at ease. — Why would anyone want to be at war with Poland?

He himself, however, believed differently: Yes, everything was pointing to an approaching war. Hitler would not stop when a valuable country like Poland was within reach.

— What are you worried about? After all, you are not a Jew. You were baptized in church. Everybody knows that.

— How could you, Michael! How about mama Hanna? How about Leon, Mindlya, Gersh, and the rest of them? This is my family! They are all in my heart, and I fear for all of them.

— Yarinka, you just have to be distressed, don't you? Is everything they write in the papers true? Why would they kill Jews? What good can it bring them?

He tried to set her at ease, but was very worried by the latest news.

THE GERMANS ARRIVE

The summer of 1939 was almost over. And although the weather was still warm, you could feel that fall was coming. The Carpathian Mountains were turning deep green; the air was rich with the invigorating smell of herbs.

Hanna would take a little stool out to the porch, sit down and bask in the sun. In spite of growing very old (after all, she was ninety three), her mind remained as lucid as before. She read papers without using glasses and knew everything that was going on in the world. That knowledge produced fear in her children and grandchildren, but Hanna was too old to be afraid..

And so there came September 1, 1939 — a day that brought a lot of grief and cut short multiple lives. Hanna's foreboding came true. The war began. Germans invaded Poland.

They announced over the radio that the motherland was in danger. The enemy was very strong, they said, but Poland would resist to the last breath and would not part with its land.

Mindlya flung her arms to her head in a gesture of despair.

— We are all doomed. We are going to die. Germans will kill us all.

Gersh sat with his head down. Leon held Hanna's hand and patted it gently.

Old Hanna said quietly, but insistently,

— Mindlya, give Shmul some money. He should run away and save himself. He is young, he should live.

Mindlya ran to her room, frantically opened a box in which she kept money, took out 5 zloties and brought it to Shmul.

— Shmul, my darling son, run! Save yourself. Run to the Russian army.

— Mom, how can I leave you? — he implored.

— Don't worry about us, we are old, and you are young and strong.

— No, mom, I can't leave you alone. I'll stay with you. Whatever is meant to happen will happen.

Gersh, who had been silent up until that moment, interfered.

— No, Shmul, you've got to leave. Escape before the Germans come here. Listen to me, I order you.

— Carry out your father's wish, Shmul, — Leon's voice sounded.

His mother put some bread, a few lumps of sugar, and five zloties into a bag and gave it to her son.

Everybody was crying. Rosa was hugging Shmul saying,

— We'll be waiting for you here. Someone is bound to stay alive. We'll be praying for you.

Shmul was sobbing. He didn't want to leave his family, but they unanimously pleaded with him to leave in order to survive.

Heavy-hearted, Shmul finally left his home and headed for Lvov. He wanted to at least reach Lvov and then proceed farther from there.

Being sturdy and strong, he walked non-stop, and covered a significant part of the trip during that day. As evening approached he felt tired and decided to lie down under a tree to rest. As soon as he touched the ground, he immediately fell asleep. He was awakened by noise coming from the road.

Shmul quickly got up and looked around. He saw people running with horror. They had children, cattle, and carts with them. They were frightened and anxious.

Shmul went to the road and tried to find out what was going on. He learned that a German assault force had already invaded the other side of Poland — it had only taken four hours for Poland to be taken. There was no place to go. The noose was drawn, and there was no way out.

What could he do? Shmul decided to go back home. You can't escape from fate: apparently, the family was meant to stay together in Kvasenina.

Seeing her son at the door, Mindlya flung her arms up.

— What has happened, Shmul? Why have you come back?

— Mom, we are surrounded. There is no way out of Poland. The Germans already have an assault force in place. I have seen lots of refugees. And I have also seen Germans with motorbikes, bikes and tanks. Mom, they are a huge and monstrous power. Poland will not be able to defeat them. I met a Polish officer on horseback. He told me we are not going to give even a button to the enemy. But I don't believe it. He was on a horse, and they are in tanks. I think Poland will crumble and it will fall very soon.

— I believe we should go to the woods, — he continued with confidence. — Everybody should leave. Look, there are mountains and woods around, and that is our salvation. And it needs to be done now, before the Germans arrive.

There was deadly silence hanging in the room. You could hear a fly pass by. And once again the silence was broken by old Hanna.

— My dear children, I am old and feeble. I am not able to go anywhere. And I do not want to be a burden to you. Go! Don't mind me. Go and escape. I'll stay.

— No, mom, I am going to stay with you, — Leon said quietly.

Mindlya was crying. Moisha was sitting in the corner and Shmul was standing at the door with his head down.

Gersh got up from his chair and asked,

— Where is Rosa?

— Rosa is gone to milk the cow, — Mindlya quietly replied.

— Let us all sit down and decide what to do, — Leon said quietly.
— Go call Rosa.

Rosa came into the house with a bucket of milk. She put it on the bench and approached Mindlya. Gersh sat down at the table and asked everybody to join him. Then he said,

— What do you think, Leon? Since our father's death you have always been the head of the family.

Leon lowered his head and sighed heavily.

— Things look black for us. The Germans are extremely iron-handed and I believe the young people should go into hiding. Mom and I will stay here. And you, Gersh, have got to go with them.

— Rosa, — he turned to his niece, — go to Brick. He knows the woods well. He knows where one can hide safely. Take all the necessary things with you and leave. Everything should be done quickly. I think the Germans will be here sooner than we expect.

Shmul, Moisha, Rosa and Brick went deep into the woods and the older ones stayed at home. Everybody believed that the Germans would not harm the old — who could those feeble sick people bother?

Brick found a good spot. Everyone would be able to fit in a small cave by a creek. But the place was especially great because the cave was located on a rise, and the road could be easily watched from there.

The day after they arrived, while gathering firewood, Shmul glanced at the road quite by chance, and was petrified. There was a cloud of dust hanging in the distance — it was the German army on its way to Kvasenina.

PART TWO
UNDER GERMAN OCCUPATION

L eon was right. Events came thick and fast. Although Polish patriotism was at its best, patriotism alone was not sufficient to withstand the powerful, merciless, well-armed and well-trained German army. Poland was not prepared for war with the Germans. And although France had signed a treaty of assistance to Poland in case Hitler's army should attack, it was not in a hurry to fulfill it.

The Polish People's Army was equipped smartly — all the officers, as though carefully selected, were slim, clean cut, and held their head high with dignity. Their shiny boots and leather belts, crossing the shoulder under the epaulets, added to their gallant look. Polish officers prepared for the war like they would for a parade. And nobody imagined that the German army, equipped with the most powerful and advanced weapons for those days, would destroy the Polish People's Army and occupy Poland in a matter of two weeks. Seeing almost no resistance, Hitler's army marched through Poland right up to the border with the USSR.

Polish soldiers and officers, full of hope, fled to Russia — they saw there a chance to save their own lives and to get deliverance for their beloved country. Unsuspecting, the young men trusted their fate to Russian authorities, seeing them as protectors and supporters. But their hopes were destined for disappointment. The supreme government of the Soviet Union directed in its own way. They gathered all the Polish soldiers and officers in a camp, promising to create a Polish army. But they were cruelly deceived. Instead 25,000 soldiers of the Polish People's Army — Poles, Ukrainians, and Jews — were shot to death in Katynsiy woods.

With their arms tied behind their backs with barbed wire, they were positioned one by one on their knees in front of a pit and shot to death in the back of the head. The dead bodies were thrown into the pit. Realizing that they had fallen into a trap, many of them made an attempt to escape, but it was too late. Everything was prepared for mass destruction. No one was supposed to live. The People's Commissariat of Internal Affairs didn't like to leave witnesses behind. The woods would cover all traces of the crime. Flowers and trees would grow on the grave. And the weeping of the mothers, wives and fiancées would not be heard.

But eventually the Katynsky woods would reveal its brutal secret. On the site of the mass grave a cross would be put up as a symbol of a human tragedy.

Germans in Kvasenina

Shmul dropped the firewood he was gathering when he saw the German soldiers. He wanted to get a closer look at them so he rushed down the mountain over hedge and ditch, slipping and scraping his body against tree branches.

The soldiers were driving motorbikes and trucks. They seemed very intimidating in their iron helmets with machine guns hanging on their chests. Upon hearing German speech close to where he was standing, Shmul held his breath. The soldiers had come up to the trees to relieve themselves. They were joking and laughing, sharing cigarettes. Shmul understood every word — it was not for nothing that the rabbi invested Herculean efforts in him. He tutored him for so many hours that he even went bald from the effort (at least that's what old Hanna believed).

Shmul recovered his breath. After relieving themselves, the Germans went back to their motorbikes. There were three men on each motorbike. The convoy started moving forward. After waiting for the last truck to disappear around the turn, Shmul rushed back to his family to tell them what he had just seen.

Suddenly he heard his name. Assuming that it just hadn't happened, he went on walking. But then he heard somebody call him by his name again, and this time it was very distinct. He stopped, looked anxiously around and saw his neighbor Pushak in the bushes.

— What are you doing here, Mr. Pushak? — he wondered.

— We are hiding horses from the Germans. Everybody says that Germans take away horses. That's why we have to stay in the woods. And what are you doing here?

— I just went to get some firewood, — Shmul lied.

He did not want to say that they were hiding in the woods, and he especially did not want to show their hiding place. You never can tell. How did he know what thoughts were inside the man's head? So he decided to join his fellow villagers where they were pasturing their horses.

They all gave Shmul a friendly greeting, invited him to the fire and gave him some baked potatoes. Everybody tried to tell what he had heard or seen. Nobody knew anything for sure, but there were rumors circulating that the Germans would not stay there for long, and that pleased everyone.

Back at the cave, Moisha could not stay in one place for long. He ran around in the woods like mad. Everything seemed so exciting and fascinating. He climbed the highest fir trees and watched the village from there. He saw the Germans go through the yards and catch chickens, and saw women ask them not to take away the food, pointing to young children. But neither crying, nor pleas helped. The Germans just laughed and rudely pushed the women away.

At night Moisha would sneak to his house to get food cooked for them by Mindlya.

Germans behaved quite decently apart from mocking old religious Jews wearing beards and long Jewish sideburns. Once they caught two old men and cut off their beards with a knife, enjoying the whole process. It pleased them to watch the old men cry. After having fun to their hearts' content they ran the old men off the road, kicking them. One of them fell down and couldn't get up, but a German soldier kept kicking him. He angrily yelled at him in German.

— Sheeny swine, get out of here or I will shoot you. And never let me see you again.

All the soldiers surrounding him laughed crudely. The show seemed very entertaining to them.

To everyone's amazement the other old man helped him get up, shielding him with his own body. Accompanied by the obscene shouts of the Germans, the old men walked away, holding each other tightly.

LIFE IN PARADISE

After a few short weeks, the Russian army started an assault on the Germans. The German army started retreating quietly and discretely. Everybody, especially the Jews, were looking forward to the coming of the Russians, whom they considered their saviors. Since World War I the Russians had a reputation for good nature and compassion.

One night there was a clatter of hoofs in the streets of Kvasenina. It was the Russian horse cavalry. Residents came out to the road waving their hands and welcoming the arrival of the Russians. Military men on horseback wore ancient great-coats. The poor quality of the Russian uniforms struck everybody. Compared to the Polish soldiers, the Russians looked extremely shabby. However, nobody was really concerned about it. The important thing was that the Germans had left their village.

The Russian soldiers asked the residents questions about the Germans and marked information on their road maps.

The villagers treated their liberators to apples and pears. Someone brought out a jug of milk, and Leon gave them a jug of sloe gin which made the soldiers extremely happy. The young soldiers left before long, and the next day the combat army entered the village.

Hanna sat on the bench as usual. Mindlya was busy in the kitchen. The door to the house opened and a few Red Army men appeared in the doorway.

— What can I do for you, young men? — Mindlya asked with a smile.

One of them, a guy with the black mustache, smiled and replied,

— Could you boil some potatoes for us, hostess?

— Sure, sure, — they heard Gersh's voice. — Come on in, dear guests.

— Mindlya, — he went on addressing his wife, — lay the table, and I will set potatoes to boil.

Mindlya was fussing around putting milk, cottage cheese and bread on the table.

Leon came into the house.

— Oh, dear guests, God bless you, — he said. — Do sit down and help yourself. You are welcome to all we have... Tell us about your life, about the Soviet power.

Smiling the young soldiers talked about everything they knew.

— You will now have a regional union, a regional executive committee, a regional committee... In other words, you will be living in paradise.

Mindlya stopped and looked at the young soldiers in disbelief. They must be kidding! That's understandable — they are young. Shmul was about their age. He was probably going to be drafted into the army, too, and then some family would give him a warm welcome, too, just like they welcomed these young Russians.

Shmul, Brick, Rosa and Moisha had returned from the cave when they saw the Russians arrive. They ran into the house and were so curious to listen to those brave guys.

— Well, lady, — one of the soldiers addressed Mindlya, — give us glasses, please. We'd like to drink a warmer-upper.

With that, he took out a metal flask.

Mindlya put out some little jiggers and ran off to get some pickles.

The young man stared at the jiggers in amazement.

— Lady, — he said again, — do you happen to have anything bigger?

It was Mindlya's turn to be amazed,

— Bigger?!

— Give us mugs. Have you got mugs?

— Yes, I have, — Mindlya replied, and put mugs on the table.

The military poured vodka into the mugs filling them almost to the brim.

The soldiers raised the mugs, and happily said, "To the host's health, peace and happiness to this house!" They gulped the vodka down, put the empty mugs back on the table and enthusiastically started to eat pickles.

Mindlya looked at them with her mouth open.

— Gersh, they are going to die now, and we will be on trial for murder, — she said coming out of her stupor.

Gersh stood nearby, pale as a wall, and looked at the guys with concern. But they were vigorously eating and joking as if nothing had happened.

— Why stand quiet, hostess? No need to be scared. Russians are amicable people. We have liberated you from the Germans and the Poles, now you will be living in paradise.

But Mindlya and Gersh did not hear anything. They were anticipating the results of the soldiers' drunkenness with fear.

After a substantial meal the soldiers warmly thanked the hosts and left.

Gersh looked at his wife.

— They must have lied to us. It was not vodka, but water! What pranksters! Youth! What can you say?

And he sat down on the bench next to Hanna, breathing a sigh of relief.

Soviet Power in Kvasenina

Russian authorities held meetings in the Kvasenina school. They explained to people how well they would be living from then on, especially women, upon whom it was impressed that from then on they would be equal with men. And although nobody was able to comprehend what equality they talked about (as if women and men had not been equal with the Polish capitalist regime!), nobody dared to argue. Why argue? They just listened and went away.

The meetings usually ended with slogans like "Long live the Soviets!", or "Long live comrade Stalin — dear Father to all the people!" Henceforth Stalin was to become the dear father to all the residents of Kvasenina. But no one minded, thinking "Better Stalin than Hitler." And everybody applauded vigorously.

Leon was appointed to work in forestry. He had a good head for the business and was made a foreman. Leon took Shmul as his assistant, and arranged for Rosa to work in the logging enterprise store.

Skillful and efficient Rosa did almost all the work in the store by herself. She was both a sales girl and a cleaning lady. The store was squeaky clean and attracted customers with its artfully-decorated shop windows. The goods were neatly spread on white napkins, tins were arranged in a pyramid form, and bottles were placed according to height.

Shmul's duties included logging and shipping timber to the sawmill.

It became known to all, of course, that both of Mr. Lihtman's sawmills were confiscated by the Soviet authorities; but, nobody knew where Mr. Lihtman had gone.

Weird things had begun to happen. People were disappearing and no one knew where they were.

Private shops with all their goods became state property.

One day an announcement appeared saying that all those wanting to go to Poland should fill out an application and then they would be sent to their historic native land. Many people, especially the educated ones — teachers, doctors and lawyers of Polish origin — decided to go back to Poland. While running away from the Germans, many Poles had left behind their families and relatives. They missed their families dearly and dreamt of a reunion.

All the applications were accepted by the new authorities in Dobromil. People were told to gather in the square by the city hall to leave. On the set day at nine o'clock in the morning the square was filled with the departing people. They were told to line up, take their things with them and walk to the railway station, where freight trains were waiting to take them to Peremyshl. People walked quickly and happily, inspired by their hopes. Families stuck together, helping each other with the luggage and kids.

There were armed soldiers with red flags waiting for them at the railway station.

Boarding began. Everybody was in a hurry to get on the train and settle down comfortably. However, it turned out that there were more passengers than there was space in the cars. Many of them had to travel standing on their feet. It was stifling and hard to breath. Nevertheless, those departing were not disheartened. Peremyshl was close at hand, so they could bear it.

After the boarding was finished and the platforms were empty, the freight train's car doors were tightly shut and locked. The train began to move out of Dobromil.

In spite of the fact that something strange had happened right in front of their eyes, the people who were seeing them off left the station full of rosy hopes.

Several months later news from "the other side" came. By order of Soviet authorities the train full of "people's enemies" was sent not to Poland, but to Siberia. People there tried to survive in inhuman conditions and only the strongest were able to send news about their situation.

Years later, the few people who had miraculously survived the Soviet concentration camps were able to tell their tales of the inhumanity.

They told the stories in a circle of faithful friends, quietly, so that no strangers could overhear them.

SHMUL JOINS THE SOVIET ARMY

Shmul worked hard hoping to save money for Rosa's wedding, and Mindlya and Gersh handled the estate. After Gersh got asthma, he was no longer able to do the heavy work. Shmul had to do the work of two. Fortunately, Brick helped Shmul a lot. He was always ready to help Shmul.

One extremely cold January day in 1940, Shmul came home from work expecting to rest, get warm and have dinner. It was unusually quiet in the house.

— What's up? — he wondered.

Everybody kept silent, sitting at the table with their heads down.

— What's up? — Shmul repeated his question in bewilderment. — Has someone died?

— Shmul, you have been drafted into the army. You are to go to the Dobromil military enlistment office tomorrow at nine in the morning.

Distressed, the youngster sat on the bench. He did not expect this.

— I'll go with you, son, — he heard his father's voice. — I am sick, and you are our primary breadwinner. The Poles have given you deferment. I think the Russians will, too.

Everybody was hopeful again. Mindlya began to set the table.

All of a sudden the door sprang open and Brick showed up in the doorway. There was terror on his face. They all froze and looked at him questioningly.

Brick proceeded a few steps into the room and blurted out,

— I've got a call-up paper to come to the military enlistment office. I am to go to Dobromil tomorrow at nine in the morning.

Once again the room was quiet. Rosa sat down on the bench, placing her hands in her lap. Fear settled in her eyes.

Brick approached the girl.

— Rosa! Rosa, did you hear me? I am to go to the enlistment office.

— Yes, Brick, I heard you, — she said as tears rolled down her face.

— Will you wait for me, Rosa? The Russians have drafted me for three years. I'll be back. I am coming back and we'll have a big wedding. I have saved some money. I'll leave it all to you, just wait for me.

— You don't have to leave me anything, Brick, — Rosa begged him. — I will wait for you. I love you.

Brick nestled his face in her hands. Rosa cried. Shmul hung his head down. Everybody sat there as if they were at a wake.

In the morning Shmul, Gersh and Brick, with Brick's parents, went to the enlistment office. It was in the same huge stone building not far from the catholic church, here not long ago the Polish recruiting center used to be.

When they entered the room, they saw red flags, portraits of Soviet leaders and a gigantic portrait of Stalin, framed with red flags with the state's seal. The two friends were amazed. It was the first time in their life they had seen so many flags.

The Russian authorities were as grave as a judge. When Shmul's turn came, Gersh made an attempt to say something about his illness, but the Russian superior interrupted him in mid-sentence and said sternly, — The Soviet power has need of brave soldiers. We will teach him military art. He will serve his term and come home. And you, father, don't worry. He won't be alone, and you won't be either. We will take care of you. You will be a soldier's father. Be proud, father!

Gersh listened to the superior with his head down.

Shmul met Brick at the door.

— How was it?

— Nothing much. They will call us one by one and process the papers.

A few hours later his turn came and they heard,

— Leventhal! Shmul Leventhal!

Shmul got up and responded,

— Here!

A military man took him into the office.

A commander sat at a table perusing some papers. Looking up he said,

— Are you Leventhal?

— I am, — said Shmul.

— Not "I am", but "Yes sir, comrade commander!" You will be a Soviet soldier now. Date of birth.

— Nineteen eighteen.

— Nationality?

— A Jew.

— Place of birth?

— Kvasenina, Poland.

— Well, now it is the indissoluble Soviet Union. Everlasting, — the superior said.

Shmul was silent.

— Why are you silent? Respond.

— Yes sir!

— Learn.

— Yes sir, comrade commander, — Shmul repeated.

The superior wrote something down, then glanced at Shmul and asked,

— Can you read?

— Yes sir, comrade commander.

The superior gave him a book in Ukrainian and said,

— Read!

Shmul began to read. After reading a few sentences he stopped and looked at the superior.

He nodded approvingly,

— Great, you read well. What else do you know?

— I know Hebrew, Yiddish, German and Polish, — blurted out Shmul.

The superior looked at him with respect,

— Where did you learn them?

— From a rabbi at school, — answered Shmul openly.

— What kind of school is this? — the superior wondered.

— All the Jews in our area went to study with the rabbi. Our parents paid him to teach us.

— Look at these bourgeois prejudices. Our schools are all free. Study all you want. This is what I am thinking: we are going to send you to Officer School. You will make a good Soviet officer.

Shmul's jaw dropped in surprise. He had not expected that.

The superior got up from his table and gave Shmul a paper. It was an assignment to the Officer School in Odessa.

— Wait here, I'll call another commander, and he will talk with you. With those words he left the room.

A few minutes later he came back followed by another commander, one that was shorter and broader. "Probably, with a higher rank", — Shmul thought.

— Well, young man, do you want to be an officer? — he began.

Shmul just opened his mouth to say something, but he did not get to say a word.

— I understand. I fully understand your wish. Can you read and write?

— Yes sir, comrade commander.

— He knows Hebrew, Yiddish, German and Polish, not to mention Ukrainian, — the commander familiar to Shmul said.

— What are Hebrew and Yiddish?

— These are Jewish languages — the old and the new one, — the first commander explained.

Shmul looked at him attentively and it seemed to him that he recognized some distinctive features he had missed before and he realized the commander was a Jew.

— Yes, Hebrew is the old Jewish language, and Yiddish is the European Jewish language, — Shmul repeated.

— Hmm, — the second commander said reading Shmul's biography. — I can see that everything is OK with you. You can forget about the Jewish languages, you won't need them any more, but you will have to learn Russian. And since you are an educated man, you will manage to do it in no time. There is just one thing that's not all right. Who gave you this name — Shmul?

— My parents did, comrade commander.

— It's no good, it is not customary. What kind of an officer can Shmul make? It's just laughable. You need to change the name, by all means. Here, for example, Alexander — it's a good name. You probably haven't heard of Alexander the Great, have you?

— I have, comrade commander.

— You have? There you go. Try to be like him. He was a good commander.

— Change his name, — he told the first commander. Cross out "Shmul" and write in "Alexander". And what is your father's name?

— Gersh, comrade commander.

— Gersh? It means "Grigoriy" in Russian. So write there "Alexander Grigoryevich Leventhal". Sounds beautiful. Now you can be an officer. Send him to the Officer School in Odessa.

He patted Shmul on the shoulder and left the room.

Shmul was taken aback. He still couldn't grasp the fact that he was going to be sent to study to be an officer.

They were all permitted to go home, but the draftees were to be back in the enlistment office at nine sharp the next morning to be shipped, first to Lvov, and then further to their destination. It turned out that four people from Kvasenina — Brick Zusman, Shmul Leventhal, Vasiliy Belay and Michael Glade — had been assigned to Odessa for officer courses.

Mindlya and Rosa baked cookies and rolls, and put them into a bag for Shmul. Mindlya cried and hugged her son. The heart of a mother felt that it was the last time that she would see him.

— Mom, why are you crying so hard? I am only going to school. It's just for three years. And here you are, saying good-byes as if I am leaving for good. I will come back, I will. I'll study in a Russian school. After the rabbi's school, it will be a piece of cake.

He cracked jokes trying to show that there was nothing terrible going on, but there was grief in his heart. A sense of heaviness entwined his heart like a snake. He felt like crying, and was just hanging in there trying to keep from breaking down.

He had never left his family before. He grew up at home and now he was expected to go so far to a strange country which was supposed to become his own. He was going to learn a language which was also supposed to become his native one. He was overwhelmed with dread, but how could he show it to his parents?

Hanna sat quietly on the bench trying not to be in the way. Shmul came up to her and sat down on the floor next to her. Hanna stroked his tousled hair and said,

— Shmul, I probably won't see you again. I am old. Just remember, while I am alive, I will be praying for you. And when I am gone, I will beg the Lord to help you travel along this hard road of life.

Tears rolled down Hanna's old eyes.

Gersh stood there stoically, although it was obvious that it was not easy for him.

In the morning they all sat in one cart and went to Dobromil.

Brick said good-bye to Rosa and his parents. He asked his parents to be a family for Rosa and her family. Rosa cried bitterly, sobbing as if she knew that she was saying her last good-bye to her fiancé.

The truck was taking the boys to a far off country. All the people seeing them off were waving their hands — only Mindlya reached out her arms as if wishing to embrace her beloved son one last time.

IN OFFICER SCHOOL

After Shmul, who had now become Alexander, was taken from Dobromil by truck, everybody went back home to Kvasenina. Mindlya kept right on crying and Gersh moodily paced the house.

But life went on, and everybody began to get used to Shmul not being at home any more. All the household chores were on Gersh and Mindlya now. Moisha, a young prankster, always found a way to wiggle out of household chores. But as he was the youngest, everybody treated him like a child, forgiving him all his mischief.

Soon they started to receive letters from Shmul. They had to send their replies in the name of Alexander Leventhal to a military unit in Odessa. Rosa sent home-baked bread to Shmul and Brick in one package. Everybody tried to send a gift for the young soldiers, something to remind them of their home.

Every time Alexander received a package from home he was happy in spite of the fact that he had to follow the strict barracks law saying "If you get a package, you must share it with friends!" It was so nice to receive news and gifts from the family, even though there was almost nothing left for him after the sharing.

The Officer Cadets, capitalists now living in a socialist society, were kept on a short leash. They would be given more responsibility and held to a higher standard than other recruits, but they still were not completely trusted.

Study did not come easily to Alexander at all. He learned to read and write Russian fairly quickly; however, conversational Russian was quite difficult for him. Learning Russian reminded Alexander of the rabbi and his school and he would smile at the memory.

Brick was not as persistent and forbearing with his studies as Alexander, and after a while he was switched to serve in an active unit of the Soviet army. Nevertheless, he often visited Alexander to talk to him or to share the treats sent to him from home. Each of them counted the days and weeks remaining until their return home. They dreamed of walking through their dear Kvasenina in the military uniform of a Soviet soldier, and having gaggles of girls run after them.

But Alexander dreamt only about the girl next door — Rivka. He thought about her long black braids and amazingly large eyes. He recalled going to the field to pick poppies and cornflowers, and buying her candy and buns at the fair; and how her father got angry when Shmul kissed her on the cheek, and how Rivka's mother calmed her husband down by reminding him of their own youth.

When he got back home, he would immediately send his mother and father to seek Rivka's hand in marriage. And he and Rivka would build a house on his father's land. His father had written Shmul to tell him that the Soviet authorities had given their family some more land, but put heavier taxes on it. It was getting more and more difficult for Gersh to work the land. Age had begun to show on him. Shmul had it all figured out. He would take care of the land and they would all live happily together in Kvasenina.

Alexander dreamed of becoming Shmul again, because it was so hard for him to get used to his new name. When the commander would call "Alexander Leventhal" Shmul would stand there for a moment wondering who was being called up. If there had been another Leventhal in his unit, he would have never figured out that he was the one being called.

Eventually Shmul got used to being called Alexander. By this time he had learned to shoot accurately and how to read political information. At first he was absolutely unable to distinguish between Stalin and Lenin, but then he got it: Stalin was a Georgian, and Lenin was a Jew. That was a secret the guys from distant Siberia had let him in on. They might have been kidding, but Alexander remembered it. And why wouldn't he? All Jews seemed like family to him, and there was Lenin himself who was a Jew. Pity he wasn't born in Kvasenina, or he might have been his cousin. Everybody was family there — distant family, but still relatives.

The Beginning of the War in Kvasenina

Summer days were going by unnoted. There was no particular news in Kvasenina. Everything was as usual — the villagers worked in the fields, tended to cattle and were busy with their households. Life was quiet and peaceful.

Soviet power established its own rules in the village. The village headman, Soltysa, who had been appointed by the Polish authorities, was replaced by another man — comrade Pidpenko. Priest Gukevich, well known in Kvasenina for many years, disappeared. A new school opened in which children were taught in a new way, and the Russian language was a credit course. Gradually, the residents of Kvasenina began to get used to all the new and strange things.

June was especially sunny. The air was full of the scent of flowers and grass. Life was running its appointed course, until one night a loud rumble was heard. At first people thought that there was a thunderstorm coming, but it was soon clear that this was no thunderstorm.

On June 22nd at 4 a.m., Germans attacked the Soviet Union. A few hours later they were walking along Kvasenina roads. There wasn't even time to think about evacuation. Kvasenina and all the surrounding near-border villages were occupied in a matter of three hours. The residents were in terrible shock, especially the Jews. Nobody had expected a war to break out.

In the very first days everybody saw the changes. Ukrainian guys decided to help the Germans establish the new order. The first thing they did was to unseat comrade Pidpenko and lock him in a barn. Power was taken by such activists as a stable groom named Opryshko. Opryshko knew no German, so he invited a man named Korostenskiy to assist him. Korostenskiy had learned German as a long-time war prisoner during World War I. They were brazen men who thought it their duty to establish order until the Germans appointed their own men or maybe even left them in power.

Then they gathered all Jewish teenagers from 14 to 16 years old and forced them to shatter rocks that they used to fill holes in the roads made by the rain. "Laborers" were taken at gun point, using weapons which the volunteer assistants to the Germans had confiscated from hunters.

The young Jews were locked in a barn for the night. They were not given anything at all to eat. The youngsters ate only what their families could bring them from home; however, the guards carefully checked all the packages and confiscated what they liked most.

Fortunately for those poor lads, a unit of German soldiers was marching past their place of work one day. They briskly walked along following a brave young officer. Noticing the group of teenagers working on the road under guard, the officer stopped his unit, came closer and asked severely in German,

— Who are you and what are you doing here?

The guards were bewildered. None of them knew German. The officer repeated his question louder, but the guards just shifted from one foot to another. And then one of the laborers stepped forward. Taking his cap off and keeping his head low he said,

— Herr Officer, they have brought us here to crush rocks for some reason.

The officer addressed the youngster.

— By whose order?

— Nobody's, Herr Officer. They decided to take power until the German authorities arrived.

— And why don't they answer my questions themselves? — the officer inquired angrily.

— They don't know German, Herr Officer.

— In that case translate to these dummies that I order you all home. German authorities, if they want to, can establish the order themselves.

The young boy turned to the guards and interpreted the words of the officer. They stood there with their heads low while the laborers, without hesitation, ran away.

Several days later the Germans moved to Kvasenina. New order was established and new authorities were appointed. Opryshko was officially appointed headman, and Korostenskiy got to be his assistant. A new priest came and the church was opened again. That made the villagers very happy.

But for the Jews, everything changed. They lost all their rights. The law was very strict: all the Jews were to wear a yellow hexagram and had no right to walk along the sidewalk. At the sight of a German, they were to stop and give him a low bow. The Jews were to give up all the valuables they had. And if any German walked into their homes and saw something he liked, he could take it for himself. The Jews did not have a right to complain, and any Jew could be killed without a trial or investigation.

During the first week of his "ruling", Opryshko formed a police brigade to search the houses of Jews, which couldn't be called anything else but legal robbery in broad daylight. The policemen entered the Jews' houses and took everything they wanted. If someone began crying or begging for mercy, the poor thing was publicly punished on the spot: they tied him to the gates and beat him half dead with a whip. The Jews were mortally frightened and waited in terror for future developments.

LEGAL ROBBERY IN BROAD DAYLIGHT

One day Gersh Leventhal was pasturing a cow in his field when he saw the headman approaching him on horseback. His heart felt trouble coming, but he didn't know what to do.

Opryshko came closer to Gersh.

— Hey, Yid, give me the rope!

— What rope, Mr. Opryshko?

— The one you are holding in your hands!

— The cow is tied by this rope.

— What imbeciles these Yids are! Give me the rope with the cow! — Opryshko laughed viciously.

— Mr. Opryshko, have mercy, — Gersh quietly asked.

— What? — The headman growled menacingly. — Why do you need a cow? You are all going to be killed anyway...

Gersh kept holding the end of the rope tied to the cow's neck.

— Well, are you going to give it to me or do I need to talk seriously with you? — Opryshko leered.

Hanging his head low Gersh gave the rope to Opryshko.

— Well, move it, — he yanked the rope pulling the cow after him.

The cow waggled her head as if she knew that she was being taken from her favorite master.

— Come on, don't kick out. Move along! — the headman barked. — Gersh, hit her on the back.

Gersh hung his head so low that the hat covered his face.

— Don't you hear me, mangy Yid? — Opryshko hit Gersh heavily on his back with the whip.

Gersh went up to the cow and softly patted her on the rear saying,
— Well, dear, go, follow him.
And tears rolled down his face.

Gersh came home very upset. As she looked at her husband, Mindlya immediately realized that something bad had happened.
— Gersh, what's the matter with you?
— Mindlya, Opryshko has taken our cow away, — he replied quietly.
Mindlya sat on the bench.
— What a disaster. What are we going to eat now? — Gersh gave way to tears.
Mindlya hugged her husband and whispered in his ear,
— Don't cry, Gersh, we've got another cow. We'll get by.
— Do you know what he told me? — Gersh asked.
— What?
— We are going to be killed anyway. We don't need to eat.
Mindlya sat with her arms down.
— Don't believe this vicious man, Gersh. He is a bandit. God is merciful. He will protect us from trouble. We have never harmed anyone. Why would we be killed?
— For being Jews, — Gersh said quietly.
Early in the morning the next day Korostenskiy showed up in the doorway of the Leventhals' house.
— What are you staring at me for? — he growled from the door. — Gersh, come and bring out the cow.
— What cow? — Gersh was in the dark.
— Your spotted cow, — Korostenskiy explained.
— Mr. Korostenskiy, have mercy, — Mindlya implored. — What are we going to eat? You are taking away our last provider.
— You will all be killed anyway. If not me, then somebody else will take your cow, — Korostenskiy snarled.
Everybody was silent.
— Well, will you give it to me nicely or should I help you? — the headman's assistant inquired.
Gersh got up from the bench and went to the barn. Tears were rolling down his checks. Could he ever have expected this to happen? What would happen next?

NEWS ABOUT SHMUL'S DEATH

Life for the Jews was getting tougher and tougher by the day. There was an extreme shortage of food. Everybody was half-starved. Three months after the beginning of the war Michael Glude showed up in the village. Everybody wanted to know how it happened that he came back alive and well, and where the rest of the guys were who served with him.

When she heard the news that Michael had returned to the village, Mindlya immediately decided to go see him. Putting a warm scarf on her head she hurried to his house. Approaching his door she timidly knocked on it. Michael was the one to answer.

— Mrs. Mindlya, come on in, — he invited her.

Mindlya entered timidly and crossing her hands on her chest, she said quietly,

— Michael, I have come to find out about Shmul. Do you know anything about him?

The guy stood in front of Mindlya shifting from one foot to the other. He looked embarrassed and frightened.

— Mrs. Mindlya, — he finally said, — He was wounded in the head and died in my arms. I buried him right there, on the Romanian border, with these hands.

And he reached out his hands to Mindlya.

The woman who hadn't expected such an answer, backed away. Having lost her tongue, she stared at Michael. His words sounded like thunder from the clear sky.

And Michael, turning away from Mindlya, began to tell her what a big fight they had had over the river Prut and how the Germans had seized the area he and Shmul were defending, and how under cover of the night he decided to come home. He found peasant's clothes in one of the empty houses and changed, leaving his military uniform under a bush in the forest. He moved only at night, afraid to be seen either by the Germans or the Russians.

Mindlya looked at Michael with her eyes wide open. Everything Michael had told her about Shmul was rejected by her mother's heart. Her mother's heart was saying, "Don't trust him, and do not believe him. Your son is alive. You are his mother, you would have felt it if he had been killed".

Without saying a word she left his house and went home.

Tears rolled down her face, and her hands clutched the head scarf.

When she arrived home, everybody looked at her questioningly. Without taking off her outerwear she sat on the bench. No one said a word. There was deadly silence in the house.

Rosa was the first one to speak,

— Mom, what has Michael said?

Mindlya looked at her daughter with cloudy eyes and replied quietly,

— He buried our Shmul. He was killed on the Romanian border.

Gersh wept, grabbing his head with his hands. Moisha who sat next to him, embraced him by the shoulders and said,

— I don't believe him. I believe Shmul is alive. My heart tells me that my brother is alive.

Wiping the tears off her face Mindlya whispered,

— I, too, believe that he is alive. I don't see him dead. He is alive.

Old Hanna did not say anything. She just sat there silently.

RIVKA'S DEATH

Terrible news shocked the village the next day. Rivka had gone to Dobromil to get some food. Somebody had promised to give her some sugar in exchange for a few valuables.

All the valuables she had were just a little ring and earrings which she inherited from her grandmother. The girl took them with her and went to Dobromil. There by the church a policeman stopped her and pulled her into the Gestapo. After a while Commandant Filus arranged a "show" for the residents of Dobromil. Half-naked, beaten almost to death, Rivka was pulled by ropes like a dog across the square to the gallows. She hung there for two days with a sign that said "Jew" on her chest. The policeman who had taken her to the Gestapo was rewarded with a can of jam.

Rivka's mother mourned her daughter; however, no one dared to go to Dobromil to get her body.

Mindlya went to her neighbors' house to try and console the desolate mother in her grief. She hugged the woman and whispered quietly,

— I thought Rivka was going to be my daughter-in-law. And everything turned out so badly. Yesterday when I was told that Shmul had been killed, I was as heart-broken as you are now. But I did not see my son dead, and my heart feels that he is alive.

The women cried, hugging each other.

Every day more and more terrible news came. The Jews got frozen with fear from listening to similar stories. Everyone had just one question: Why? The answer was always the same: they were only guilty of being born Jewish. Half a Jew, a quarter Jew, even the tenth generation of that strain was to be eliminated. The Jews were to be wiped off the earth.

LAST DAYS IN KVASENINA

The Germans ordered all the Jews of Kvasenina to leave their houses and move to Dobromil.

That night all the Leventhals gathered at the table. Old Hanna, who was over ninety six years old by that time, sat on the bed. Everybody was silent. Leon was the first to begin.

— We are leaving our home. We are allowed to take only things we are able to carry with us.

— Leon, where are we going? Where are they moving us? — Mindlya wondered.

— They say it will be to work, but I don't know where, — Leon replied quietly.

— Leon, I am not going anywhere. I'd like to die in my own house, — It was Hanna's voice.

— Mom, we are going to Dobromil. We have relatives there. We will stay with them, and then we will see what happens next, — Gersh said.

Hanna agreed.

Everybody was very anxious while they were packing. Leon put all his best things in a trunk with Shmul's possessions, items Mindlya had carefully saved for his return from the army.

— Moisha and I will take this trunk to the priest, — Leon said. — If anyone comes back, the Holy Father will give it to him. The Germans will not touch him because he is Christian. We will carry the trunk at night. Put all the valuable things into it, whatever we cannot take with us.

— What if he doesn't give it back, Leon? — Gersh was in doubt.

— How could he not? He won't commit such a sin, — his older brother assured him.

In the dead of night Moisha and Leon took the trunk with the things to the priest.

The priest opened the door and muttered,

— Come inside quickly... Has anyone seen you?

— No, Holy Father.

— That's good... What have you got here?

— Holy Father, we have brought our things for safe keeping, — Leon said. — If anyone from our family returns home, please give these to him. If no one comes back, then better you keep them than anyone else.

— Sure, sure, don't worry. Everything will be safe, — the priest muttered. — Here, put the trunk in the corner and leave discretely, so that nobody sees you go.

Moisha and Leon placed the trunk where they were told, said good-bye and left the house.

Leon walked with his head lowered; thoughts were jumbled in his head. What should they do next? His nephew interrupted his painful thoughts.

— Uncle Leon, I did not like that priest one bit.

— Why not? — he wondered.

— He didn't look us in the eyes and tried to get rid of us as soon as possible. I think he is ransacking through our things as we speak.

— Yes, Moisha, I think so, too, — Leon replied. — But we didn't have any other option. Maybe he has at least a little bit of conscience. After all, he is a Holy Father.

With that thought, they went back home.

The next day the door flew open and the headman Opryshko appeared in the doorway. Under the Polish and Soviet power Opryshko was just a stable man. Now, his power had gone to his head. He performed his duties with great zeal, trying to suck-up to his new superiors and trying not to betray the "high trust" of the new power. The headman's visit to the Leventhals' house was another example of his abusive ways.

Gersh stood in front of the "guest" as pale as a wall.

— What can I do for you, Mr. Opryshko?

— Where is your bastard?

— There are no bastards in my house, Mr. Headman, — Gersh tried to object.

The headman did not like the answer and hit him on the face with his whip.

Gersh doubled up with pain. Screaming, Mindlya rushed to her husband.

Meanwhile Opryshko confidently entered the house.

— Where is Moisha? — he asked strictly.

Moisha stood in the corner. Rosa shielded him with her body.

— Aha! You are hiding, skunk!

He pushed the girl away with such force that she fell down. The headman began to beat Moisha with his whip.

— Mr. Opryshko, have mercy, he is just a kid, — Rosa implored.

— Liquidate the Jews in their mother's womb! This is our motto.

Opryshko bared his teeth and, grabbing Moisha by his thick hair, dragged him out of the house.

Mindlya fell to her knees in front of the headman and begged him with desperation in her voice.

— Spare my child, Mr. Opryshko. Do not destroy the innocent soul. Take me instead of him.

— Old fool, — the answer was, — who needs you?

Mindlya stayed on her knees.

— I am taking him to work in the forest, to log timber, — relented the headman.

Everybody felt relieved.

— Mr. Opryshko, when will he be back? We are to leave Kvasenina in two days, — Mindlya implored from her knees.

— He will catch up with you there, don't you worry, — Opryshko roared with laughter pushing Moisha ahead of him.

They had barely got out of the house when Hanna yelled to her granddaughter.

— Rosa, put bread and whatever else we've got for Moisha to take with him for the trip.

The girl quickly put everything she could find into a bag and wanted to rush after her brother, but Mindlya stopped her.

— No, Rosa, I will run. I am his mother. They will let me give him some food for the road.

Mindlya grabbed the bag and rushed to overtake the headman.

— Mr. Opryshko, wait! Mr. Opryshko, — she implored out of breath. — Please let me give Moisha a little bit of bread for the road.

— Get out of here, — the headman responded and threatened her with the whip.

— Mr. Opryshko, — Mindlya didn't give up, — I will be grateful to you forever. After all, you have children of your own. I will just give him a slice of bread, and God will repay you for that. Please, let me do it; he won't be much of a worker without food.

Opryshko grinned widely.

— You Yids should be taught to work under whip. Otherwise you don't get it. The Germans will establish the order for you!

With that he hit Mindlya with the whip with terrible fury. Clothes did not protect the body of the elderly woman. There was a bloody band spreading on the woman's white blouse.

When Moisha saw that, he rushed to his mother's help.

The headman got even more furious and began to whip them both wherever he could strike.

Mindlya gave Moisha the bag with the food and whispered,

— Run, son, run.

She was trying to put her body under the blows.

Moisha grabbed the bag and ran as fast as he could.

When Opryshko saw that the boy was running away, he dropped Mindlya and ran after the escaping boy. Soon he caught up with Moisha, grabbed him by his hair and began to whip him.

When he got tired of beating his humble victim, he growled like a wild animal. All beaten up, with bruises all over his body, holding his bag with the bread tightly to his chest, Moisha could barely drag his feet.

Moisha joined all the Jewish teenagers between the ages of fourteen and eighteen who were gathered in the church yard. The newly-appointed Ukrainian policemen carried whips and rifles and surrounded the teens. They counted the boys and then took them to the forest to log trees.

Beaten and bloody, Mindlya came home.

Gersh looked at her with horror, not knowing what to say.

Hanna asked Rosa to bring her some water and began washing off her favorite daughter-in-law's wounds.

— They will kill us all, — Mindlya whispered.

Leon was silent. Gersh sat on the chair silently, keeping his head low.

— What should we do? They will kill my children, — Mindlya cried. — They don't consider us human. Where are they taking us? Tomorrow we will have to leave our house.

— They will take us to work, — Leon said quietly.

— What work, Leon? — Hanna raised her voice. — Can I go to work? No, my darling son, they are going to kill us. The young must go to the woods.

— You see, mother, the policemen behave even worse than the Germans. Who would have thought that Opryshko could be such an animal? — Gersh said.

— We have all lived so well together, we haven't offended anyone. Why are they doing it? They are beating women and children almost to death. What will happen to Moisha? He doesn't have any warm clothes. They took him with whatever he had on. You should have seen him beat Moisha. How will he be able to work when he has been so beaten up? — Mindlya cried. — What will happen now? We are not even able to find out where he is!

IN THE GHETTO

Early the next day Opryshko burst into the Leventhals' house again — this time, entering like a bandit without even knocking. He stood in the middle of the room wearing German boots made of good leather, and barked,

— Come out!

— Mr. Opryshko, — Rosa tried to say something.

— Shut up, sheeny brat! — he barked and hit her with the whip.

Rosa screamed with pain and at that moment Mindlya rushed to her and pushed her aside. She stood in front of the headman fearlessly looking him in the eyes.

Opryshko was struck dumb: he did not expect such a rebuff.

Recovering, he rapped out,

— Come out one by one. You are permitted to take only the most valuable items that can be carried.

Everybody kept silent.

— What's the matter? Have you gone deaf? Be grateful that I am providing a cart for you. You will be driven to Dobromil, but I can always change my mind and force you to walk like cattle.

Roaring with laughter, he left the house.

Hanna took her small bundle, turned to her sons and said,

— I'd rather he killed me here and I would be with your father. After all, my whole life was in Kvasenina. Why do I need to go somewhere else?

— No, mom. You are our support. You have given us wise advice so many times. We need it so much now, — Leon said quietly and looked at his brother.

Gersh nodded in acknowledgement.

One by one they began to come out of the house. Each of them held a bundle of possessions.

The headman stood by the gate, grinning and waving his whip.

With their heads low the sons led their mother to the cart, followed by Mindlya, who held her head high and had Rosa tightly by her hand.

She did not feel any fear at that moment. Always timid and obedient, she did her best fulfilling her duties as a mother, wife and daughter-in-law. She worked diligently all those years and raised the children. And what was going on? Her children were being taken away from her one after another. And who were these strangers? Why were they deciding their fate? Mindlya did not think of herself. Fear only attacked her when she thought of Moisha and Rosa. Would there be another chance to see her youngest son?

They were all placed in the cart and taken to Dobromil in accordance with the German order.

In Dobromil

There was a ghetto formed in Dobromil — an area designated for Jews to reside in. All Dobromil Jews were forced there. They were forbidden to leave the specified area or to communicate with the local residents. The ghetto territory was under barbed wire and was guarded by the Ukrainian policemen.

The ghetto was located between the synagogue and the catholic church. A high stone wall separated it from the whole world on one side with the barbed wire on the other.

There were rumors that all the Jews from Kvasenina would also be placed in the ghetto. But the rumors did not prove true.

The cart with the Leventhals stopped by the catholic church. Everybody was ordered to get off. Leon was glad and whispered to his brother,

— Gersh, we will now go to our relatives. It's right around the corner. Take mom under her arm and let's go there quickly, and then we'll see.

Without hesitation the sons scooped old Hanna under her arms and almost carried her around the corner with Rosa and Mindlya running after them.

They managed to pass out of any strangers' view. They came to the house owned by Hanna's first cousin once removed, a distant cousin of the Leventhal brothers.

Leon knocked on the door. Nobody answered. He knocked again. There was a rustle behind the door and they heard a quiet question.

— Who's there?

— It's me, Leon. Open up.

The door opened and Leon and the others quickly came inside. It was difficult to tell in the dark who was in front of them.

— Leon, — they heard from the corner, — I am here, Leon.

Leon followed the voice and finally he saw his cousin's wife, Sara. She was sitting on the bench.

— We are asking you to help us. We don't have a place to stay, — he bowed to the woman.

She was silent.

— Mrs. Sara, we ask you for shelter, temporarily, until we find a place to stay, — Gersh repeated.

Mr. and Mrs. Fluger looked at the Leventhals in silence.

Everybody was confused.

Hanna broke the silence.

— What is going on here, Mr. Fluger? We were in the village and we don't know anything.

— We cannot tell you any good news. Our situation is terrible, — Mr. Fluger finally responded in a dull voice. — We are being bullied and killed. And the local residents seem to be out of their minds. The policemen are killing the children and the old. We have been ordered to come to the city hall with our things in three days. I have no idea what they are going to do with us.

That news shocked them all. Their last hopes were shattered.

Hanna asked for permission to sit on a chair. Mindlya sat on the floor next to her.

— What should we do? — Leon asked.

— I don't know, — Mr. Fluger replied. — I do know one thing: we are doomed. What I saw with my own eyes goes beyond imagination. They force everyone to the railway station where freight trains are waiting. They force everybody into the cars and send them somewhere. You know Leon, it's over a mile from the city hall to the station. They follow them all under police escort. Those who resist are shot. Those who are not able to walk are shot, too. The road to the station is the road of death. And the Ukrainian policemen rage like wild beasts.

That news completely stunned the Leventhals. Everybody sat very quietly not knowing what to do.

— You may stay here. I just don't know whether it will help you in any way.

They had dinner together. They all sat quietly with their heads down as though at a wake.

The next day did not bring anything good. Leon went out into the street hoping to find a place for the family to stay, but it was not possible: nobody wanted to even talk with him.

Everything in the town had changed drastically. Jews had no right to walk on the sidewalks now. They had no right to enter restaurants and cafes. Everyone had to wear yellow identification hexagrams on their sleeves.

The town crawled with policemen and Germans. The Commandant of the town was known for his bloodcurdling violence. The Gestapo was now in the building that used to be the military enlistment office.

Frequent executions were held in the town, but the executioners most loved to bully Jews. The Jews were afraid to leave their houses, but it didn't help much.

Finally, Leon had some luck and found a place to stay: a Pole, Mrs. Pogranichnaya, rented her basement to him for 30 zloties. Mrs. Pogranichnaya was a kind woman. She felt sorry for the Jews, although she was afraid to say it aloud.

A building that used to be the Dobromil police department, 2004

The next day Mindlya, Gersh and Rosa moved into the rented apartment, and Leon, with Hanna, stayed with the Flugers.

On Friday morning Leon decided to try to get some bread. As usual, he dressed and went out. He heard wild screams a block away from where he was and hid in one of the doorways of the nearest house. What he saw from his hide-out terrified him.

The Jews were herded like cattle. If anyone stumbled and fell, he was shot at once. Those who attempted to run were shot, too. The guards — Germans with machine-guns and specially trained German Shepard dogs — did not hesitate for a second to pull the trigger. The police, formed of local Ukrainian residents to assist the Germans, beat the people with whips and clubbed everybody without exception — the old, children, pregnant women, women with babies in their arms — after which they were shot.

Hiding under the stairs in a corner, Leon was waiting for the massacre to end; but unfortunately it lasted for a long time.

All those poor people were forced into the wide open synagogue doors. When the space inside was filled up completely, the big beautiful doors with two stars of David on them were shut tight and locked. The policemen and the Germans with the dogs surrounded the synagogue.

Local Ukrainian residents hid in their houses, too. Only the most curious peeped from behind the curtains to watch what was going on. They saw the policemen pour gasoline on the walls and doors of the synagogue. They heard the people locked inside praying loudly.

The whole town froze, waiting, refusing to believe what was happening.

There were dead bodies lying on the road. The policemen dragged the bodies to the synagogue making a big pile out of human bodies, which was also doused with gasoline.

Silence came. Eternity froze in that moment.

One of the policemen threw a burning torch on the bodies by the synagogue doors. Black smoke shot into the sky mixed with the screams and coughing of the people burning alive. Wishes, screams and cries were addressed to God and the people. But nobody heard them. Nobody wanted to hear them.

The Germans were laughing hard watching what was going on and the policemen, like helpful dogs, were running around the synagogue

watching carefully so that no living soul was able to escape from the burning building. The brave ones, who broke the windows and jumped out of the synagogue trying to escape, were shot on the spot with amusement.

A terrible medieval spectacle was played out in the town. The fire in the center of Dobromil burned with angry flames and the evil black smoke from it covered the autumn sun.

HERR FILUS

Death flew over Dobromil like a tornado. The death cries and moans of the wretched echoed in the hearts of the people. The bells sang in the Ukrainian Christian Church while the priest, Father Pachkivskiy, knelt in front of the icons. Reaching his hands to the faces of saints, he begged God to help those poor people. Tears streaked down his cheeks. But neither God, nor saints heard him.

The next day ten trucks appeared in the square near city hall, into which young men were pushed by force. The Ukrainian policemen were wildly trying to please the Germans. They beat anyone they wanted with no reason at all, and they shot the old and the disabled without warning.

After the packed trucks left, there was an order for all the people to leave the square within three minutes. Whoever lingered or did not run away within that time period would be shot. Upon hearing that, people rushed away from the square leaving behind the dead and the bodies of severely beaten people who were not able to move. The Commandant personally shot those still alive with his gun.

A young woman with a crushed head laid there with her arms widely spread. There was a two year old girl squatting beside her. Holding her mom's jacket the little girl was weeping.

Inserting a new magazine into his gun, the Commandant shouted to a policeman in broken Russian-Ukrainian (he had studied it in Germany),

— Make the brat shut up.

The policeman ran to the crying girl and kicked her with all his force. His foot was in a German boot with an iron toe and the child's body flew up in the air and fell away from her mother like a ball. The

Germans and the policemen were laughing loudly. The Commandant liked that entertainment very much.

— That will be my target. Throw her up in the air.

The child did not cry any more. The girl's lifeless body was thrown high in the air and Filus' bullet hit it. Wild laughter and shots drowned out the death moans of the dying. Blood and dead bodies were everywhere.

Dobromil's Commandant was an especially cruel and merciless executioner. Everybody respectfully called him Herr Commandant Filus. His favorite dog was always in his office with him — a specially trained German Shepard. With a fierce bared-teeth display on its muzzle, it carefully watched everybody present, ready to attack at his master's order and tear apart another victim.

Filus formed a Jewish committee and a Jewish police brigade. It helped him to get information regarding all the residents of Dobromil and about who owned what valuables.

On his order, all people who owned furs were to bring them and give them to him, and if anyone tried to hide anything from him, he or she was immediately executed by hanging at the market place in the center of the town.

The Jews were evicted from their houses and placed in a ghetto, which was located behind the burnt synagogue. Every day people were taken from the ghetto in big trucks to an unknown destination.

MOISHA'S ESCAPE

Opryshko herded Moisha and the other boys like cattle to and from the forest. He whipped them on their backs with gusto and malice. Back-breaking labor and starvation drained the boys of their last strength. At night after the end of the working day they were herded like cattle behind the fence of the former Osinskiy sawmill, which was located away from Lyatsk (now it is Solyanovatky).

Exhausted and starving they fell on the ground. Moisha still had a little piece of bread left in his bosom. He went aside and tried to eat it so that nobody would see him.

Suddenly he heard a familiar sound. At first he thought that he heard wrong. But the sound — a bird's song — came again. It was the way he and Peter had communicated in the woods. Moisha began to move cautiously toward the sound. He stopped, looked around and crawled again. Finally, almost above his ear he heard a whisper.

— Moisha, it's me. Do not look around. I have brought you something to eat. I will leave, and you will crawl to the bush and take it. I will come again tomorrow. If I am not here, check this place anyway. I will leave a bundle with the food. Moisha, your family has already been taken to Dobromil. People say that from Dobromil they will be sent to work. I will let you know where they are.

Moisha had not expected that. He sat on the ground as if turned to stone. After recovering a little bit, he crawled to the bush. Reaching with his hand into the vegetation he felt around for the bundle and took it out. Quickly untying the knots, he took the food out of the cloth and was stunned: Peter had brought him some salt pork and some rye bread. He did not hesitate for long. He began to eat the food greedily. At that moment nothing in the world was tastier to him than a slice of poorly baked rye bread and a piece of salt pork. Moisha ate and prayed at the same time, asking God for forgiveness.

After everything was eaten Moisha got thirsty. He searched under the bush, but found nothing. Not far from the place he sat there was a puddle of water. Moisha crawled to the puddle and, trying not to disturb the dirt, put his lips into the water.

Suddenly he felt someone step on his head and literally push his face into the water so that he could not breathe. Who knows how it would have ended, if Peter hadn't come to his rescue. He was watching everything that was going on from a hill and saw Korostenskiy — Opryshko's assistant — sneak up on Moisha. Seeing that Korostenskiy was trying to suffocate his friend, Peter rushed down the hill and, with all his might, pushed the unsuspecting bully aside.

Rescued, Moisha jumped up and began gasping for air. Korostenskiy, not expecting the attack, fell down, and Peter rushed back to the forest like the wind to be out of harm's way.

After he recovered Korostenskiy yelled to another policemen for help. As he did not understand what had happened, he began to tell them about some mysterious evil power that had pushed him to the ground.

— What nonsense you are saying, Mr. Korostenskiy, — one of the policemen shrugged his shoulders in bewilderment. — There is no evil power here.

— Yes, there is, — Korostenskiy repeated stubbornly. — Who else jumped on top of me if it wasn't a devil?.. And where did Moisha go?

The policemen looked around, but Moisha was long gone. Gasping he ran into the depth of the woods. He knew the area very well and could orient himself in the thicket even with his eyes closed. He reached the brook and ran down the hill in the water. He stopped only when he heard someone call him by name.

— Moisha, Moisha, stop! It's me, Peter.

Breathing heavily he peered into the darkness.

— Moisha, don't run, they are afraid to go into the woods when it is dark.

Still breathing heavily, the fugitive sat down on the ground.

Emerging from the darkness Peter sat next to him.

— Thank you, Peter, — Moisha said. — He would have suffocated me, if it hadn't been for you.

— He may have, — his friend agreed. — Do you know what Opryshko has done?

— What?

— He threw a grenade into the rabbi's window at night.

— What are you saying? — Moisha did not believe him.

— Oh yes, I saw myself how he sneaked to the rabbi's house at night, pulled the grenade's ring and threw it into the window. Then the explosion came. The rabbi and his little children are badly crippled. Nobody got killed, but they have been badly injured. And there are no doctors here. Just your Rosa took some herbs and concoctions to clean their wounds. And when she was leaving, Korostenskiy stood on the road waiting for her. And when he saw her, he beat her bloody...

— Peter, what is happening? — Moisha asked with numb lips.

— I don't know. I just know that people have gone crazy and hate the Jews.

— But why? Peter, what have we done to them?

— They say you crucified God, — Peter said.

— We haven't crucified anyone. We are regular peasants. Who made that up? Probably, Opryshko, — Moisha protested.

— No, that's what the priest in the church has always said. What, you didn't know? But I think they are now using it to rob honest people. Look, when Opryshko and Korostenskiy came to your house to search, what were they looking for?

— I don't know, — Moisha answered quietly.

— But I do. Money and gold, that's what! — Peter shouted.

— Keep it down, Peter, or they will hear us, — Moisha implored. — Where would we have money from? What gold?

— But they are saying that Yids have got money and gold, and that if pressured enough, they will give everything up.

— Are you nuts, Peter? What are you saying? — Moisha whispered.

— It's not me; it's Opryshko who is saying it. Everybody in the police department says it, — Peter corrected. — Moisha you cannot return to Kvasenina, they will kill you there.

— I know that. I will go to Dobromil to look for my mom. They are probably at the Flugers' place. They are our relatives.

— You don't understand, — responded Peter after some thought. — The Germans have burnt the synagogue down in Dobromil — the one downtown by the city hall. And do you know how they did it? Let me tell you. They forced all the Hassids into it together with the rabbi, women and children. They packed the synagogue so full the door wouldn't close, and then splashed some gasoline on it and lit it on fire. If only you had seen and heard what was going on there. Coughing, screaming, begging, praying. And what do you think the policemen did? They laughed and shot at the doors and windows, so that no one could escape. There are only ruins there now. Every day someone gets killed. Don't go to Dobromil, Moisha.

— But where should I go? There is nowhere for me to go, Peter, — Moisha whispered.

— I've heard that all the village Jews are going to be killed, too. I beg you, do not go to Dobromil.

— I want to go to my mom, — Moisha objected stubbornly. — Whatever happens, happens. If we are killed, at least we'll be killed together.

— Oh, Moisha! You are so stubborn. Okay, let's go to Bald Mountain, — Peter finally agreed. — You will stay there while I find your family. Then you can join them.

95

— Thank you, Peter, — Moisha said. — I've always known that you are my true friend.

The boys got to Bald Mountain. Moisha hid behind the rocks, and Peter went scouting.

MOISHA'S RETURN

The reunion was touching. Mindlya had already lost hope of seeing her youngest son again. When she saw him in the doorway, she almost fainted.

Without saying a word the son ran up to his mother and hugged her and wept like a baby. Mindlya kissed his curly hair and tears rolled down her cheeks. Gersh cried quietly and noiselessly. Peter stood by watching the scene.

After they all calmed down, Moisha told them about his adventures. After Mindlya heard his story, she gave him whatever food she had. They had run out of money. Besides, The Germans forbade selling food to Jews. If they found out that somebody had helped the Jews, they executed the whole family by shooting them on the spot. People were afraid to even talk with Jews in the streets. Mindlya turned to Peter.

— Son, I am asking you, you are the only one who helps us. Please, try to sell my coat. Someone might trade it for a loaf of bread.

Peter nodded, took the coat out of Mindlya's hands, and disappeared.

— Moisha, what should we do? — Gersh addressed his son. — You have seen more than us. We are trying not to go out, but this way we will soon die from starvation. In Kvasenina we at least had something, but here we are completely isolated from the world.

Moisha looked at his father and said firmly,

— We have to go to the woods. That is the only way we can get away. Look, dad, the local residents hate us. Why, I cannot comprehend, but they are even worse than the Germans. What have we done to them? Opryshko beats me every day. Not just me, but the others, too. Korostenskiy tried to suffocate me. Why? They hate us. We can't expect help or mercy from them and to stay here...

Soon Peter came with a loaf of bread and a piece of salt pork.

They all were shocked: bread was excellent, but the salt pork?

— I traded it for what I could, Mrs. Mindlya. There was nothing else available. By getting pork it showed that I was trading for myself, a Ukrainian, and not for Jews.

Mindlya looked at the food and did not say a word. Moisha interrupted the silence.

— Mom, we need to eat. Give up your prejudices. Shmul and I always ate salt pork with the other kids when we went to the pasture. And see — nothing bad has happened to us. We need to survive.

With her head down Mindlya listened to her son. Peter took out two potatoes and handed them to Moisha.

— I stole that. The lady didn't want to trade it for potatoes.

— Look, mom, we've got to survive, — Moisha went on. — Peter will go back to the village and tell Yarinka, and she will send us something. I am sure she has not forgotten us.

Peter nodded in agreement and soon disappeared.

Moisha's return brought joy and gave everyone hope.

PETER'S HELP

Exhausted and groggy, Peter arrived at Yarinka's house. When she saw him at the door the young woman was shocked.

— What's the matter with you, Peter? You look awful. Are you hungry? I've got some soup. Sit down. I'll give you some food.

Peter took off his cap, put it on the bench and sat at the table.

— I have come from the Leventhals, Yarinka. They are in Dobromil.

The woman sat silently on the bench.

— They are really starving. They asked you to send them some food if you can, — he continued.

— Sure, sure. How are they? I am so worried about mother Hanna. She is so old. I wanted her to stay with me, but Opryshko said that he would kill both me and my children if she did. What is going on with this world, Peter? — Yarinka cried. — Opryshko walks under my windows every day and threatens me with the whip. Once he called me a Yid's foster-daughter. But my Michael told him nicely not to call me that anymore. He reminded him that everybody knows I am a Christian and that every Sunday my family goes to church. However, I don't think it makes any difference to him. He is a bandit, and that's all there is to it.

Peter nodded his head.

— If only you had seen him beat these Jewish boys, Yarinka! He is really just a thief with power.

Peter ate the soup, but put the slice of bread Yarinka gave him in his bosom.

— Well, Yarinka, I've got to go, — he looked at her with his blue eyes. — Are you going to give me anything to take to them? They are dying of starvation.

— Sure, sure, — the hostess ran around the house putting some bread, cottage cheese, beans, and apples into a canvas bag. — Tell them I will come to Dobromil tomorrow with my husband and will bring them more.

The boy nodded.

— Be careful, Peter, — Yarinka instructed him. — Go through the woods and gardens. Don't walk along the road.

Peter tied up the bag, placed it on his shoulder and, carefully sneaking out of the house, went through the field to the woods.

Late that night he went to the house where the Leventhals were staying. Upon hearing the secret sign, Moisha opened the door. He was very happy to see his friend at the door.

— Here. I have brought you a package from Yarinka, — the boy said taking the bag off his shoulder.

They all rushed to the bag, but Moisha stood in front of the guest and looked at him with gratitude.

— Thank you Peter. Thank you for everything, — he whispered hugging his friend.

The two friends sat in the corner watching Rosa's and Mindlya's happy faces. They divided the food and put some of it in a package for Hanna and Leon. Moisha and Peter snuck off to the Flugers' with the package.

Hanna was very glad to see Moisha and his best friend. She asked about everybody in Kvasenina.

When Peter said that Yarinka would come to Dobromil the next day and was going to visit her to bring some food, old Hanna was very concerned.

— It's very dangerous, Peter. She can get killed, and she has two young children. I am already old, and it's time to leave this awful world. But she has got to live for her children. Peter, go back to Kvasenina and tell her not to come here. It is too dangerous.

— Yes, dear Peter, tell her to stay away from Dobromil, — Leon seconded his mother. — If anyone finds out, she will be killed. But I'd like to ask you to do something, Peter. I left all our valuable things with the priest in Kvasenina. Go there and ask him to give you some things and sell them or trade them for food. There is some money there, too. If you could buy some grain, Yarinka would be able to bake bread.

— Mr. Leon, why have you given him your valuable things? — Peter wondered. — He doesn't like Jews at all. He won't give anything back. He just pretends to be a saint. But actually, he is as much of a bandit as Opryshko.

— What are you saying, Peter? — Leon was taken aback. — After all, he is a priest. He cannot take such a sin upon his soul.

— I think he is a bandit, — Peter insisted. — But I will try to do something for you. We will see what will come of it.

With these words the boys left and melted into the darkness.

HANNA'S DEATH

Mindlya looked at the food and smiled. It had been a while since Gersh saw a smile on her face. He looked at her and knew what she was thinking.

They went to bed late. Mindlya fell asleep in her husband's arms still smiling. She would have some food to give her family in the morning. She had already planned how to divide the food so that it would last for a long time. Her sleep was deep and undisturbed.

In her dreams she saw Shmul, who came home and helped her around the house. She hugged her son and asked him where he had been and how he had lived without them. But a dog's angry barking scared Shmul and he left Mindlya. She ran after him and asked him to come back. That's as far as her dream went.

She woke up because somebody was holding her hand. Gersh was sitting by his wife and looking at her.

— Gersh, I saw Shmul and I hugged him and talked with him. He looked well.

Gersh was silent.

— Why have you woken me? — Mindlya continued. — I felt so wonderful there.

Gersh nodded and said quietly,

— You were calling Shmul's name all night long. I'd like to have this dream. I miss him so much. I believe he is alive and that Michael Glude lied about everything. I saw in his eyes that he was lying. My son is alive. Alive!

Glancing towards Rosa, who was sitting on the bench, he added,

— And Brick is alive, too. I know it for sure. They are fighting the Germans together.

Mindlya got up, dressed and began cooking. She made stewed fruit from the dried apples and gave everyone a slice of bread with cottage cheese. The Leventhals had a feast for breakfast that morning.

Moisha swallowed his portion in a second. Nobody wanted to go out. They were all afraid of the Germans.

All of a sudden the sounds of roaring cars, stamping boots and barking dogs were heard outside. Everybody froze. The streets were filled with wild screams together with rapid orders in German "Quick, quick!" Bullets sang in the air and shots were heard.

There were sharp blows on the door with a boot. Mindlya began praying. Moisha grabbed the rest of the bread and put it in his bosom.

The Germans started yelling.

— Come out! Get out now! Moisha grabbed the backpack and shouted to Gersh,

— Dad, they are driving us out of the house. Take the suitcase.

— Moisha, I will not be able to carry it, — Gersh answered.

Then the door fell down with a bang and two German soldiers with machine-guns on their chests ran into the room.

"Out, quick!" — they yelled pushing everyone out of the house.

When they got outside they saw a terrible picture. People were being pushed out of the houses and driven somewhere. Soldiers were yelling and shooting. Mindlya was holding on to Rosa. Moisha was helping his father. Gersh was terrified. There were dead bodies on the road. Gersh asked with horror in his voice,

— Do you think Leon and mother Hanna are okay?

His question was not answered.

The Germans herded people like cattle. They didn't give them a minute's break. Suddenly Mindlya tripped and fell, but fortunately, Rosa managed to grab her by the arm. Mindlya got up quickly and they almost ran along the road.

They managed to collect themselves near the catholic church, where they saw a terrible picture: the Germans were putting people against a wall and shooting them.

Everybody was shaking as if they were sick with a fever. It was difficult to believe their eyes. What they saw could not possibly be real. But it was heartrending reality.

People walked the road of death. Koliyova Street was covered with bodies. Residents stood along the street and watched the spectacle. Some of them smiled, happy at somebody else's misfortune; others looked on with empathy, but were not able to help the poor people.

When the Germans burst into the Flugers' house, Hanna was sitting on the bed and Leon was standing by the window listening to the crying and moaning of the poor people outside. Deep in his heart he hoped that they would avoid that fate. But he knew better.

The doors swung open widely and a tall young officer with a gun in his hand appeared in the doorway.

He entered the house and barked out,

"Out! Quick!"

Leon ran to his mother trying to help her get up from the bed. But the German pushed him away and confronted Hanna.

She looked at him calmly with her green-blue eyes and said in good German,

— I am ready to die. Go ahead and shoot!

Upon hearing the German language the officer was stunned and lowered his gun. He quickly recovered and raised his gun again and took a shot.

The woman's dead body fell from the bed.

Witnessing this scene, Leon leaned against the wall, almost fainting. But the German did not give him any time to think, pushing him out of the apartment. Leon joined the stream of people walking on the road. He walked along, not seeing the road or the surrounding people. He couldn't get a hold of himself. He kept seeing the image of his mother's murder.

The stream of people carried Leon along the road of death to the railway station. He saw a young guy lose control and start running, and witnessed the dogs catch up with him and tear him to pieces in front of everyone while the German soldiers laughed wildly.

The bloody spectacle was horrible. There were dead bodies everywhere. Blood was streaming like water. And the living envied the dead.

Lihtman's sawmill was halfway to the railway station. It was impossible to recognize it. Surrounded by barbed wire, with the watch towers placed all around, it looked like a prison.

THE ROAD OF DEATH

Grinding his teeth Leon walked along with the rest of them. Where? What for? Suddenly he heard his name. Not believing that somebody was calling him, he went on walking without looking around. And then he felt someone pull him by the sleeve. As if waking up he turned his head and saw a gray-haired man in a hat. He held a small suitcase in his hand and leaned on a cane. It was obvious that the old man was an educated person.

— Mr. Leon, — the old man repeated. — Sorry for bothering you.

Leon looked at him in bewilderment, not knowing who the man was or what he wanted.

— It's Gud. Itsik Gud, — the old man introduced himself.

At first that name did not ring a bell, but a few minutes later he realized who was next to him. It was Matilda's husband! Leon even slowed down for a bit at the realization, but the old man pulled him along.

— Please do not stop, Leon. The Germans shoot those who fall out of the pace.

They walked side by side. Leon's heart beat so loudly that Itsik Gud could hear it.

— Mr. Leon, — the old man went on after a while. — You probably want to know why I am here without Matilda and your son.

Leon stopped again, but Mr. Gud pulled him by the sleeve.

— Please, don't stop. Matilda and your son are out of danger. My friends saved them. They are already on their way to America.

Kolieva Street – the "road to death", 2004

— What are you saying, Mr. Itsik? — Leon said in quiet amazement. — I have never had a son.

— No, my dear Mr. Leon, you had and you still have a handsome son. Mrs. Matilda gave birth to him after your affair with her. We went to Italy and it was there that Aaron was born.

When Leon learned that news, he began weeping.

— You are a mean person, Mr. Gud, — he whispered. — You stole my happiness. And now, when my life has come to an end, you are telling me that I have a son whom I have never seen and won't ever see now. You are a cruel man, Mr. Gud.

— Mr. Leon, don't be angry with me. I gave your son the kind of life you would have never been able to give him. I married Matilda according to the custom. And it was you, Mr. Leon, who interfered in our life.

— I interfered in your life? No, dear Mr. Gud, it's you who interfered in our life. You crushed our love and took my happiness, — Leon shouted.

— No, dear Mr. Leon. I did everything according our customs and I lived with Mrs. Matilda as our ancestors told us to. We raised a handsome boy who looks exactly like you, in a great environment and gave him a decent education. I left him money in a Swiss bank. Matilda fell in love with me for being a good father and husband, but she has not stopped loving you to this day. We have never talked about you, but I know that she still loves you.

Leon could not breathe. He had a lump in his throat. There was a flame burning in his chest.

— See, Mr. Leon, — the old man continued. — Our roads cross again. I think we will leave this world together.

Leon did not respond. Tears were streaming down his cheeks. He no longer noticed Mr. Gud. He cried, walking in the crowd of people not knowing where they were going.

Mr. Gud stopped talking. He cast glances at Leon, and seeing the expression of grief on his face, almost regretted that he had started the conversation.

Itsik Gud walked calmly and confidently. He knew that his life was over and he was not afraid of death. The important thing was that he was sure that Matilda and Aaron were safe. The money in Switzerland would provide good support.

Mr. Gud was not aware that the train carrying Matilda and her son had been seized by the Germans. All Matilda had managed to do was send her son with a family to France. She went to Dobromil, hoping to find shelter.

Matilda decided she would go see her "devoted" maid, Zosya. She knocked on the door quietly and Mrs. Zosya appeared in the doorway.

— Mrs. Matilda! — she exclaimed in amazement. — Where have you come from?

— Quiet, Zosya, quiet. Let me in and I will tell you everything.

Zosya stepped away from the door letting her former mistress into the house. She was petrified looking at Matilda.

— Zosya, help me. Hide me. I will pay you well. I don't have any other place to go. I don't know anyone else here besides you.

— And where are Mr. Itsik and your son?

— I have no idea, — tears filmed her eyes. — God, what terror is going on. Zosya, hide me.

— How much money does mistress have? — Zosya asked, this time in a steady, cold voice.

Happily assuming that Zosya had agreed to help her, Matilda began to unbutton her jacket.

— All the money and jewels are sewn in right here, — she said anxiously while taking off the girdle.

Zosya took the girdle and began to feel it. Her fingers felt coins and stones and her face became more cordial.

— Come in, Mrs. Matilda, — she said finally. — Is that all you have?

— Yes, dear Mrs. Zosya, that's all I have with me. But I also have some money and gold in Switzerland. When this nightmare is over, I will make you very rich.

Zosya was silent and deep in thought.

Matilda did not know what her former maid was thinking, but she hoped for the best.

Zosya was thinking that if anyone found out that Matilda was staying at her place they would both be shot. If she kicked Matilda out of the house, she would not get her jewelry. And Zosya knew that Matilda had very valuable stones.

Grabbing the girdle, Zosya ran to the next room and quickly hid it behind an icon in the corner.

Matilda was surprised but assumed that act meant Zosya was agreeing to save her.

— Mrs. Matilda, you must be hungry, — Zosya asked returning from the other room.

— Oh, God bless you, Mrs. Zosya, — Matilda said. — I haven't had a bite since yesterday.

— I've got some boiled potatoes. Have a seat, — Zosya put a plate with potatoes on the table and went to the cellar to get some pickles.

Matilda lit into the food.

When she finished eating Zosya gave her a towel.

— Mrs. Matilda, you'd better go to the cellar, and I will call you to dinner at night. This way it will be safer for both of us.

Matilda kissed Zosya's hand.

— I knew it, Zosya. You have always been my guardian angel.

And with these words she went down into the cellar.

Matilda's heart sank when she heard the clang of the locking bar above her head. She tried to convince herself that it was just Zosya and calmed down; but she soon heard the stomping of jackboots and dogs' barking. Matilda flattened herself against the wall.

The locking bar clanged again and the opening to the cellar was released. Matilda heard Zosya's voice.

— She is down there, Herr Officer. Get out, Mrs. Matilda, they have come for you.

Matilda continued to press herself into the wall, as if the wall could protect her.

There was a machine gun burst. The German was shooting into the cellar.

— Get out, quick! — the officer yelled.

Leaving the wall and barely understanding what she was doing, Matilda began to climb the stairs.

When she reached the last step someone grabbed her by the hair, hurting her, as they pulled her ahead.

Everything happened in a second. Blows showered on her body. There were no more thoughts left. It was surprising, but there was no pain, either. Matilda's insensible body was pulled to the church's wall. She did not notice anyone around her. The dogs were biting her legs and tearing her body to pieces. There was just one thought in Matilda's head: "I hope the end comes soon."

Then she saw the beastly bared teeth of Filus' dog and felt it drive its sharp fangs into her throat. Matilda's body was sprinkled with gasoline and burned to ashes at the same place where the dogs attacked her.

The only person Matilda counted on was Zosya, the devoted maid, but she had miscalculated. Zosya called the Gestapo when she saw Matilda on her door step. Her son Aaron, who had become a member of the French insurgent army, was killed in France in 1944 while fighting the Germans.

Mr. Gud never learned any of this.

Leon tried to walk faster in order to get away from Itsik Gud. Gasping, he thought about Matilda. Everything flashed back to him — all the days of their happiness and the months and years of grief. Matilda's image and her beloved features were never gone from his memory. Unaware that he was almost running, Leon continued on his way.

He came out of his stupor when he got to the station. The yelling of the Germans and the barking of dogs brought him back to reality. Recovering, Leon looked around. A vast number of people — the old, women, children and teenagers — were gathered in a crowd. They all were anxious. Babies cried for food or drink. Their mothers were desperate but unable to help them. He saw a woman with a baby in her arms, going from one person to another asking for some water for the baby who was dying in her arms.

Finally, she approached a policeman, got on her knees and asked him for some water. The policeman was confused, but a young German officer came to his rescue. Taking his gun out of the holster, he shot the woman in the forehead. The other shot was to the baby's forehead. People around them rushed aside. The policeman got as white as flour. Apparently he hadn't lost all human feelings and was not able to take such scenes calmly. He stepped aside and threw up. Embarrassed by his weakness he tried to clean himself up.

Freight train cars were already waiting on the tracks. Everything was ready for boarding. Mindlya and Rosa held hands. Gersh and Moisha were next to them. Mindlya was praying and watching what was going on around them.

All of a sudden a German officer walking among the sitting people stabbed at Moisha's back with his finger. The boy looked back, but didn't move. Immediately a series of blows showered on his head. A policeman who was following the officer started to beat Moisha with a whip and yell.

— Trash! You were told to get up!

Moisha managed to stand up despite the ongoing beating. Mindlya and Gersh watched everything in terror.

Pushing and hitting him, the policeman led Moisha to a group of teenagers. The boy wanted to turn around and look at his mother and father for the last time, but the blows hitting him on the head and shoulders did not allow him to do so.

The locomotive gave a long whistle, and the Germans together with the policemen began to force people into the cars. The boarding was accompanied by the sound of whips, shouts of "Quick!", shots, children's cries, and the moans of the dying.

Those who didn't obey were shot on the spot, and those who wanted to ask a question were shot, too. People were herded into the cars like cattle. After they packed the cars full, they locked them. There were dead and wounded on the ground who were finished off with point blank shots.

The selected teenagers were driven to Lihtman's sawmill where they joined other young boys of the same age. The guards accompanying the teenagers were just as cruel as the policemen. Soldiers beat everybody without exception, and those who resisted or lingered were shot without warning.

The cars packed with people stood at the platform. Moans, prayers, and requests for help could be heard from them.

The policemen and the Germans stood aside. The German guards stood there rigorously maintaining "order". Every third soldier had a German shepherd on a leash.

A handsome blonde German officer went along the cars making sure they were locked tight.

The policemen stood in small groups discussing the events, smoking and laughing. One of them said,

— See, the Germans are people of order. They know how to treat Yids.

— Shut up, Michael. It's sickening, — responded the other.

— Why would I shut up? Now Ukraine will be free — no Yids and no communists. The Germans will help us. Our land is rich. We will live well.

The other policeman did not say a word; he stood there quietly with his head down.

A third one joined their conversation.

— They say the Germans are forming an SS army. They equip you with everything.

— Yes, that's true. Ukrainian men are warlike. Remember the Cossacks? That's who we are — Cossacks. We are defending our land, — Michael said proudly.

— Defending it from whom? — the silent policeman wondered in bewilderment.

— From Yids, of course. See, how many there are now? There was no escape from them whatsoever, from this evil tribe, — Michael spat in anger.

— Michael, I don't understand. There are women and children here, — He shut up at once when he saw the look on his colleague's face.

— Women? Children? These are Yids, stupid! Yids!

And stepping onto the platform, Michael began to shoot at the cars full of people. Screams and moans rose to the sky. Blood poured to the tracks, but Michael went on shooting with hatred until he emptied his entire magazine. Nobody dared to stop him. On the contrary, loud approving laughter from his friends encouraged his initiative.

Michael's bullets hit people, killing or wounding them. Rosa and Mindlya fell to the floor covered with the dead bodies and the wounded. Sticky blood was running all over them.

— Mom, why are they doing this to us? — Rosa whispered.

— I don't know, my child. I don't know anything any more, — Mindlya answered with bitterness.

— Have you seen your father? — she asked suddenly.

— No, mom, I haven't seen him.

Gersh lay, hit with bullets, close to them; but among such a number of people — dead and alive — it was difficult to see him. Rosa and Mindlya heard the train start. Now where? They did not know. But the uncertainty no longer bothered them. The living envied the dead.

When the train came to its final destination, the doors were opened. The mother and daughter, smeared in blood, quietly sat close to each other on the floor of the car. Prisoners in striped clothes with a yellow star on their chest silently unloaded the cars. The dead were pulled out and placed on a cart in a heap. Looking indifferently at the strange and already peaceful faces, Mindlya was suddenly stunned: she saw Gersh. His body lay on the top of the pile with arms spread. She instinctively rushed towards him, but a blow to her face stopped her halfway. She fell on the ground and the prisoners pushed the heavy cart to the side. From her knees, Mindlya's eyes followed her beloved husband on his last mile. Leon's body lay on the same cart, unnoticed by anyone. That was how the life of the Leventhal brothers came to an end.

IN THE CONCENTRATION CAMP

Women were herded to a barrack and told to line up two at a time. Rosa and Mindlya stood side by side holding hands. Fear filled their hearts. At the sight of what was going on they were preparing themselves for the worst.

Several women in SS uniforms with black raincoats entered the barrack. Each of them held a whip in her hand.

Mindlya squeezed Rosa's hand tightly and whispered,

— Whatever happens, let's try to stick together.

Rosa nodded in agreement.

Then an order in German was heard.

— Quickly! Go into that room, ten people at a time.

Right after that the order was repeated in Polish,

— Quickly, into the room. Ten people at a time.

A big door on iron rollers slid aside and everybody saw short-haired women in striped prisoner uniforms with hexagrams on the chests. Each of them had scissors in her hands and there were heaps of different color hair next to them. A few SS women in black leather gloves were walking among them drumming whips on their hands.

One of them hit a woman standing in the front with her whip and yelled,

— Why are you standing? You have been told to go, cad!

The SS woman had yelled in perfect Polish. She was a Pole. She whipped the women viciously, herding them into the room like sheep. In the room they were pushed into a chair, where the short-haired women cut their hair.

Because Mindlya and Rosa stood together, they were seated on chairs next to each other. They continued to hold hands, but when the

SS woman saw them she began beating them on the hands with sadistic pleasure.

The mother and daughter let go of each other's hand, but the SS woman did not stop beating them. Blows were showered on their heads and shoulders, and everybody saw Mindlya lean her body forward to protect Rosa from the whip's blows.

The short-haired women cut hair quickly, roughly and carelessly. Rosa watched the locks of her thick black hair fall to the floor. She felt the woman cut her hair and it seemed as if she had cut it to the skin. Tears streamed down her cheeks.

She saw a lock of grey hair and wanted to turn her head to where it fell, but the woman cutting her hair pulled her head so hard that Rosa's eyes dimmed.

It was difficult to recognize Mindlya and Rosa among all the bobbed women who ran out of the barrack. Mother and daughter tried to run side by side, but it was very difficult. They were not allowed to talk or hold hands. If someone fell behind, they were beaten with whips.

They were lined up again to be counted. This time there were soldiers with machine guns and dogs standing on each side. Trained dogs displaying fierce bared-teeth sat ready to pounce at any moment.

Looking around discretely Mindlya saw a sight that made her heart sink. The area was surrounded by electrified barbed wire. There were guards with machine guns across their chests standing on the watch towers. SS men with dogs were guarding the prisoners.

Fear squeezed her heart. Where were they? Who were these people and what did they want from them? She was more scared for Rosa than for herself. Rosa was young and had her whole life ahead of her. She hadn't been married yet and hadn't known a man's caress. Her fiancé was in the Soviet Army. Was he still alive? If only she had been allowed to, she would have given her life to save her daughter. But nobody considered their wishes.

Judging by the behavior of the SS men, Mindlya realized that they all would die soon. They were considered slaves with no right to live.

Mindlya looked at Rosa and her heart bled. She hardly recognized her daughter. Her hair was cut very short making her almost bald; uneven clumps stuck out in different directions. Only her eyes were telling her "Mom, it's me, your daughter Rosa."

Tears rolled down Rosa's cheeks and her hands shook.

Mindlya found the strength to whisper firmly and confidently,

— Hang in, Rosa. We are together. There are two of us, don't be scared.

Her daughter nodded in agreement.

The SS woman counted the women and told them to go to the gates where two German officers and soldiers with metal plates on their chests waited for them.

Barbed wire gates opened and the guards led the women up the road beside the camp. On the right stood a high smoke stack, out of which thick black smoke was rising.

Rosa and Mindlya tried to stay close to each other. On both sides there were German guards with dogs. They growled viciously and were ready to attack their victim at the first order.

Mother and daughter leaned against each other closer and closer. It somewhat calmed them both.

The prisoners were taken to an underground facility where they were all told to undress. Rosa and Mindlya neatly put their belongings into one pile. A metal door on rollers slid aside, and they all saw a large area resembling a bath house with multiple shower heads in the ceiling.

There was an order first spoken in German, and then in Polish.

— Everybody go into the room and take a disinfecting shower.

Rosa hugged Mindlya.

Mindlya tenderly embraced her daughter, kissed her on the fore-head.

— Don't be afraid, my child, we are together. We are so fortunate to be together.

Embracing each other they entered the shower room.

The prisoners were forced inside quickly with harsh yells. The whips were being used and women were weeping, but Mindlya and Rosa no longer paid attention to that. They stood in the center of the room embracing.

Then the door was closed with a loud clang. The women heard a terrible noise as if something was rolling along the walls. At that moment the light went out and the space began to fill with gas. Somebody shrieked hysterically. Somebody coughed. One could hear curses on Germans and words of prayer.

Mother and daughter cuddled even closer. Hugging her daughter, Mindlya whispered,

— I love you so very much, Rosa. Please forgive me for everything. We leave this life, but remember the main thing: we are together.

Rosa kissed her mother on the cheek and replied,

— I love you, too, Mom. Forgive me, too. I am happy that we go together and I am happy to have a mother like you.

They cuddled closer and began to lower themselves to the floor.

The guards opened the door and began to pull out the bodies. The prisoners were throwing the bodies on the wooden carts which were then taken to the crematorium.

One prisoner asked another,

— Help me. I can't manage to get this one out.

When the other prisoner came and saw the two bodies joined together, he said with sadness,

— Do not separate them. See how they hug. It's a mother and daughter. Let's leave them as they are.

They carefully placed the two united bodies on the cart, paying respect to the mother's and daughter's love.

FOOD FOR MOTHER HANNA

After Peter's visit Yarinka was restless. Despite the warnings of Peter and her family members, she decided to put together a bundle with food and go to Dobromil.

When Yarinka's husband, Michael, came home, the first thing that he saw was a bundle of food on the table.

— Yarinka, you are going to Dobromil to the Leventhals, aren't you? — he said.

— Yes. I'd like to take some food to them. We will get by somehow. After all, we are in our own house, but they... Everything turned out so terribly. What a misfortune, — Yarinka muttered.

Michael sat on the bench and sighed heavily.

— Look, Yarinka. If you do this, the Germans will kill us all. They destroy everybody who helps the Jews. Opryshko is angry with us already. I implore you, do not bring trouble on our heads.

— Michael, what are you saying? Mother Hanna raised me; she got us married, and gave us a piece of land. Everybody else turned away from us, but she helped. And it is my turn to help her.

— You won't be able to help her, you just won't. You won't help her, but you will destroy us, — Michael didn't give up.

— Let's go to bed, — Yarinka offered. — Morning brings wisdom.

Getting up at dawn she began to get ready to go to Dobromil.

Michael sat on the bench and shook his head hopelessly,

— You'll die, Yarinka. And you have got a family and children. Think about us.

— Michael, no one will find out, — his wife responded. — I will give them the bundle and come right back home.

— In that case I'll go with you, — answered Michael. — I just cannot let you go alone in these times.

Yarinka hugged her husband, looked him in the eyes and said,

— I love you, Michael. I love you more than life.

— I love you, too, Yarinka. That's why I am asking you not to go to Dobromil.

But nothing could stop the young woman. Taking the bundle prepared the day before she said,

— Michael, why are you so worried? There is just a little bit of food here. Nobody will find out. You will see.

Michael shook his head hopelessly, and they both left the house.

When they reached Dobromil, Yarinka and Michael went towards the catholic church and suddenly came across a stream of people walking along the road. They were the Jews who were being herded to the railway station.

Yarinka stopped and clung to her husband.

— Michael, what is this? Where are they taking them?

— I'll ask around. Let's get away from here, out of harm's way, — responded Michael and pulled his wife aside.

At that moment they saw the Germans place a group of old people at the church's wall. The elderly looked exhausted and starved. Some of them shook with terror.

Three large Ukrainian policemen approached them and began to shoot them point blank. Hit by bullets they fell to the ground, and the policemen were already forming another group of poor people sentenced to execution.

— What are they being killed for? — Michael asked a man standing next to him.

— No idea, — the man replied quietly.

It was obvious that the man felt uneasy at the sight.

— Don't you know, mister? — responded a woman standing nearby in a singing voice. — These are Yids. That's what they are killed for.

There were no other people willing to continue the conversation. Michael pulled Yarinka away from the nightmare that was going on in the center of Dobromil.

When they reached the street where Hanna was supposed to be, they saw with surprise that there were things scattered in the street, along the road and in the yards of the nearby houses. Dead bodies lay among them.

Approaching the house, they leaned on the fence looking around in terror. The young woman began to shake as if in a fever.

Michael took Yarinka by the hand and whispered,

— Don't go there. I feel in my heart that trouble waits.

No sooner had he pronounced that than the head man Opryshko appeared in front of Yarinka and Michael.

— Aha, bitchy tribe, — he said. — Have you come to visit your family?

— What are you talking about, Mr. Opryshko? We have come to Dobromil to buy some salt, — Michael muttered.

— You say to buy salt? And what does this Yid's foster daughter have in her hands? — and he pointed to Yarinka. — Untie the bundle and show what you are hiding. All your Yids have been taken to the station and put into the freight train cars a long time ago, — he added, smiling viciously.

— Where were they taken? — Yarinka asked in a trembling voice.

— To hell, where they will all die. And you should be taken there, too, — and he hit the young woman heavily with the whip.

Yarinka let the bundle go, bent over and covered her face with her hands.

Merciless blows hit the woman one after another. Realizing that Opryshko would not stop until he beat Yarinka to death, Michael rushed to protect his wife, placing his own body under the blows.

— Mr. Headman, have mercy, — Michael asked. — You were at our wedding. You know that Yarinka has been christened. We were wed in church. I beg you, have mercy!

Yarinka got in the corner under the fence like a chicken.

— Do not destroy a Christian soul, Mr. Opryshko, — Michael went on taking the blows. — Better let us go and you won't regret it. We will repay you for it.

The hand with the whip stopped in midair.

— Repay? With what?

— You will see, Mr. Opryshko. Please let us go!

— Well, be careful, — the headman took mercy, — if you deceive me, I'll put you under the ground.

Michael grabbed Yarinka by the hand and pulled her after him. She silently ran with him. They stopped to catch a breath only after reaching Bald Mountain. But even there they could hear shots and the screams of people.

Holding his wife tightly by the hand Michael walked steadily to Kvasenina.

When they got home, Yarinka fell into a dead faint, and Michael began to clean her bloody wounds. Although his shirt was bloody all over, he seemed to be oblivious to his own pain.

The children sat in the corner quietly, watching everything in silence.

— Yarinka, we need to go to the forest, — Michael said, when his wife came around. — Opryshko will kill us. We need to leave right away.

Together they packed what they could, took the kids, and in the dark went through the gardens to the forest. They didn't know then that they would not return home to Kvasenina in 1944.

SALT MINES

After the trains departed, the Germans and policemen went to Lihtman's sawmill, where they began to form a working team from the young men selected from the crowd at the station.

Moisha was sitting hunched over on a rock when someone pulled hard on his backpack. The boy jumped up and turned to face the assailant. It was a big tall policeman. Moisha looked him right in the eye.

— What are you staring at, brat? — the policeman hissed. — Give me your backpack or I'll shoot you!

Moisha took the backpack off his shoulder and handed it to the man.

The policeman hastily looked into the backpack hoping to find gold and jewels, but was extremely disappointed with what he saw.

Disappointed, he shook out the contents of the bag onto the ground, kicked it with his foot, spat and left. Moisha rushed to pick up the desiccated apples and slices of bread and put them in his bosom. Hungry boys who sat nearby saw the food and ran to pick up whatever they were able to grab off the ground. A moment later there was not even a crumb on the ground.

Moisha sat with his head down, agreeing with Peter too late. His friend had been right when he advised him to hide in the woods.

The boys were formed into a line and herded to Peremyshl under intensive supervision by the guards — Germans with machine guns, dogs and policemen. Those who got exhausted and fell down were shot in the head. Those who tried to sit down in order to catch their breath were shot, too. Hungry and exhausted, many young boys fell to the ground where they would be shot by one of the guards. The policemen loved shooting helpless victims.

The guards were having fun betting on how long each prisoner would last. They would wager for money or cigarettes, and they laughed loudly while shooting each youngster.

After the prisoners arrived in Lyatsk (what is now Solyanovatka), they were divided into two groups — "strong" and "weak". The "strong" ones were taken further to Peremyshl, whereas the "weak" ones were sent to the salt factory. Under the Polish authorities, they mined salt in the salt mines, which was then boiled and sold all over Europe. The boys were happy, thinking they would work at the salt factory. But it turned out that there was a different task prepared for them: they were supposed to haul out the dead bodies of people who had been thrown in the mines by the communist authorities.

The deep mines were filled almost to the top with human bodies. It was an awful sight. Some of the boys were screaming hysterically upon seeing such a horrible scene. Some began to throw up at the sight and smell of half decomposed bodies. But there was no alternative; they were either going into the mine to pull the dead bodies out or getting a bullet in the head.

Who were those people killed by the communists?

After the mines were cleared, the local residents came to identify the belongings of their missing relatives and friends, who had been ar-

*The monastery that housed Polish priests prior to their execution
by a firing squad, 2004.*

rested by the Soviet authorities. Priests, who lived in the monastery by Gerburt's castle, had not escaped that sad fate either. They were taken, viciously tortured and thrown into the mine half dead. Occasionally, prior to being thrown into the mine, victims were knocked senseless with clubs.

After the bodies had been pulled out of the mines, immense funerals were held. Priests from all over Poland came to hold a burial service for the innocent souls. Lots of angry words were said. Many speakers expressed their anger with the communists, calling for vengeance for the murdered ones. They called for a pitiless battle against the Soviets for the freedom of Ukraine; for the forming of a Ukrainian Liberating Army and starting a merciless war with the Soviets. And nobody paid attention to the people guarded by the Ukrainian policemen and German soldiers with dogs, who were right there behind a barbed wire fence.

Exhausted and hungry, the prisoners who had worked on getting the bodies out looked at the rally from afar. Many of their comrades had been left inside the mines. They had no strength to get out.

The funerals were over. A huge oak cross was placed at the site of the tragedy and three oaks were planted as an eternal memorial to the people murdered by the Soviets.

While the local residents were mourning their family and friends, a large number of Jews were heading to the exact same place under armed guard. They were feeble old people, women with babies in their arms, children of different ages. People walked with hopelessness written on their faces. They saw how brutally the Germans and the policemen were disposing of them and they did not hope for anything good any more. Those who fell behind were killed. Those who fell from hunger and exhaustion were shot without warning. It was hard to say who was more fortunate — the living or the dead.

The local residents looked at the file with contempt as if they were the cause of their misfortune. Some even threw rocks at the exhausted travelers. The file moved forward slowly, leaving behind the dead bodies of the old, women, and young children. The stream of death led to the salt mines where dozens of strong men in police uniform with clubs in their hands were waiting for them. Nobody understood why they were there or what was going on.

After the first party of people was lined up at the edge of the pits, they were pushed into the salt mines one by one. When the people saw

Former salt mines, 2004. Here, in 1941, thousands of Ukrainian and Polish Jews were shot to death or buried alive.

what was going on, there was panic. Teenagers tried to escape by running, but the dogs and bullets caught them fast. Women screamed and cried, trying to shield their children with their bodies. But nothing helped the poor people. They were all thrown into the mines along with the children. After the execution was over, moans and the sighs of the dying emerged from the mines for a long time.

The young boys behind the barbed wire in the area of the salt factory saw it all and were frightened to death wondering their fate. The German officer gave the young boys an order to line up and go towards Peremyshl. Those who no longer were able to walk were taken to the mines and thrown in half dead. Many walked hanging on by the skin of their teeth, well aware of what awaited them if they fell. Moisha was in that group. He, as well as the other boys, became witnesses to the barbaric liquidation of Jews in the salt mines in the very heart of free Ukraine.

The huge cross erected in memory of the priests and other Christians murdered by the communists at the salt mines still stands today. But there is no Star of David or memorial in memory of the Jews who died there at the hands of the Nazis. Nobody took their bodies out of the mines. Nobody said prayers over the innocent Jewish souls killed in this huge mass grave. To this day these mines are full of Jewish bones. Only the local residents remember the ones murdered by the Soviets and nobody ever talks about how many Jewish women, elderly and children were buried alive in those mines.

PEREMYSHL PRISON

Moisha and other young boys who remained alive were herded to Peremyshl. Where did they get their strength? There was just one thought in his mind: "To survive... To survive no matter what."

In Peremyshl the boys were forced into a prison. The cell was gloomy, damp, and completely empty. There were not even any board-beds in it. A very small window with iron bars was located high under the ceiling. In order to look out into the street you had to stand on somebody's shoulders.

Several hours after their arrival the minors were forced into the yard and lined up. No one knew what awaited them.

This time fate was quite merciful: they were each given a slice of barely baked rye bread and a little bit of soup. Everything was swallowed at once. The Germans counted the boys once again, and after that the Polish policemen took them to unload train cars. When the doors of the cars were opened, Moisha saw a pile of clothes and footwear. There were tiny baby things in the pile, too, like shoes and toys. The yelling of the Germans and the policemen brought him out of his stupor.

One group of boys was told to unload the cars, and all the others were to sort the clothes. Some things were smeared with blood. But everybody tried to work hard without paying attention to anything. There were sounds of policemen's whips hitting boys here and there and one could hear angry yelling by the guards. However, they had already gotten used to the humiliation, insults and beatings, and only thought about one thing: how to survive.

Moisha worked without raising his head, scared to get another blow of the whip. Suddenly he saw painfully familiar colors on one of the things. He pulled it by the sleeve and froze — it was his mother's sweater. The boy did not know what to do. His first instinct was to hide the sweater, but the blow of a whip stopped him. He lowered his head and went on working, aware that he was being carefully watched. But the thought of how to keep the sweater was stuck in his head. After all, that was all that remained in memory of his mother.

No matter how hard Moisha tried to throw the sweater aside, it was nevertheless placed into the pile and taken to be sorted.

After the long work day the boys were again herded to the prison. They were again given a slice of half-baked bread and a spoonful of soup each. It was swallowed in a second. When they came to the cell the boys fell down from exhaustion. They had only one desire: to sleep.

At night their sleep was disturbed by the loud roaring of trucks which drove into the prison yard, and soon the air was filled with loud and desperate children crying. One could hear the Germans laughing, shooting, and dogs barking. Moisha asked the boy sitting next to him to help him look out of the window to see what was going on. A few boys were willing to do it and they raised Moisha up to the window.

What he saw there made him slide down almost unconscious. The boys looked at him in bewilderment, but Moisha was not able to say a word. Then other brave boys decided to have a look with their own eyes at what was going on beyond the window. What they saw there left them speechless for a long time.

Young children were being unloaded from trucks in the prison yard. For the most part they were two and three years old. The soldiers threw the kids like fire wood. They took them by the legs and battered their heads against the wall. Sometimes they threw the kids up in the air and shot them like moving targets. Others were attacked by dogs which cheerfully tore the kids apart. Screaming, crying, yelling and laughter were heard until morning. None of the prisoners was able to sleep a wink. Everybody knew the same fate awaited them. Hope of survival vanished.

In the morning the boys were pushed out to clean up the yard. The scene was horrible. There were tiny crippled bodies lying all over the yard drenched in blood. Many boys fainted at the sight and were immediately shot. Others gasped for air trying to prevent vomiting. Almost fainting, Moisha picked up the children's bodies and put them on the cart. Tears were rolling down his cheeks, and his body shook as if in fever. He no longer had the desire to survive. He wanted to die. The children's bodies were brought into one pile, gasoline was poured over them and their bodies were ignited.

The boys were lined up again and counted. They all stood with their heads down. Nobody wanted to look at the fire. The smell of burnt flesh was nauseating. The living envied the dead.

In the cell nobody talked. They all sat there half-conscious. Moisha held his head in his hands and cried bitterly.

There were three brothers in the same cell with Moisha — twins Abrumka and Motik and their older brother Gersh, who was two years older than the twins. Besides being from the same village as Moisha, they also had the last name of Leventhal and were Moisha's distant relatives. The brothers tried to stick together at all times, helping each other and sharing each crumb. Moisha envied them. If any of his family was there with him, he would have a chance of surviving.

The next day the boys were taken to unload cars full of soap. It was very hard work. The boxes felt like they were full of rocks, not of soap.

A small piece of soap fell on the ground. One of the twins picked it up and put it in his pocket. He didn't notice that a German guard saw everything. A whistle sounded and there was an order to line up.

They were all lined up in a row. The German walked along the row and pointed to Abrumka with his finger. The boy stood with his head low. The German barked,

— Step forward!

The boy stepped forward and immediately two huge policemen picked him up under his arms and dragged him to a pole. He was tied to it so tightly that the ropes bit into the skin of his hands and legs. The German walked along the line of boys looking with approval at the work of the policemen and playing with his whip. When he approached Abrumka, he put his hand into the boy's pocket and took out the soap. After walking along the line with the soap, he said,

— Only work will make you human beings. And this is how we will punish thieves.

He tore the shirt off the poor boy who was scared to death.

Policemen stood on both sides with their sleeves rolled up and whips ready.

The German yelled,

— Begin!

And the policemen began beating the boy industriously. His screams went right to the hearts of his brothers who were watching the atrocity along with everybody else, but there was nothing they could do to help poor Abrumka. Silent tears rolled down their faces. They tried to lower their heads more to avoid seeing their beloved brother being tortured.

Pieces of skin flew everywhere. Blood splattered out of the injured body. Soon the cries stopped, but the policemen continued beating the limp lifeless body as if enjoying it. Soaked with blood like butchers they heard the order,

— Stop, he is already dead.

Grudgingly, they stopped waving their whips, and one them threatened the boys in the line with his bloody murder weapon and said viciously in Polish,

— This will happen to each of you!

And both executioners roared with laughter.

They were ordered to resume work. Scared to death, the boys went to unload the cars, hanging their heads low. And the boy's bloody body hung on the pole until that evening.

HANS

A few days later a group of boys, including Moisha, were sent to work on the gas line. It was hard work especially since it had gotten much colder outside. Hands were freezing, and the wet soil seemed beyond lifting. The Germans guarding them during that time were not as cruel as the prison guards. Some of them — those who were being punished for something — worked with the prisoners. The food was also much better than in prison, and there were almost no murders. At least people were not killed in front of them. The boys were taken to the ghetto for the night, and brought to work in the morning.

Since Moisha spoke German, he was one of the few who could communicate with the Germans. Some used him as an interpreter when they wanted to communicate with Poles. A German by the name of Hans treated Moisha with special kindness. He took him to the village and asked him to interpret to the villagers. When he entered each house he would ask for bread, eggs, or boiled potatoes. While Moisha spoke, Hans put on a very authoritarian face, and all the Poles tried to oblige in order to stay alive. After leaving the village far behind them, the German gave Moisha some food. Moisha was happy to get an extra piece of bread. He was ready to do any kind of work so that Hans would take him along.

One day Hans motioned for Moisha to approach him. Looking around to check if there was anybody listening, Hans quietly said,

— Moisha, we have already finished our work. Everything you were supposed to do is done.

He stopped talking for a while, sighed and continued.

— We have an order. Tomorrow at dawn you will all be shot. Nobody will survive — no one.

Moisha looked at Hans in shock. His knees shook. His hope of survival disappeared with Hans's words.

— Look Moisha, — he heard as if from afar. — I will take you to the village and you will run away. I will let you go.

Moisha could not believe his ears. He stared at Hans silently.

Hans repeated what he said.

— Do you understand me, Moisha? It's your last chance to escape.

Moisha came out of his stupor and responded.

— I have nowhere to go. I am scared. I am afraid of everything. Everybody hates us. I don't know what to do.

Hans looked around again.

— Take your friends with you, just be careful, or it will fail. I will come to take you in an hour. Be ready. This is your last chance to survive.

Hans left, and Moisha ran to the friends which he had made there and explained the situation to them. Only two boys — Yarmak and Shpreher — believed him and agreed to go with him. The rest refused, saying they had nowhere to go and at least they were fed there. They were sure they would be kept as laborers because the Germans needed workers.

An hour later, Hans came back. He yelled at Moisha harshly and pushed him with a gun-butt. Moisha pointed to Yarmak and Shpreher who stood next to him. Hans pushed Yarmak with the gun-butt, too, yelled "Quick!" and herded the boys forward.

When they reached the village, he went into one of the houses and ordered the hostess to give him some food. The peasant hesitated, but Hans yelled at her menacingly and she immediately brought out a pot with boiled potatoes. The German began smiling and nodded his head.

— Good, good.

When he came out of the house he spoke quietly to Moisha.

— Run to the woods and hide there. And do not go to the village. They will report you. Run now while my hands are full of potatoes. Run.

Moisha grabbed a potato from Hans's hands and rushed towards the woods. Yarmak and Shpreher ran after him, leaving Hans alone in the middle of the road.

The boys ran fast jumping over fences, afraid that Hans would change his mind and run after them. Finally they got into the forest and stopped, gasping.

Moisha told them to stick together and follow him as their leader. They agreed. The leader took his group to look for a creek with water.

Making sure nobody was chasing them, the boys climbed high in the pines to see what was going on in the village. Everything was quiet and peaceful.

Soon it was twilight. The boys shared the potato which Moisha had grabbed from Hans. It was time to settle for the night. They decided to gather fallen leaves in a pile under thick bushes and get inside the pile. That's what they did. The boys spent their first night of freedom cuddling each other. Early the next morning they were awakened by a noise. Frightened, they jumped to their feet. Moisha decided to climb the highest pine to see what was going on. Noise and shots were coming from the labor camp. Hans had told the truth: all the minor-laborers were shot. The dead bodies were thrown in a pit dug by the victims themselves and covered with sod to hide traces of the crime.

MOISHA AND THE "FOREST BROTHERS"

The boys thanked God and Hans for their salvation. At that point they were facing lots of problems: how to survive in the mountains without warm clothes, fire, or food, and without even a knife to protect themselves from wild animals. Moisha decided to go to the woods by his native Kvasenina. He felt they would be safer in a place where he knew every tree and rock, but it was not easy to get there.

The boys ate acorns all the time. It was the only food they were able to find. Finally, Moisha decided to go to the house nearest the forest and ask for some food.

— Wait for me here. If I don't come back, you will be on your own.

— I will go with you, Moisha, — Yarmak replied.

— No, we cannot risk that much. Climb a tree and watch what's going on.

The boys climbed high pines and Moisha began to sneak to the house.

When he approached the house, he looked in the windows. He saw only the forester's family there, and knocked.

— Who's there?

— Mr. Forester, it's me, Moisha Leventhal. Please open the door.

The door opened and the forester appeared in the doorway with a gun.

— Moisha, what has brought you here?

— Mr. Forester, please give me some food.

— Come in, quickly.

Moisha came into the house.

— How many of you are there?

Moisha did not want to answer that question. — Please give me and some other boys something to eat.

Woods around Kvasenina and Dobromil, 2004

The forester put some pickled cabbage into a bucket.

— Come tomorrow, all of you. I'll make some food and will feed you all. Right now I don't have anything besides pickled cabbage.

Taking the bucket with the cabbage Moisha asked,

— Have you got any matches? We are so cold.

The ranger gave him a box of matches, but by the expression on his face Moisha understood that the forester was scheming something.

It was time to run out of harm's way fast. And Moisha ran as quickly as he could into the woods holding the bucket of cabbage tightly.

Reaching the pines where he had left his friends, he stopped and whistled.

The boys came down and lit into the treat. In a moment the cabbage was gone.

PETER IN HIDING

After visiting the Leventhals in Dobromil, Peter was going home deep in thought. Suddenly all the memories came back.

He did not have a happy childhood. Who knows how his life would have turned out if he hadn't met the Leventhals. They had always been kind to him, and he valued his friendship with Moisha and Shmul very much. He did not know his mother — she died in childbirth — but Mindlya and Hanna treated him like their son. They surrounded him with kindness and love. What was going on in the world now? Why had the attitude towards the Leventhals changed so drastically? They had never harmed anyone. On the contrary — they had helped so many people. Hanna was known as a healer in the village. She treated people with herbs and helped women to deliver babies...

With these thoughts, Peter entered Kvasenina. As he was passing the Leventhals' house he stopped because he heard some rustling. There was somebody inside the house! Without hesitation, Peter ran into the house hoping to see one of the family members, but to his astonishment he saw Opryshko and Korostenskiy there. The headman turned his head to Peter and spoke in a displeased tone.

— What are you doing here, trash?

— Nothing. I was passing by and heard somebody rummaging in the house, and came in to look.

— Hmm, — the headman responded. — Have you looked? Now leave. You have no business her.

— Sure, Mr. Headman, — Peter agreed. — You are right. I will leave now. But what are you doing here?

— You, brat, — Opryshko growled. — How dare you interrogate me!

Peter was gone in a flash.

Opryshko opened his mouth in surprise: the boy disappeared so suddenly.

— Damn boy, — the headman said, disappointed that he hadn't been able to take out his anger on the boy. He turned around and continued his work.

But Peter had no intention of leaving. Rushing out the door, he hid under the window. He was very curious to find out what the "officials" were doing in the Leventhals' house.

And then he heard Korostenskiy's voice.

— Mr. Opryshko, I cannot find anything here.

— Look thoroughly, fool. They must have gold. After all, Leon was a businessman. He had a profitable business and he dressed well. Where is it all? They only took some clothes with them. And I took those when they got off the cart. Everything should be here, — Opryshko responded irritably.

— What if they already sold everything, Mr. Opryshko? — Peter heard Korostenskiy's voice again. — It's dark. Why don't we come again tomorrow?

— Are you scared? — the headman got angry. — Sure, we'll leave, and what if someone else comes to look for the gold? Everybody knows Yids must have gold. What is this tribe — Yids?

— My Grandfather once told me they are a people chosen by God, — Korostenskiy said.

— Chosen where? In a ghetto or a concentration camp? — Opryshko laughed.

— Look what the Germans make out of them. Have you heard what recently happened in Dobromil?

— No, Mr. Opryshko. What happened in Dobromil? — his assistant wondered.

— Did you known the hat maker? The one who made the best hats? All of Peremyshl ordered hats from him. So, he was hiding in the bell tower of the catholic church and somebody found out. Do you know what they did?

— No, I don't, Mr. Opryshko. But I know there is an order from the German authorities that whoever finds a Jew, or even better brings a Yid to the Gestapo, will get a reward. Usually they give a big jar of marmalade.

— It's true, — the headman nodded in agreement. — Klim and Stefan Belinskiy got it. They caught this little snotty Yid Abrumka Gud. He was about twelve or so.

Peter stopped breathing beneath the window, listening intently.

— And where did they find him, Mr. Headman? — Korostenskiy asked.

— Nowhere, he came to them himself, — Opryshko responded. — If one is hungry enough, he will go into any trap. This Abrumka kid was part of the group being led to the salt mines to be thrown in and he ran away from the pack. The convoy was heavy — both Germans with dogs and our policemen, and yet they missed him. But he did not run for long. One night he knocked on Klim Belinskiy's door and asked for a piece of bread. Klim is cunning. He invited the boy in and promised to hide him in the cellar. The boy believed him. Klim locked him in the cellar and ran to the Gestapo. They came and took Abrumka. They say the Commandant ordered the dogs to attack him by city hall and they tore him to pieces. Yes, the dogs killed Abrumka and Klim Belinskiy got a big tin box of marmalade. He said it was very sweet and tasty.

Korostenskiy sighed heavily. He seemed to be envious of Klim Belinskiy's good fortune and asked immediately,

— So what happened to the hat maker, Mr. Opryshko? Did the one who tracked him get marmalade, too?

— Sure he did. Do you know what a spectacle Filus made of the hat maker? The residents of Dobromil will remember that show for a long time.

— Do tell me, Mr. Headman, — Korostenskiy was interested.

— They brought two strong horses, — Opryshko began with enthusiasm, — and tied them to a wagon. And they tied the hat maker between them by his arms and legs. You should have seen this Yid beg them crawling on his knees in front of Filus, who just kicked him with his boots. When he was tied up to the neap, he no longer howled, but just said prayers in his language. One of the policemen drove the wagon and he rode the horses along Koliyova Street — to the station and back without stopping. If you could only see what was left of the hat maker: just his arms and legs, tied to the drawbar of the cart.

— And where did the body go, Mr. Headman? — Korostenskiy wondered puzzled.

— What a fool you are, — Opryshko got angry. — The horses trampled it into the road. It's impossible to talk with you. Look for the gold, stupid, it's late already.

And they continued to search the empty house.

After Peter had listened diligently to all the news, he decided it was time for him to get out of there. His heart was pounding — he was still in shock from what he had heard. What would happen to Moisha and his family now? They would probably all be killed and would die a painful death.

He ran along the street to the priest's house. There was light in the windows of his house, so it was apparent that he was not asleep.

Peter approached the door, took off his cap, crossed himself and knocked.

— Who is there? — he heard in response.

— Holy Father, it's me, Peter. I have come to tell you something, — the boy replied.

The lock unlatched noisily and the door opened. The Holy Father stood in the doorway in a long white shirt.

— Holy Father, I have brought to you a request from the Leventhals.

The priest did not let him finish, but grabbed him by the shirt and pulled him into the house.

— Are you nuts? What are you blabbering? And right in the street, — he growled at Peter, shutting the door behind him.

— Holy Father, please forgive me if I said something wrong. Mr. Leon asked me to ask you to give me some things that he and Moisha left with you for safe keeping. I will take those things to them to Dobromil tomorrow. They are really starving there, — Peter stammered.

— What's that? What things? Don't you know the laws? All connections with Yids are forbidden. Any person who helps them will be punished severely, — the priest growled.

Peter, pale and frightened, looked at the Holy Father.

— Go home, — he heard an abrupt change of tone, — and I will think of something. I will let you know tomorrow morning what to do.

With those words he pushed the boy out into the street and banged the door shut behind him.

Peter went home with his head low. The house he had inherited from his grandparents had a straw roof and was so old that it had almost grown into the ground. Nevertheless, he had a place to spend the night. He entered the house, sat on a stool by the window and began crying.

After a while, without undressing, he lay on a make-shift bed covered with straw, which served both as a featherbed and a pillow. Exhausted by his emotions and gloomy thoughts, the boy resigned himself to broken sleep. He was dreaming of the mother he had never known. She hugged him tenderly and begged him to escape to the woods away from people. She stroked his hair, but he suddenly felt pain. Peter opened his eyes.

Opryshko was standing in front of him. Peter wanted to get up, but the headman held the boy's thick forelock tightly in his fist.

— Well, brat, I've got you! — he hissed.

Half asleep, Peter was unable to understand what was going on.

Opryshko pulled him off his bed and began beating him vigorously with a stick.

— Why, Mr. Opryshko, — the boy implored. — What have I done? Please spare me!

— Oh, you don't know, do you? Haven't you visited the priest? Didn't you want to rob him? — Opryshko growled.

— No, no, Mr. Headman. Have mercy. I did not want to steal anything. I just asked him...

— Shut up, brat! I will take you to Dobromil and will send you to Germany to work. Only labor will make a human being out of you.

And with these words he dragged Peter out of the house.

Two policemen were already waiting outside. They were residents of Kvasenina and Peter knew them well.

— Well, boy, — they laughed, — you will go to Germany to work. It's better than hanging out here pointlessly.

The boy's hands were tied and secured to the fence. Everything happened so fast that he was still in shock. His thoughts were confused, but suddenly he remembered his dream and his mother's words. He had to run to the woods! But how could he get out of the hands of those bandits? He sat on the ground and saw a piece of glass. He picked it up inconspicuously and put it into his pocket. The rope was tied so tight that it had cut the circulation to his fingers.

Peter turned to the policeman standing next to him,

— Mr. Motse, please loosen the rope a bit, otherwise blood does not come to my fingers. If my fingers get numb, what kind of a worker will I make?

Motse glanced at the boy's fingers. It was true, they had turned almost bluish. He loosened the rope. Peter sighed with relief, thanked him and asked for some water.

The policeman gave him some water and said with empathy,

— You are an orphan, Peter, that's why they bully you.

The boy began to feel the ropes on his hands. He felt that they were tied loosely and that he could get out of them. But if he tried to escape at that moment, they would catch him. He began to make a plan of escape.

At that moment Opryshko appeared on the road leading a horse by the bridle. Coming closer, he took the rope the boy was tied with.

Peter implored,

— Mr. Opryshko, don't let me die! How will I be able to run after the horse?

Without responding, the headman mounted the horse and pulled the rope.

There was nothing else left for Peter to do but to follow him. Opryshko proceeded through the village proudly looking around and the villagers nervously watched the scene from their yards.

They soon left the village behind and continued on their way along the country road. Peter walked behind the horse and the road seemed endless to him.

— Mr. Opryshko, please give me some water, — he asked, but the headman only grinned in response.

— Mr. Opryshko, what kind of a worker will I make if you drag me into Dobromil half dead?

After those words the headman stopped the horse, got down and gave Peter an iron flask with water. Peter began drinking greedily. Opryshko looked around and spit through his teeth.

Peter drank the water, all the while observing everything around with one eye, trying to come up with a plan on how to escape from the headman.

When Opryshko noticed that look he hit the boy with the stick.

— You'd like to escape, brat, wouldn't you? No way! You will never run away from me!

He began beating the boy with the stick. Peter tried to back away, but the rope would not let him.

— What, tied up? — Opryshko grinned through his rotten teeth. — Let's go to together. I'll show you what power is.

And he hit him with the stick with all his might on his back. Peter bent over trying to protect his head from the blows. The headman went on beating the boy for over a mile until he got tired and decided to catch his breath.

Opryshko sat down on the grass and took out some tobacco, planning to roll a cigarette and have a smoke. The beaten sixteen year old fell exhausted on the edge of the ditch. There was one thought stuck in his head: How to escape?

Gradually he freed one hand from the rope, and then the other. He lay quietly on the ground pretending to be asleep.

Finally, Opryshko got up and kicked Peter,

— Enough lying here. Get up. Go ahead.

Peter got up pretending that his hands were still tied.

Opryshko approached the horse in order to mount. And the moment he set one foot in the stirrup, Peter stuck a piece of glass into the horses butt.

Feeling severe pain, the horse rushed ahead and broke into a gallop dragging along the headman who was stuck in the stirrup. Peter ran towards the forest like the wind.

When the boy finally stopped to catch his breath, he was already far from the road. He began looking for a place to hide.

Meanwhile some kind people stopped the horse and helped Opryshko free his foot from the stirrup. The injured headman returned to his village late that night. He stayed in his house for a whole week licking his wounds.

Peter's first night in the woods was a nightmare. He made himself a bed in a deep hole on the very top of a mountain. He dreamed of his mother who fed him and begged him not to go to the village. He dreamed of old Hanna who smiled at him kindly. He also dreamed of Abrumka Gud. He played with the stones, waved and invited Peter to play with him.

A rustle close to his improvised bed woke him. Afraid of attracting attention, Peter almost stopped breathing. Soon the noise went away and after waiting a while the boy decided to leave his shelter. He looked around, got out of his hideout and saw two human shapes below. They were teenagers like him looking for a safe shelter in the woods.

Peter did not know what to do. Should he call to them? Should he let them go? It was scary and uncomfortable for him to be in the forest alone. It would be much easier for the three of them. But after thinking it over for a while, he decided to wait and follow the young boys.

When he sneaked closer to them he recognized them. They were from Dobromil. He did not know their names but he had often seen them at the market place. It looked like they had escaped from the ghetto.

He followed the guys carefully so as not to frighten them off while they were moving towards the village Yurkovo.

Peter oriented in the woods very well. He knew where he was and which way was the best and the safest. When he realized that the boys, who did not know their way around the forest, had chosen a dangerous path, he at last decided to show himself and warn them.

— Don't go there. Germans are there! — he said to them in a low voice.

The youngsters stopped, stunned with fear and surprise.

— Don't go there, — Peter repeated. — You need to go through the upper end. Nobody goes there, but everybody travels in the lower part. Any person who sees you there will report you.

The boys, still in shock, continued to stand there as if turned to stone.

— What are you staring at? Haven't you seen a living man? I am in the same boat as you. I have just escaped from the headman, damn him!

Peter spat on the ground in anger.

— And who are you? Where are you from?

AT LIHTMAN'S SAWMILL

Recovering a bit from the fright, the boys began to tell him their story. Itsik Buk and Dolik Gruver were forced to go to Lihtman's sawmill along with other Jews. Young and healthy boys were taken to one side, but the rest of them were kept on the Northern side in a

Site of Lichtman's sawmill, 2004.
Here, in 1941, thousands of Ukrainian and Polish Jews were shot to death
or buried alive.

large barrack where they used to keep the wood. Women and young children were also placed into the barrack. They were all kept with no food or water. Some fell down from dehydration and were immediately shot.

About 300 feet away, over the barbed wire, there was the river Vyrva. At that time it seemed like a shallow mountain creek. But everybody knew it was a deceitful illusion. In the spring, when the snow melted in the mountains, the creek turned into a fast and furious river. It was especially dangerous during rains.

The water was tempting and some brave hearts forced by thirst tried to get to it through the barbed wire. Their attempts failed — the Germans watched the prisoners carefully. The desperate ones were shot then and there, and their bodies were hung on the barbed wire as a deterrent for others. Everybody knew that death was awaiting anyone attempting to quench his thirst.

In one of the former warehouses a pregnant woman sat among the boards. It was the youngest daughter-in-law of Mr. Lihtman, the former owner of the sawmill. Old Lihtman knew his factory like the palm of his hand and would have gotten out of there long ago, but he could not leave the young woman alone. At night he would go out and bring back food for her. He had a devoted and trusted person on the outside, who helped him with everything. It was a young woman by the name of Paraska. She had been working for Lihtman since childhood, was a nanny to his grandchildren, and all the people at the sawmill loved her for her kind heart and skillful hands. Mr. Lihtman generously repaid her with kindness and supported her whole family who resided in Nizhenkovichy. During those tough times that woman helped Mr. Lihtman selflessly.

The labor started unexpectedly. He gave the woman a piece of wood to bite on to prevent her from screaming, and he snuck out to meet Paraska and ask her to come and help him deliver the baby. They took sheets and made their way back to the woman in labor. Soon the woman gave birth to a son. The healthy and strong baby announced his arrival into the world with loud crying.

At any other time that event would have been the happiest for old Lihtman, but at that moment the infant's cry sounded like a defiance of death. And Mr. Lihtman covered the baby's mouth with his hand.

The mother saw that and reached for the boy.

— Hand him over to me. I will nurse him and he will be quiet, — she implored.

Old Moisha Lihtman gave the baby to his mother.

She took him tenderly and put him to her breast and the baby, as if feeling the danger, calmed down at once.

Paraska looked at that and her heart was filled with compassion. But Moisha said strictly,

— Paraska, take the baby and go home. We will come tomorrow. If not, go to the old place. And please hide my grandson from evil people.

Hugging the baby, Paraska disappeared, and old Lihtman began to help his daughter-in-law. But all of a sudden it occurred to him that he should have first helped Paraska go through the secret passage, so he left his daughter-in-law and ran after the nanny. But she was already out of danger and in a safe place. She cuddled the baby to her large bosom and he was peacefully asleep. Sighing with relief Lihtman went back. But he suddenly felt fear.

There were screams and shots. He hid waiting until everything got quiet. When he reached the place where his daughter-in-law was hiding, he was shocked. The young woman lay in a pool of blood with her head shot. Apparently, someone did hear the baby crying and reported it. Immediately a unit of guards was alerted and they quickly found the woman. Without hesitation Moisha sneaked out of the sawmill's territory and hid in the thick underbrush by the river.

That whole story immediately became known among the prisoners. Somebody recognized the young woman. They all began to discuss the incident.

While all the forces were busy looking for Paraska and the baby, Itsik Buk and Dolik Gruver got out of the sawmill unnoticed and hid in bushes along the river. The young men did not have a plan. They had no idea where to go or what to do. The whole world seemed to be against them. The only decision they could make was to sneak into the woods. They needed to wait until dark, but the forest would be their refuge.

They were sitting quietly in their hide out when there came noise from an area quite close to them by the yellow bridge. The Germans and the policemen were herding the Jews from the sawmill. Shots, screams and children's crying sounded in the air. Itsik and Dolik stayed put in the bushes. They pushed themselves into the ground and held their breath watching what was going on.

The Germans made the prisoners dig a trench. The old, women, and children — everybody who could hold a spade began working. Nursing mothers had to put their babies on the ground and dig with the others.

Suddenly Itsik and Dolik heard a suspicious sound near them and immediately saw the gray head of an old man staring at them in surprise. The boys guessed that it was one of the Jews who had escaped from the sawmill. Moisha Lihtman pressed his finger to his lips and crawled closer, and they began watching the scene together.

What they saw was horrible. After the prisoners had dug a deep trench from which they could not get out of on their own, they were lined up with their backs to the trench. In front of them stood a line of soldiers with machine guns across their chests. The people realized they were digging a grave for themselves. Mothers hugged their children tightly. People were crying, begging, and praying to the sky. There was panic and fear in the people's eyes. Dogs' barked and single shots killed the ones who tried to escape.

And then they all heard the steady voice of a man. It was attorney Karitan, a respected and distinguished resident of Dobromil. He held a two year old child in his arms and he stood on the edge of the trench with his head held high.

When they heard Karitan's self-assured voice, the people quieted and began to listen to his words. Holding his son in his arms, the distinguished attorney stepped forward. His voice was a bit shaky, but it sounded loud and clear. The words he was saying were clear and understandable to everyone. He asked everybody to remain calm, and reminded them about the prophets who had predicted the fate of the Jewish people. He called on them to hold hands, pray and accept death with dignity from the hands of their executioners.

The Germans began shooting and the people started to fall into the trench. The dead and the wounded all fell together. There were over nine hundred people shot point blank by the Germans — young and old, children of various ages. When the execution was over, the officer walked along the edge of the trench and when he noticed any wiggling bodies he personally shot the wounded.

But the moans of the wounded and the crying of the children who had fallen into the trench alive continued. The officer waved to a policeman who sat on a tractor and he began to push soil over the living and the dead, burying everybody alive in the trench. By and by, the moans and crying of the buried subsided. But when the tractor made its first pass pushing the soil over the trench, the ground began moving under it. Those alive were trying to come out to the surface.

The tractor began to move back and forth, leveling the ground and crushing the victims underneath. It got quiet. The Germans left in a line, and the policemen formed a group to have a smoke and discuss the incident.

One of them addressed the tractor driver.

— Well, Mr. Gyk, you have done a great job today.

Gyk looked around, but did not respond.

— Today will become history, — another policeman said.

When Gyk noticed the residents of nearby houses standing by their fences and looking at him in disapproval, he growled,

— What are you staring at?

He was as white as flour. It was obvious that everything that had happened went against his beliefs.

— Go away! Get into your houses, quick! — another policeman yelled at the crowd. Spitting on the ground, he turned to Gyk.

— Well, stay here for another couple of hours. If you see anyone trying to come up, drive over the trench a couple of times, so that there is no trace left of these Yids.

The policeman left with his subordinates, and Gyk stayed in his tractor. He was smoking a cigarette. It was obvious that he was very stressed.

That scene was carved forever in the boys' and old Moisha Lihtman's memory.

They lay pressed into the ground as if it were their shelter. They waited until Gyk drove his tractor away. Then Moisha told the boys,

— I need to disappear and I advise you to do the same.

— How can we do it? And where should we disappear to? — Gruver whispered.

— To the woods, make it to the woods, guys. Have you seen what is awaiting us? Save yourself whatever way you can.

And with those words he disappeared in the bushes.

The boys had waited until dark and crept to the woods, where they soon met Peter.

After listening to that ghastly story, Peter asked,

— Did you know the Leventhals from Kvasenina?

— Shmul who traded cattle? Yes, we knew him.

— How about his brother, Moisha, his mother, his sister Rosa?

— No, we didn't know the rest of them, just Shmul.

— Shmul is fighting in the Russian Army, — Peter said. — If only I could, I would join the Russian Army to fight the Germans.

— So would we, — the boys answered.

MISTER ZALEVSKIY

After Moisha and his friends gulped down the cabbage, they began to think about what to do next.

Moisha was their leader. The warning he had been given by Hans, the German, constantly reverberated in his head: "Do not go to people, do not go to villages, and do not ask for food — you will be betrayed to the Gestapo."

But what else was there to do? They had no winter clothes and no food. Thinking it over again and again he realized that there was nothing left to do but wait until dark and go to the forester for the food he had promised to give them.

When he reached the opening in the forest where the forester's house stood, Moisha decided to climb a high pine first and watch what was going on. Later on he thanked himself many times for that precaution. As soon as he settled on top of his observation post, he saw policemen walking around the forester's yard. The host himself came out on the porch and, with a wave of his hand, showed them the area of the forest where Moisha had gone the night before. It was clear that the forester had immediately called the policemen so that they could catch the escaped boys.

Moisha held his breath. Yes, Hans was right. Moisha, afraid to move, sat in the tree until late that night. He saw the policemen's torches light up the darkness while they were searching the area.

Finally, after he had made sure the policemen were gone and the danger was over, he climbed down the pine tree and began to creep carefully to the shelter where his friends were waiting.

When they saw Moisha come back with empty hands, the boys got very upset and began asking him questions about what had happened.

Moisha told them what he had seen and gave his conclusion.

— It'll be all over for us if we go to any houses and ask people for food. No wonder Hans, the German, warned me against it.

— What should we do then?

— If that's the situation, we will die of hunger and cold...

— Winter is coming, and we don't have any clothes, or shoes, or food...

— In summer there are at least berries, but what is there in winter? — the boys interrupted each other.

— We cannot even start a fire because it will attract attention...

The situation was very grave. Moisha sat there with his head down, and the rest of them looked at him as if he could solve all their problems at once.

"The leader of the pack" knew one thing for sure: they had to go deep into the woods immediately, before the policemen with dogs began a massive search.

The boys agreed with Moisha and they began to move into the depth of the woods.

They walked for half the night. Moisha knew the area very well. As children, he and Peter had visited all the secret places and caves there. There was one cave which he and his friend especially liked.

Moisha decided to take a rest in that cave, and think about what to do next. He knew that there was not much space in it, but the boys would be able to huddle together to keep warm and fall asleep.

Moisha was the first to climb into the darkness, but as soon as got in the cave he stumbled on something warm.

He jumped away in fear and the thing he stumbled on did the same. His heart just about jumped out of his chest in fear. But then he heard a human voice.

— Who are you?

— And who are you?

— No, you go first — tell me who you are!

That voice seemed very familiar to the boy, and he blurted out at once,

— I am Moisha, and who are you?

— I am Peter.

Moisha did not believe his ears. It turned out that he had come across his best friend in the cave.

— Peter, it's me, Moisha! Don't you recognize me?

Peter rushed to hug his friend.

— Moisha? Where did you come from? They say that your whole family was shot. Have you come from the land of the dead? And where is your family?

— I don't know, Peter, I don't know anything. Have you got anything to eat? It's really bad without food. My friends are here, also. We escaped from the ghetto, and those who stayed were all executed.

Peter rustled in the darkness and put something into Moisha's hand. Feeling food in his hand Moisha quickly put it into his mouth without looking at what it was. It was a piece of salt pork with bread. Moisha was chewing hungrily, and Peter said with a grin,

— Go ahead, Moisha, eat. I am not going to tell Grandma Hanna.

When he finished Moisha responded.

— Peter, Grandma Hanna was shot by Filus, Commandant of Dobromil, right in her bed. She refused to go to the train cars.

— What happened to the rest of them? — Peter asked after some silence.

— I don't know... They may have been killed or put in the camps... I have no idea. May we join you in this cave?

— It's a bit tight here, Moisha, but the more the merrier, — Peter answered. — Go call your friends. Morning will bring direction. We will sleep and then decide what to do.

The boys cuddled up with each other, got warm quickly, and fell asleep. They were so exhausted they could have slept for days. But shots coming from nearby woke the boys about noon.

What was it? Had the Germans or policemen managed to track them down?

Their hearts beat so loudly that it could be heard from a distance of a few feet. A dog was barking very close to them.

"Is this the end? Is it really the end? — the thought was burning in Moisha's head. — Such a pity. I survived so much, have been through so much to get caught so stupidly."

Suddenly there was a man's voice saying sternly,

— Who is there — come out. Do not be afraid if you are a good person.

Moisha was the first to come out of the cave. A huge man in a vest stood in front of him. He held a rifle in his hand.

— Who are you? — he asked, this time kindly.

— We hid in this cave from the cold, — Moisha answered evasively.

— Sure, from cold. You must have escaped from the ghetto. Don't be scared. How many are in there?

Moisha didn't know what to answer.

— You must be hungry, aren't you? — the stranger asked again.

The boy nodded. The man put his hand into the bag hanging on his side and took out a piece of bread.

Moisha could not believe his eyes. With shaking hands he took the bread not able to understand whether he could take a bite or call his friends first.

— Well, call your friends, — the stranger helped out.

— Hey, guys, come out, don't be afraid, — Moisha called.

The boys emerged one by one like shadows.

— My name is Mr. Zalevskiy, — the man introduced himself. — I am a hunter. Do not be afraid of me. I was a prisoner of war during World War I, then got married and stayed in this area. I have sons your age. Don't be afraid, I won't betray you. Share this piece of bread and wash it down with water, and when it is dark come to my place and I will give you something to eat. We will talk there.

— Thank you, Mr. Zalevskiy, — said Moisha. — Please, if you will, divide this piece of bread for us. Otherwise we are so hungry that we'd probably fight for each crumb.

Zalevskiy nodded and divided the bread into equal portions. Then he took out two apples and divided them, too.

The food was consumed in a moment.

As he listened to the boys' story about everything that had happened to them, he nodded compassionately. After that he said,

— You should not go and ask people for food. They will report you. I will give you rifles. When the Russians retreated, they abandoned a lot of weapons. I picked up everything and hid it in a hole in a forest clearing. I will teach you to shoot. You need to learn to hunt animals. We don't know how long the war will last, but it looks like it will be quite a while. I'm afraid this is not very good news for you.

The boys listened to the hunter keeping their heads low.

— Mr. Zalevskiy, what do you think, will the Germans win the war? — Peter wondered.

— No. I am sure they will lose it. They treat prisoners of war and Jews very badly. The policemen created from local residents commit

atrocities. Power obtained like this will be unable to win the war. They are ferocious brutes and they don't even hide it. And you boys must live to tell about all the atrocities they committed.

When it got dark the boys went to see Mr. Zalevskiy. He lived outside the village Yurkovo, in a house surrounded by forest.

Their hostess met the boys with a pot of boiled potatoes and the baked meat of wild boar. The boys began to eat hungrily, but Mrs. Zalevskaya did not let them overeat,

— Do not eat a lot, guys, or your stomachs will hurt. You can take all the leftovers with you.

Mr. Zalevskiy looked at the boys, frowning. He was pondering how to help the children.

— Listen to me attentively, — he said finally. — You cannot stay in that cave. Sooner or later you will be found there. You need to dig a hideaway by a creek. In winter it will be possible to walk along the creek without leaving tracks. The hideaway should be made under a big hollowed-out tree, so it is possible to make a hole for fresh air. We will begin digging tonight. I know one suitable place.

— For now you will eat game, — he went on. — I have shot a few wild boars and put the salted meat in barrels. The barrels are buried in the forest. I will show you one. You need to divide the food. Do not think that it is easy to get game in the forest. If the Germans find out, and the people here are such that they will report you without hesitation, then I will be hung along with you.

The boys listened to the hunter holding their breaths.

They tried to do everything the way Mr. Zalevskiy had instructed. They learned to shoot. They learned to catch rabbits. They avoided coming out of their hideaway when there was a lot of snow around, so as not to leave tracks. And everything would have been fine if one of the villagers hadn't snitched on Mr. Zalevskiy to the police. Hunting was strictly forbidden by the Germans. The policemen caught Mr. Zalevskiy's oldest son. The boy was beaten day and night, but did not betray anyone. On the third day he was hung in the square at the center of the village. His body hung there for three days.

Mr. and Mrs. Zalevskiy hid in the forest hideaway with their five other children. By that time, Moisha, Peter, Yarmak, Shpreher, a boy name Berger, the Feniky brothers and the son-in-law of Kvasenina rabbi Volkenfeld, lived there, too. Shpreher had lost his hearing and hardly ever left the hideaway. Mrs. Zalevskaya mourned her son, and her husband dreamed of avenging his death. In that manner the Zalevskiys stayed with the boys for half a year, saving themselves until the Russian troops arrived.

When the cannon's roar got closer, they all got extremely happy, but Mr. Zalevskiy continued to warn the boys,

— Do not go to the village — you will still be killed there. The local residents are very mad at Jews. When you do leave the woods, go immediately to the Russian Army. This is the only way you will survive.

The Feniky brothers did not follow Mr. Zalevskiy's advice. They came from a rich family. In their village, Yamnoye, they had buried some jewelry. They hoped to dig it up and start a new life. But as soon as the brothers showed up in the village, their fellow villagers caught them and hung them in the center of the village, even though the Soviet Army had already liberated it.

Berger was killed when he returned to Poland, also after it had been liberated by Russian troops.

To the Soviet Army

Following Mr. Zalevskiy's advice, Yarmak, Shpreher, Peter and Moisha began to make their way to the Russian troops who were passing through the nearest village.

On their way they suddenly came across Ukrainian militants with machine guns on their chests and grenades tied around their waists.

When they noticed the boys one of the militants asked,

— Who are you?

— We are escaping from the Russians, — Moisha answered.

— Where are you going?

— Abroad.

— That's good. Would you like to join us?

— We need to go to the village first.

One of the militants looked at the boys with suspicion.

— Are you Yids? You look like them with your faces and all.

Peter stepped forward.

— You know, I'd like to see one myself. But, fortunately, they have all been caught and liquidated.

The militants laughed cruelly, and Peter continued.

— We will just run to the village, get some food and go abroad. We will probably see you there. God bless you, brothers. Long live Ukraine!

The militants bolted upright and barked,

— Long live Ukraine!

With that, the boys left.

After walking away from the militants, they started to run, trying to reach the village without encountering anyone else.

Upon entering the village they saw Russian soldiers who pointed their machine guns at the strangers when they noticed them.

— Stop, who's there!

The boys raised their hands and responded,

— Don't shoot! We are friendly. We have been looking for you. Take us to the commander.

The soldiers searched the boys and took them to the commander. They told him everything that had happened to them. After listening to them the commander lowered his head, deciding what to do with the unexpected reinforcements.

— All right, — he said finally, — you will eat and you will fight in our unit. Are you ready?

— Yes sir, comrade commander! — the boys answered in chorus.

— Good. You will have a meal, a hair cut and then off to the Russian army. We need people.

That's how military life began for Moisha, Peter, Yarmak and Shpreher. The companions in arms fought shoulder to shoulder, helping and supporting each other through tough times. They bandaged each others' wounds and rushed back into the fight. The desire to avenge everything they had seen and experienced gave them strength.

PART THREE
AT THE FRONT AND IN THE REAR

June 22, 1941 was warm but rainy. It was getting easier and easier for Alexander to serve in the army. Citizenship training had already been mastered. The most important thing was that he now understood the slogans "He who was nothing, will become everything" and "Workers of the world unite!"

The school's political instructor, Captain Azotov, painstakingly explained the new material to the "westerners" — that's what they called soldiers from Western Ukraine. At the end of each explanation he stressed that the Soviet Union was the most powerful and humane country in the world.

Captain Azotov paid special attention to Alexander, considering him very bright. He especially valued the young man's fluency in the German language. The captain often said to Alexander,

— Well, you are a clever cookie. So young and you already speak so many languages. You will be very useful to us. I have already mentioned you to some people here, and they took quite an interest in you. There is only one thing that needs to be done — educating you well politically. Otherwise Pilsudsky is still stuck in your head.

— Comrade Captain, — Alexander responded quietly, — I was raised with a different background, in a capitalist country. I was never aware of the things you are teaching us here. I could only work, and never made much sense of politics. Actually, you could say, I didn't make any sense of politics whatsoever.

— That is exactly why we are going to educate you, so that all the bourgeois prejudices are gone from your head.

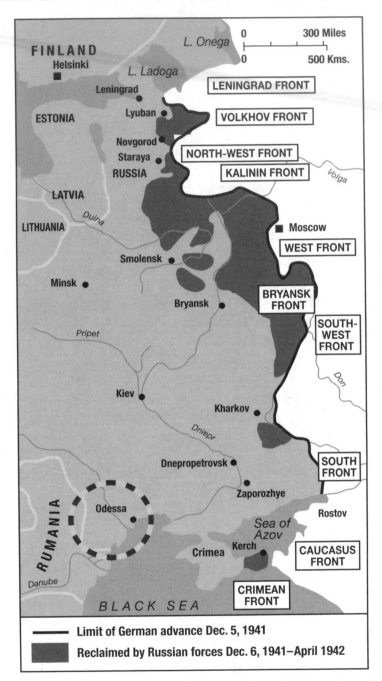

The beginning of Alexander Leventhal's war trek. He graduated early from the Odessa School of Military Officers.

Alexander nodded, but he was thinking: What the hell did he need politics for? He'd rather go home, to his mom, to Rivka, to Grandma Hanna. Boy, did he miss them! As soon as he got home, he would get engaged to Rivka. Her father had almost agreed to it, even though he had an older daughter not married yet. According to custom, the younger sister was not supposed to be the first to get married. Maybe her sister had already found herself a fianceé by now? And if she hadn't, then he would talk one of his friends from Dobromil into marrying her. He might even pay him something for that.

Alexander was so deep in dreams that he missed what the political instructor was saying. The political instructor was pontificating slogans, making a point to the "dumb westerners" about how happy the Soviet system made them. What a joy it was to live in such a wonderful country as the Soviet Union, where all men were friends, whereas in a capitalist country a man was a wolf to another man.

Alexander woke from a stupor upon hearing the last word the political instructor said, which was "wolf".

— Where is a wolf? What the hell? — he nudged the guy next to him and asked once again, — Where's the wolf?

The guy was bug-eyed.

— What wolf?

— The one the political instructor is talking about.

— Not a clue. Who even cares? Just listen and that's it.

Alexander calmed down.

Division Commander Komaldinov often came to inspect them. He was Tartar by nationality. He would move around the parade ground with an air of importance looking over the lines of soldiers. Everybody stood straight, not moving, sprung to attention, trying to make a good impression.

After the tour Komaldinov would give the command "At ease!", and everybody would heave a sigh of relief.

Once he came up to Alexander and asked harshly,

— Name!

Alexander sprang to attention and fired off,

— Cadet Alexander Grigoryevich Leventhal, Comrade Captain!

— A Jew?

— Yes sir, Comrade Commander!

— As you were.

Alexander relaxed.

The commander approached the political instructor Azotov and whispered something into his ear. The latter glanced at Alexander.

There was a command "Dismissed!", and everybody ran wherever.

Alexander went to the barracks and sat on the bed. His fellow villager, Michael, came up to him and asked him,

— Why the sad face, home boy?

— I don't know. Somehow I don't have a good feeling about all this. I can't wait to go home.

— Sure, — agreed Michael Glade, — It's not much longer now. It'll all work out.

At night everybody went to bed, but Alexander had trouble getting to sleep. He laid there thinking of his family. And then he heard a whisper,

— Hey, Leventhal, can you hear me?

— I can, — Alexander turned his head, — What's up?

— Nothing much. I am just curious, why do you think he asked if you are a Jew?

— No idea. Why?

— Well... I have read in the paper that the Germans kill Jews. They are liquidating Jews with no exception. Do you think it's true?

— I don't know, — Alexander replied, — but it sounds like its true.

— Listen, friend, it's great that the Russians occupied Western Ukraine, otherwise you would be in a deep-six.

— What's a deep-six? — Alexander didn't understand.

— They would have killed you and all your family.

— Maybe they would, and maybe they wouldn't. Maybe they don't kill everybody, but only those who are guilty, — Leventhal didn't want to believe it. He was a very kind and peaceful guy by nature and tried to find good things in everything.

His bunkie stopped talking and soon they were both fast asleep.

THE FIRST FIGHT

The cadets completed many practice drills. Alexander learned to get ready in three minutes. Three minutes — and he was ready in the line up. Once they were alerted and forced to move somewhere with the order "Forward!" But nobody knew for sure where forward was, and where back was. Everybody thought, "I can't wait until this alert is over!" But to the cadets' big surprise, sound-off did not follow. A war had begun. It was 1941.

— Right face! March! — The command sounded and everybody marched ahead.

They walked for a long while. Since he was used to walking, Alexander could determine quite accurately what distance they had covered. After twenty five kilometers the cadets were allowed to rest. Everybody got a ration.

After the meal the cadets were lined up by rank and the Division Commander and the political instructor began to grant accelerated promotions. Everybody was very surprised by it, but no one asked any questions. The ceremony was simple and brief: they shook each cadet's hand and said that as of that moment he was a sergeant of the valiant Red Army and the new sergeant would respond energetically and proudly with,

— I am serving for the Soviet Union!

After the ceremony was over, the Division Commander, Comrade Komaldinov, came to the front of the formation.

— Comrade officers, sergeants and privates, it is my unfortunate duty to inform you that today, on June 22nd at 4 am, Germany committed a treacherous attack on our Motherland. Nazis marched into our territory without declaring war, terminating the non-aggression treaty. Heavy fighting is going on at the borders. But ours is the just cause. We are going to defend our land from the enemy. We will vanquish the enemy in his lair. We are leaving now for the South-Western front to help Comrade Budyonniy vanquish the enemy at the Romanian border. Each of you will get ammunition and a ration kit. You need to know that the whole country is now watching us, and so is Comrade Stalin personally. We cannot fail their trust. And we have been entrusted with the most precious thing we've got — our Motherland. We'd rather die than let the enemy trample on our land. Long live our Motherland! Long live the Communist Party! Long live Comrade Stalin! Hurrah, comrade soldiers!

And the platoon unanimously yelled "Hurrah!"

Alexander could not believe his ears. Could that be true? Was it really a war?

"God! What a disaster! Who would have expected it? How are things in Kvasenina? They are so close to Germans there. What's going on there? I'd like to find out..." — thoughts were tumbling about in Alexander's brain and all jumbled together in Alexander's head.

At this point, somebody thrust rounds into his hand. He stared at the ammunition with the unseeing eyes, and then shifted his glance to the person who gave it to him.

— Give me more, comrade, — Leventhal said in a weird voice.

— It's not allowed. When you kill a German, then take his weapon from him, — the man answered gravely.

Alexander heard his reply as if through thick fog. He saw Germans in 1939. He remembered German soldiers armed to the teeth. Was it really possible to stop them with a rifle and ten rounds?

"I need to tell the Commander, — flashed through his mind. — They may be missing something. Maybe, they haven't seen what the German power is like? They are in tanks, airplanes, on motorcycles, whereas we are on foot with a single rifle and ten rounds". Leventhal stepped forward.

— Well, go ahead and report! — allowed Komaldinov.

— Comrade Commander, I saw Germans in 1939. They occupied our village for two weeks. And then the Russian army liberated us.

— You see, sergeant, you were liberated in 1939. That means our army is more powerful, and now we will crush them, — Komaldinov said loftily.

— Comrade Commander, they've got great power — tanks and machine guns. They are all on motorcycles, — Leventhal continued in agitation. — We need ammunition and something more powerful than a rifle.

— What are you saying, sergeant? I hear propaganda in your words. You don't believe in our victory, do you? — The political instructor Azotov asked harshly.

— I do! I do believe in victory, — Alexander whispered fearfully. — I am just asking for some more ammunition, comrade political instructor.

— You will get your hands on some ammunition in the battle, — hissed the political instructor. — You'll fight much harder knowing you need to get yourself weapons.

Alexander squirmed, and at that moment he heard the Commander's words.

— You Jews should be hiding under women's skirts instead of serving in the army.

The commander roared with laughter.

The political instructor began to laugh, too, in support of the Division Commander, setting an example for the others. But very few in the line-up followed the Commanders' example. Most of them stood there quietly, with their heads low.

Completely ashamed, the newly-made sergeant hung his head down and went back into the line.

Before long the platoon marched in the direction of the Romanian border. Their march lasted for seven days and seven nights. Halts were really short. No sooner did the soldiers manage to find fire wood and water than there followed a command to move on. Rations were passed out once a day.

Hungry and exhausted, with their feet turned to a bloody mess, they finally reached the Romanian border. There they were to go into combat with the Germans.

Soldiers halted in order to redo their foot wraps and get rifles ready for combat. Some guys smoked. And then terrible explosions blew up close to them. It was German artillery beginning the shelling.

Some men managed to lay flat on the ground. Others got wounded. A few were killed. Grabbing his rifle, Alexander ran cowering to a trench, where soldiers of the Budyonniy regiment were in position.

They glanced at him.

— You're new, aren't you?

— I am! — the young sergeant responded.

— You keep your head down, or they will make a hole in it in no time. You won't be able to mend it, — the Red army man advised, laughing.

— How should I fight then? Where do I shoot? — Leventhal was at a loss.

All those who heard his baffled question began to laugh.

— You will learn. The war is not your aunt, it won't spare you.

— Stop talking, — ordered a young commander, looking through a pair of binoculars. — The Germans have started to cut across the river. To arms! And don't you let a single German jerk step on our land.

Everybody became one with his rifle.

It was the young cadets' first battle.

Well armed and trained, the Germans did their best to cross the river and secure the waterfront territory, but the Soviets fought hard. The Germans were amazed at the Russians' bravery. The Russians were amazed at the Germans' endurance. The river was red with blood, but Germans were still crawling out like zombies, as if appearing with the wave of a wand.

By nightfall, the Russian soldiers were hungry, just about weaponless, and had no medical care. One couldn't only wonder at the bravery and courage of the soldiers crawling over the battle field under cover of night to gather German weapons, grenades and ammunition. They also took German marching bags hoping to find medication and food.

The village of Tsyganka looked lifeless. All the residents hastily abandoned their houses, taking with them only what they could carry. Houses with straw roofs stood empty, and only uncared— for chickens were seen in the yards. The hungry soldiers made their way to the houses hoping to find some food. In one of the houses Alexander found a barrel with brinsen cheese. It was a godsend. After packing as much as he could carry into his bag, he rushed to the trenches. Gasping for air, he took the rucksack off his shoulders.

— Guys, I have brought some food! — he yelled.

Everybody rushed to him, but the commander spoke strictly.

— You all go and take your defense positions. I will divide the food myself and distribute it.

The commander began dividing the cheese into small pieces, so that there would be enough for everyone.

That night, Alexander went through the whole trench in search of somebody he knew or one of his fellow villagers, but he didn't see any. That really surprised him — he didn't see them among the dead, but he wasn't able to find them among the living, either. They couldn't have been transferred to a different area. Where did they go?

As he was going back to his position, he came across a fellow villager who had been drafted before him. Alexander was very glad to see him and shook his hand with a lot of emotion.

— Mr. Melnik! I am so glad to see you.

— Shmul, my friend! Drop this "mister" thing. I am glad to see you, too. I am famished. Do you by any chance have anything to eat?

Alexander happened to have some dry crumbs in his pocket. Turning his pocket inside out, he poured out the crumbs onto his palm.

— Give me your hand, — he addressed Melnik, — Let's share everything there is equally.

After pouring half the crumbs into the hand of his fellow villager, Alexander began to lick the remains off his hand. Upon finishing his meal, he turned to Melnik,

— What do you think of the war, Mr. Melnik? What will happen next?

— I don't know, — answered the man. — We are in need of weapons, ammunition, and food.

— Have you seen anybody else from our area, Mr. Melnik?

— I didn't, but I know that many have deserted.

— Deserted?

— Ran home. Home is a stone's throw away from here.

Alexander lowered his head.

THE WITHDRAWAL

In the morning machine guns opened up again. Once more, the Germans went into the assault. And once again the Soviet soldiers held off the attack. Wounded and half dead, everyone who was able to hold a rifle, fought. The water in the Prut River turned a bloody color. The bank was piled up with the dead bodies of the soldiers from both sides. The men of the Red Army were putting up stiff resistance. And then in a moment's notice, Alexander heard a command to withdraw.

Withdraw? Why? The position they held was such a position of advantage for the Soviet soldiers. If they retreated, the Germans would easily cross the river, and nobody would be able to stop them any longer. His thoughts were all jumbled together. There was one thing Alexander knew for sure: if they gave away that river bank to the Germans, they would make a big mistake.

— Comrade Commander, permission to report, — he addressed his superior in command.

— Permission granted, — replied the latter.

— We shouldn't withdraw, Comrade Commander. We must hold the position until help comes, — Leventhal blurted out in one breath.

— You are right, sergeant, we shouldn't. But that's what the order says. And they are starting to surround us. If we don't leave, we'll end up in a noose.

— If we withdraw, how will we take the wounded? — the young sergeant asked unable to hide his confusion.

— Those that are able to walk will come with us.

— How about those who are not? — Alexander inquired. — What are you going to do with those who are not able to walk?

— We have no transport to take them with us, — the commander responded quietly.

The expression of the sergeant's face changed.

— Comrade Commander, we cannot abandon them and cast them loose. It is murder.

— Don't argue, sergeant, — the commander barked out. The order must be fulfilled. Our leaders are nothing like you. They know what they are doing. They know better.

And he walked away from Alexander.

It was obvious that he didn't feel too good about it. The wounded were moaning and asking for water. Watching everything that was going on, Alexander didn't know what to do. But somebody gave him a push in the back and he joined the line marching in step with everyone. Village Tsyganka and the wounded, doomed to death, were left behind.

Seeing the Russians withdraw, the Germans crossed the Prut River with no difficulty and began to shoot the wounded soldiers point-blank.

After Alexander's unit had covered several kilometers of road, another command arrived to win back their previous tactical positions. But just as the young sergeant had thought, it was no longer possible. The German army was much better armed and equipped. The Red Army ranks had considerably thinned out. Lots of young men died a brave death on that battle field.

Shooting their way out of the entrapment through brutal battles, the Soviet troops suffered heavy losses. Hungry, exhausted, dirty, and ragged, the Red Army men tried to stick together in groups, making their way to friendly troops.

Local residents rendered them with all kinds of help. Somebody brought out a slice of bread to give the soldiers; another gave them some milk; another gave some boiled potatoes. Women cried and begged soldiers not to leave, being afraid of ending up in the occupied territory. People blessed the soldiers for their feats, helped them to find a shortcut to the rear and informed them where the German troops had already landed and where it was still possible to pass through. The soldiers traveled through a field where rye was swaying in the wind. That picture reminded Alexander of a more peaceful time.

The commander decided to do some reconnaissance and took Alexander with him. Hiding in the thick underbrush, they carefully peered into the distance. Then Alexander saw soldiers coming in their direction. Pulling the commander's sleeve he whispered,

— Look, there are Germans coming.

— Not at all, it's friendly, — the commander replied.

But Alexander was sure that those were the Germans. There couldn't be any Russian units coming from that direction.

— Comrade Commander, it's Germans, I assure you, — he wouldn't give up.

— What a chicken you are, "westerner"! You're scared of everything. You seem to see Germans everywhere.

He got on one knee and stuck his head out of the underbrush. At that very moment a bullet sang, striking the commander's throat. Choking on his own blood, the guy dropped dead.

Alexander didn't linger. He picked up the commander's mapboard, took his papers from his breast pocket, unbuckled the holster with the gun and rounds and carefully crawled back toward his unit.

After covering a significant distance by crawling, he crouched and continued moving in short bounds. He cowered to the ground, in a hurry to warn his unit about the danger. And then he noticed a German ahead standing with his back to him.

Without hesitation Alexander jumped at the German, grabbed him by his head and jerked. The German fell down with him in the high rye grass without a peep. Leventhal quickly began to take his weapons,

grenades and ammunition. Upon taking his helmet off, he saw a picture in it of a young woman with a baby. It must have been that German's family.

Without delay Alexander pulled the helmet on and scurried to his unit well-armed. A German knife was a high-value trophy. Alexander stuck it in his belt.

When he reached his unit, gasping for air, he told them everything he had seen. After he showed his trophies, he opened the map that was in the commander's mapboard and began to study it.

They were going to use the map to make their way to their own troops, without really knowing where they were going. There were no more commanders among them. Any that remained had torn their stripes off, unwilling to assume command — being too scared to either displease the Soviet authorities and get court marshaled or fall prisoner with a commissioned rank.

Withdrawal seemed endless. After fierce battles the rows of the Red Army men thinned out. Worn-out, hungry and dirty they fought their way through to their own troops. But what was that? Out of nowhere a small automobile "Vilus" appeared on the road in a cloud of dust. An officer with the rank of major, whom the guys didn't know, sat there. He held a gun in his hand and yelled loudly,

— Buggers! Scamps! Traitors to the Motherland! Back to the fight! Cowards! I'll shoot you!

The soldiers were struck dumb. Bewildered, they stopped.

Getting out of the car the Major began to berate the soldiers.

At that moment German artillery began a shell attack. The enemy started an assault.

Seeing what was going on the officer quickly jumped back into the car and ordered the driver to go. The driver didn't need to be asked twice. Stepping on the gas he zoomed along the road. The car disappeared fast. The soldiers remained there completely confused and anxious. Nobody knew what to do. Shells were exploding all around. The soldiers lay down on the ground afraid to move.

But his lust for life told Alexander that it was necessary to battle through to his own troops, to break through no matter what. Many soldiers surrendered, but Alexander knew that captivity for him as a Jew would mean death. He wanted to live. And that meant he had to fight.

FIGHT FOR ODESSA

It took a long time for the soldiers to make their way to the rear. It seemed like an eternity until they reached familiar places in the vicinity of Odessa. Everybody was happy to break out of encirclement and make it to their own troops.

Before long they were restructured into new units and assigned to new commanders, who had never been in battle before. Alexander held a German machine gun obtained in the fight. He had given away his fallen commander's gun and the commander's personal items to his new superior upon telling him everything he could. The young commander acknowledged Alexander for bravery under fire and promised to inform the family of the slain officer.

Everyone cheered up hoping for victory. However, there was no rest for them. The enemy was bombing Odessa. Grueling battles were in process. Odessa residents were a special kind of people. They loved their city with all their heart and fought to the last. There were bloody fights for each stone, each house, and each street. Dying, they wrote in their own blood on the walls of the houses they were defending: "I am dying, but not surrendering, for Mother Odessa". Statements like these were followed with their blood-written signature.

Germans didn't expect such a response. They started to bring up massive forces, tanks and artillery. Odessa kept holding fast. In the battle for Odessa, Alexander Leventhal was badly wounded. The bullet went tore through a tendon in his right arm. Three fingers ended up crooked and he lost mobility in them. But when the medic dressed his arm and wanted to take him away from the battle field, Alexander refused to leave.

— I've still got two fingers left, and I am able to pull the trigger, — he responded. — We must stop the Germans.

At that moment a thundering explosion threw Alexander and the medic up into the air and back to the ground. Germans had opened artillery fire.

Leventhal was not able to hear anything. The ground was reeling under his feet. He was shell-shocked. The medic lay not far away. Alexander crawled up to him and felt his pulse. The man was alive, but unconscious.

Alexander tried to pull the medic to himself, but had no strength. He pressed his face into the sodden ground. There was just one thought hammering in his head: to pull through, to survive no matter what. Clenching his fists he forced himself to get up, as if through a fog he saw soldiers running to attack. And at that moment strong hands caught him and Alexander heard a whisper.

— Hold on to me, dear. Let's go, don't be scared, — it was a young nurse, who was carrying the wounded away from the battle field.

— Nurse, — said Alexander, — the medic is alive. Help him.

The sound of his own voice surprised him. It sounded like he was in a deep tunnel. But what mattered was that he was able to hear.

The nurse looked at him with disbelief.

— Are you sure you can walk on your own?

— I don't know where to go...

— Follow me. I will drag the medic, and you follow me.

Staggering from side to side, Alexander followed the nurse, seeing just the man's feet dragging on the ground in front of him.

Upon reaching the first-aid post, he lost consciousness.

LEAVE

Alexander stayed in a hospital in Odessa for just a day. After the war roads the hospital seemed like heaven. But the Germans were already assaulting Odessa, and the battles were fierce. The next day they began to evacuate the hospital. All the wounded were placed on a ship and sent to Zaporozhye, and then moved to Kislovodsk.

Alexander enjoyed his stay at the "resort", but then he felt that his condition abruptly got worse. After examining him the doctor immediately diagnosed him with jaundice. Observing the guys laying next to him in the room, Alexander considered himself quite healthy. His heart overflowed with compassion when he looked at those poor guys. Young and healthy men turned into cripples. Many of them had gone insane.

More and more often Alexander remembered the rabbi from Kvasenina. As a child he wasn't keen on going to synagogue and learning prayers by heart, but now he read them almost aloud every day, praying for the repose of some souls, and for the recovery of others. More

and more often he had dreams about his family and fellow villagers. He talked with Rivka in his mind very often, hugged her in his dreams, and thought about his upcoming meeting with his beloved.

Wounded soldiers stayed in Kislovodsk, but the Germans were advancing, and it was no longer safe to remain there. The hospital was evacuated again, this time to Baku. German bombers performed deadly air attacks on the trains carrying evacuated people. Nobody knew whether he would manage to get to his destination.

In a hospital in Baku, because of his jaundice, arm wound and contusion, Alexander was taken off the military records with an order to come to the military enlistment office six months later after a complete recovery.

One of the wounded, who was also eligible for a leave, suggested they should go to Tashkent. Tashkent was a "grain city". He could have a shot at getting a job there. Without hesitation Alexander and his wounded friend Vasily Krakhmalniy went to Tashkent.

NAMANGAN — THE "GRAIN CITY"

Alexander and Vasily went to Krasnovodsk by ship, and then took a train to Tashkent. At that time Tashkent was full of refugees. The young men were looking around in amazement. There were people everywhere: sitting, lying; many reaching out their hands begging. Typhus and famine mowed people down. The native population, the Uzbeks, was indifferent to the unwanted migrants.

Someone gave Alexander a tip not to stay in Tashkent, but proceed further to the regional center of Namangan. Alexander and his friend followed that advice.

Namangan looked almost the same as Tashkent, and was also overcrowded with refugees. From the rail station the young men went to the city party committee, showed their papers and asked for help in getting a job.

There was an elderly woman sitting in the office.

Casting a stern look at the young men in military uniform, she asked,

— What would the young men like?

— We'd like to get a job! — Vasily Krakhmalniy replied with confidence.

— What kind of work are you interested in?

— It doesn't matter. We have no preference. And we'll do anything that's required, — Alexander replied.

The woman's glance got warmer. She stood up from her table and extended her hand in introduction.

— Let me introduce myself. I'm Comrade Mineralova, the chairman of the cotton factory party committee.

— Alexander Leventhal, — Alexander introduced himself shaking her hand.

The woman went up to Vasily and tapped him on the shoulder.

— And what is your name?

— Vasily Krakhmalniy, — he said.

— Great. I'll arrange for you to be security guards in the factory, — she smiled. — But first I'll treat you to dinner, get you washed in the bath-house, and will buy you underwear. Follow me!

The young guys beamed. What good fortune to finally get settled and to meet such a wonderful person as Comrade Mineralova.

The woman treated the veterans like family. First she took them to the works canteen, and then took them to the factory bath-house, stopping on the way to get each of them a pair of underwear. She gave them bread vouchers for two weeks and vouchers for three meals a day in the works canteen. After that she brought them to the dormitory, where each of them got a bed and a bedside table. The young veterans thought they went to heaven.

Alexander met many wonderful people at the cotton factory, many who became very good friends. His roommate, Ivan Shved, was also from Ukraine and turned out to be a good guy, too.

Everything would have been great, if it hadn't been for the southern climate. The heat was unbearable. In addition, there were swarms of mosquitoes. In order to escape from the heat and mosquito bites, the guys had to sleep wrapped in wet sheets.

Somebody gave them a tip to move to Chelyabinsk. Everybody said that the weather there was the same as in Ukraine. They finally had enough money for the tickets to Chelyabinsk, but just enough money for the tickets — there was nothing left to buy food. Once again, some kind people gave them a tip to buy some tobacco and trade it for bread on the trip. Alexander and Vasily took the advice. Alexander bought a few glasses of tobacco and several sewing spools to trade for bread as necessary.

CAPITALISTS IN A SOCIALIST COUNTRY

After saying warm good-byes to all of their new friends, the guys went to the railway station. While waiting for the train, the friends were sitting on a bench, when they saw a police squad. Not expecting any trouble, the boys did not pay much attention to them. They had no idea that serous trouble was closing in on them.

The police officers approached the two young men.

— What are you doing here?

— We are waiting for the train to Chelyabinsk, — Vasily answered.

— Papers! Why aren't you in the army? — the same officer went on.

— We were wounded and have been deferred from service for six months, — Alexander explained.

After examining their papers thoroughly, the officer asked firmly,

— What have you got with you?

— Nothing much, — Vasily replied. — Just personal things.

— Open your bag, — he addressed Alexander.

Unsuspicious of anything bad, the young man untied his back-pack.

Taking out a canvas bag filled with tobacco, the policeman asked,

— What's this?

— Tobacco, — Alexander answered.

— Why do you need so much tobacco? — asked the policeman again. — Do you smoke?

— No, I don't, — Alexander answered honestly.

— Why do you need tobacco, if you don't smoke?

— We are going to Chelyabinsk, and we don't have any money to buy food. We will trade some tobacco for some bread, — Alexander frankly admitted.

The policeman looked at the young man disapprovingly and whispered,

— Follow me!

174

Alexander stood in front of the law enforcement officer in bewilderment.

— Why are you standing there? Didn't you hear what I just said? — he repeated in a stern tone. — Follow me!

The guys exchanged puzzled looks, and set out following him.

At the police station Vasily and Alexander were brought to the chief's office.

The chief was a short baldish man of about forty.

With an angry look, he ordered the two visitors to take everything out of their backpacks and put it on the table. The young men untied their backpacks and put the contents on the table. In it were two little bags with tobacco, forty sewing spools, biscuits tied into a handkerchief, a few lumps of sugar and half a loaf of stale rye bread.

— Is that it? — the chief of police asked harshly.

— That's it, Comrade Chief, — the young men answered.

Walking around the table the chief looked at the stuff spread on the table and said,

— I see attempted speculation...

— Comrade Chief, — Vasily made an attempt to object, — we were not going to sell tobacco, but just to trade it for bread.

— I am not a comrade to you, — he growled. — We'll find out what you have been doing here! There are people fighting Germans at the front, and you spread speculation here in the rear! We will put you to trial!

— Comrade Commander, permission to report, — Alexander saluted. — We are wounded veterans. Have a look. I have been wounded in my hand. I also had a contusion. Vasily was wounded in his head and his hand. See? His fingers were torn on his right hand. We are not speculators. We want to go to Chelyabinsk. We've got no food and no money, so we've decided to trade some tobacco for a slice of bread.

Casting a frowning look at the young man, the chief barked,

— Put them in the lockup. Let them sort it out there.

The young men were led from the office and taken through the long halls to the cell. The iron— clad doors screeched open. Alexander saw a gloomy room, seven feet by ten feet, with three men inside.

When the young men were pushed into the cell, they still didn't grasp what had happened to them: they had been arrested for suspicion of capitalistic activities.

IN THE LOCKUP

In the lockup the young men smelled a strong slop-pail odor. The people in the lockup gave the newly arrived a questioning look.

The young guys were in shock. The door behind them closed with a clang, but they still stood frozen without moving.

— Why stand? — they heard the voice of one of the prisoners. — It'll take a long time. Go ahead and make yourselves at home.

These words woke Alexander from his trance.

— What do you mean, it will take long? Why long? We are not guilty of anything. We are wounded veterans.

— Veterans, you say? In that case, do tell us what's going on at the front? What's your name, young man?

— Mine is Alexander, and his — Vasily... Look, he got his fingers torn off at the front, he was wounded in the head, and I had a contusion and was wounded in my hand. My fingers don't move now, — Alexander started to tell his story.

— So what's the situation at the front? — another man interrupted him.

— What's going on at the front? The Germans are beating us severely. They are heavily armed with tanks and airplanes. They all ride motorcycles. And we fight with bare hands. We can only yell "Ahead!" and "Hurray!" If you kill a German, you take his weapon and fight with it. Otherwise, there is nothing to fight with. So many people die, it's scary to watch.

The cell became quiet. Upon hearing such news, the prisoners lowered their heads. Everybody knew that the country was in grave danger. Although everyone was not particularly fond of the Soviets, they believed that Hitler was much worse.

The cell was extremely tiny. There were neither beds in it, nor bunks. They had to sleep right on the floor in their clothes, lying close to each other. If one of them wished to turn over to the other side, the rest of them had to turn over, too.

The heat was scorching and they were given food just once a day. They got grape leaf soup and a ten ounce slice of rye bread. The food was pushed through the window in the door. Each of them had his own iron bowl and a cup. They were also given something to drink once a day during the meal.

The men stood in line to get some fresh air and look at the sky through the barred window. They were not let out to go for a walk.

Three days passed. It was like they had forgotten about Alexander and Vasily. They were not interrogated and nobody seemed to care about them whatsoever.

One of their roommates in the cell was a Korean. His family brought him food. Usually it was rice pilaf with dog meat. He generously shared his food with Vasily and Alexander. Another of their colleagues in misery — a Jew from Leningrad — got some food packages from his wife. He also shared everything he had with the young men. Alexander and Vasily had no idea how those men had gotten into the lockup. And they had no idea what awaited any of them.

One day the door to the cell opened and a woman of about thirty five appeared in the doorway. Poking Alexander's shirt, she said,

— Let's have this one help.

Alexander heard an order.

— Step forward. Our cook needs assistance.

Staggering, Alexander followed the cook. He didn't realize how weak he had become during the two weeks he had spent in the cell. A bucket of water seemed like a back breaking burden.

The cook looked at him angrily.

— Jerks! You dishonor the soldier's uniform! People at the front die for you and you...

Alexander didn't say anything in response to her unjust rebuke, but each word hit him right in his heart. Years later, Alexander would recall those words and regret not explaining everything to the Russian woman. At the time, he was just happy to be let out of the terrible cell for a few hours into the open air. He didn't want to say anything to risk that being taken away.

He tried to do his best to oblige the cook with the hope of getting an extra spoon of soup or a slice of bread. But his hopes were in vain. The woman treated him almost with hatred, as if it were his fault that there was a war.

TOUGH SENTENCE

The young men were kept in the cell for twenty five days. They had lost hope of surviving. Hungry and exhausted, they could barely stand on their feet. When they were finally taken to court, Alexander could barely drag one foot after the other.

The young men were seated and everybody waited for the judge. The young men had been assigned an attorney who spent five minutes studying their case.

The judge came in and everybody was ordered to rise. After familiarizing herself with the case, the woman austerely looked into the courtroom and gave the floor to the defending attorney. The attorney, a man of about forty, wiped his forehead and started to explain Alexander and Vasily's story to the judge. He mentioned that the people sitting in front of her were veterans, Motherland's defenders, who had heroically fought with Nazis, were wounded and sent to be treated and to convalesce in order to return to the Soviet Army.

The explanation was of no interest to the judge. She kept leafing through the case. An attempt to speculate — that's what mattered to her.

The attorney requested a final statement from the defendants. The judge generously nodded in agreement.

Hanging on by the skin of his teeth, Alexander said,

— Send me to the front. I'll prove to you that I am not guilty. I was at the front from the first days of the war. Give me this chance. Please, send me to the front.

The judge screwed her face into a smile.

At that moment the attorney, who couldn't take any more, almost screamed.

— Who are you judging? These are our defenders! Veterans! What are you judging them for?

The judge cut him off abruptly.

— Your behavior is inappropriate, comrade attorney. You are in the Soviet City Court. We are the most humane country in the world. We cannot permit the existence of speculators in our country. That's it, the discussion is over.

A few minutes later she told the associated judges to leave the courtroom with her in order to make a decision regarding the sentencing of the defendants.

The attorney was nervous, but Alexander and Vasily looked at him with hope.

The door opened, and the judge with the associated judges entered the courtroom. The verdict was read. Pursuant to Article 175, Section 13 of the Criminal Code of the USSR "Attempt at speculation", the defendants Vasily Krakhmalniy and Alexander Leventhal were sentenced to five years of prison camp.

The trial had lasted just an hour.

The young men were taken out of the courtroom under police escort, placed into a transfer car and driven to prison.

IN THE SOVIET CAMP

After four months of torturous waiting, Alexander and Vasily were transported to a camp located somewhere in the vicinity of Tashkent. It was difficult for the young guys to comprehend what had happened to them. They were almost sure that they were doomed to death in the Soviet camps, and it was futile to expect rescue from anyone.

Pinched with hunger and worn-out by the heat, Alexander and Vasily lost almost all hope of survival. After being wounded in the head, Vasily was shaking as if in fever.

Vasily cried, saying over and over as if in stupor,

— We won't survive this. Why did they do this to us? We are their own... We fought the Germans. We broke out of the entrapment with such difficulty... Did we do all that just to be ground down by our own? We won't survive this.

Alexander looked at his friend with an aching heart. He was right. Everything that had happened to them was impossible to comprehend or accept. But to give up just like that? No, he was not the kind of person to wait for death quietly. No need to panic. He had to fight to survive.

Alexander put his hand on his friend's shoulder.

— Vasily, my friend, try to keep up your spirits. We must survive. Those who don't believe in life, die. And you and I are young; we are just 23 years old. Life is just beginning for us. Our whole life is ahead of us.

We've got to have faith in a better future. We have survived a lot and we will survive this misfortune, too. We will come out of this hell. You will see. I will dance at your wedding and you will dance at mine. I will have a beautiful wife. Her name is Rivka. Just hang in there, buddy, please hang in there. We will survive. We are tough.

As he said those words, he started to believe in them himself.

The camp's appearance didn't inspire any optimism. It was a vast territory under barbed wire with watchtowers placed along the perimeter. When he saw the prisoners, Alexander was shocked, unable to trust his own eyes. Behind the barbed wire people walked — dreadful, pitiful, looking like stacks of bones covered with skin. Females were on one side and males, separated from them with the same barbed wire, were on the other side.

When the gates were opened and the young men were brought to the camp commander, a more horrible sight broke upon them. Young men, boys between the ages of sixteen and eighteen with their heads shaved bald, were carrying rocks on their backs to the construction site. There were guards everywhere.

The camp commander, a young and handsome blonde man, approached the new arrivals.

— Well? Messed up, haven't you? Here you will correct your outlook on life.

Take them to the supervisor.

A worn-out man looking extremely exhausted and miserable glanced at the newcomers.

— Why are you here?

They looked at the supervisor.

— If we tell you the truth, you won't believe it.

— Why wouldn't I believe it? — the man responded. — I will. Go ahead and tell me.

— We wanted to trade tobacco for bread. We were hungry, but had no money. They convicted us for attempted speculation. Article 175 Section 13. That's it. And we are wounded veterans. We fought the Germans at the front, and battled through entrapment. And this is what they did to us. I'd rather they send us back to the front. We'd prove that we are no speculators, but veterans, — Alexander blurted out passionately.

Vasily stood there silently, just trembling like a leaf.

The supervisor frowned.

— I'll take you to your barrack, and then I'll find suitable work for you.

Then he quietly added,

— How's it going at the front?

Alexander looked at him and replied quietly.

— The Germans are thrashing us, giving us a really bad beating.

The supervisor lowered his head even more, and motioning the guys to follow him, walked towards the barracks.

The barracks were positioned like houses on a street. Each of the barracks had a number, and the prisoners had to memorize their number.

As they entered the barrack, they saw long beds made of boards and placed in two rows, one above the other. There were no sheets, pillows, or blankets.

Turning to the supervisor, Alexander asked,

— Where is our spot?

The supervisor smiled slightly.

— Two hundred people sleep in this barrack. Everybody works 12 hours a day. When they come to this barrack, they fall down on any available bed half dead. You will learn about this life. Do not leave your belongings anywhere — they will get stolen. Do not seek the truth — you will get killed. Try to get breakfast, lunch and dinner — grape leaf soup and a ten ounce slice of rye bread. If you don't get your meal in time, somebody else will eat it and you will go hungry and die of hunger. My advice — stick together.

Alexander listened carefully. When the supervisor finished, he asked him,

— How did you get here?

— I am not even sure. I was tried by the triad. This is when three parties come together — the interrogator, the judge and the prosecutor — and decide your fate. They convicted me, but didn't say how long I would serve my sentence. It means that every five years my case is reviewed. So I did my five years and they called me and said that my case had been reviewed and they added five more years. Then they would see... I was arrested with no charges made. I haven't been able to find out what these jerks did to my family. I have already reconciled myself to my fate, but my heart aches for my beautiful wife and two year old son.

Alexander hung his head.

What Alexander and Vasily witnessed and experienced in the camp was unimaginable. They worked 12 hours a day on textile machines made in the 1800s before the revolution. They made carpets out of cotton strings. They had to watch the time very carefully, so that they didn't miss the distribution of food — meals were only served at certain hours. Each man was supposed to put his cup under the ladle so that the cook could drop one ladle's worth of soup into it. They would also get a slice of bread, which they swallowed in a second and washed down with the concoction made of grape leaves.

Sometimes the prisoners tried to wrestle bread from the weak. If they succeeded the poor guy was doomed to starve to death, because once this started, the strong ones didn't stop until his last day. The guards didn't interfere. They just smiled and watched the vicious fights from the side.

Men, if they could still be called that, were gradually turning sub human. Many of them dug in the soil searching for worms, bugs and other "edible" insects. They caught rats, mice, frogs — anything alive that could be eaten. Sometimes fights would start around the kitchen scrap-heap — the inmates trying to get a place close to the garbage. Everyone tried to survive.

Alexander did his best to support his friend. Occasionally he put his own bread in his friend's pot.

— Vasily, just make an effort to hang in there, — he told him. — Try not to tremble. We will overcome all this, you'll see. There are two of us together. That means a lot.

Vasily tried to smile while he gulped down his soup.

The two men did everything together and life didn't seem so hopeless to Vasily after all. Two weeks passed in that way. The guys stuck together as if they were blood brothers. Unexpectedly, the supervisor approached them. Alexander was wary. But the supervisor, coming closer, patted Alexander on the back and said,

— Get your stuff, Alexander. I found a new place for you.

Alexander was struck dumb.

— Why aren't you moving? — the supervisor wondered. — Rejoice and let's go.

Alexander wasn't moving.

Vasily cast a frightened look at his friend.

— And me? What about me? What's going to happen to me? Please don't make me stay here. I need to be with him. We are to- gether, — he whispered.

— Don't worry, Vasily, — the supervisor replied. — I haven't for- gotten about you. But I can't take you both at the same time. I will come back for you in a week or two. You can visit Alexander — it is allowed.

With these words he led Alexander to the fire station, where the fire tenders worked. A tall man, Georgian by nationality, greeted them warmly at the door and invited them into his little office, known as his commissary. As he entered, Alexander caught sight of a few boiled potatoes on the table. At the sight of the food he almost fainted. No- ticing Alexander's reaction, the Georgian seated the dear guest at the table and gave him two potatoes and a slice of bread.

— Eat, — he said with a heavy Georgian accent, — I don't be- grudge food for a good person.

Alexander gulped everything down in a second. He was all eyes looking at the Georgian, not believing that he was so fortunate.

— Well, my dear man, — the Georgian said smiling, — your job will be to disinfect clothes. Clothes will be brought, and you will have to sort them. You will put the clothes to be washed to the right, and you will place what should go into the fire in the left heap. It will be your decision which to put where.

— Now you won't have to stay in the line for soup. We get food for our department directly from the kitchen, and then divide it among all. You will live here, in this corner. That's about it, — he concluded.

— Thank you so much, — Alexander finally managed to say. — I've got just one question: where do the clothes come from?

— Hmmm... My dear man, you, obviously, haven't been here long. You don't know yet that there are lots of people in the camp, do you? There are many thousands of people here. And a few hundred of them die every day. Typhus and hunger decimates the population of our camp. And the order is to bury people in a mass grave without clothes. Their clothes are brought to us for disinfection, — the Georgian ex- plained.

Alexander turned white. He worked his jaws.

— What's with you, young man? — asked the Georgian. — What, is that news to you?

— Yes, that's news. — Alexander nodded. — Why are they torturing everybody here? They'd be better off sending them to the front. There is such a shortage of people there.

— To the front, you say? We would all ask to be sent to the front. But it's not us who makes the decisions here. They are made for us. Why are you here — for something insignificant? You were hungry, right? Sure. As for me, I am still in the dark as to why I was brought here. I don't know where my family is now. They arrested me at night. And they tried me by the triad that night. They still continue to try me. Looks like I will have to die here. I've gotten used to it already. They try me every five years, and I don't know the charges, and nobody is willing to tell me. To the front; yes, we all would go to the front. But I'll tell you in confidence: Stalin and Hitler — they are alike, one is no better than the other.

And he hung his head low.

Alexander lowered his head and began to carefully examine his hands. Fingers on his right hand did not bend because of his wound.

"Is it really the end? — he thought. — Will my life end like this? I so want to go home, to see my mom, grandma Hanna, my father, Moisha, Rosa, Rivka, if only for a minute..."

— What are you so deep in thought about, soldier? — this question brought him out of a stupor. — Don't think. You need to live. Whatever happens, it is necessary to live.

Those words stuck in Alexander's memory.

A new life started for Alexander at a new place with new people.

A bit more food came to him, because the new cook gave second helpings, and sometimes an extra slice of bread. The Georgian got all that in exchange for some pieces of clothing, brought for disinfection.

Vasily came every day. Alexander shared everything he could with his friend. Getting a tiny slice of bread seemed to make Vasily the happiest man in the world. The fire men looked at him musingly.

One time Alexander was sent to get a new load for disinfection. He merrily pushed his wheel barrow. Reaching the assigned barrack he stopped. There was a big heap of different things rising by the doors. Alexander's heart ached. He saw a cart full of naked bodies stacked as if they were fire wood. There were women, very young girls, and young boys among them.

Alexander started shaking. This is where the clothes came from. Good God, what a mockery! What could those children possibly have done to be sentenced to such a horrible punishment?

What Alexander witnessed next shook him for life.

A big guy — a warden, holding a sledge hammer — was hitting the heads of the dead, making sure that no creature escaped alive.

Alexander began to throw up. He saw a lot of blood at the front; he saw torn body parts; but this made him shudder.

When he came back to the fire station, everybody noticed that something had happened to him.

The Georgian was the first to come up to Alexander.

— What's wrong, Leventhal? What's happened?

Alexander was not able to say a word. He was whiter than chalk, and his hands shook.

— Come on, Alexander, drink some water, — the Georgian offered.

Alexander took a sip, glanced at the Georgian, and spoke with difficulty.

— Why? Why do they do that to those children? They taught me in military school before the war that our country is the most humane one in the world. Where is the humanity? It is a crime what they are doing.

The Georgian nodded silently. Alexander cried like a baby, and the Georgian didn't know what to say. He had no words to comfort the young man.

After seeing that bloody medieval spectacle, Alexander avoided going to get the clothes.

TYPHUS

Several weeks later Alexander suddenly got ill. He had a fever and was burning up. When he regained consciousness, he saw that he was in an unfamiliar room.

A stranger approached him.

— Are you alive? I thought you wouldn't live. You have been unconscious for so many days. Are you still alive?

Alexander moaned.

— Water. Give me some water.

His roommate put a cup to his lips.

Alexander was drinking greedily. Every drop was like balm to him, bringing him back to life. He drank all the water and licked his lips.

— Give me some more, friend. How long have I slept?

— For seven days, — the roommate answered.

Seven days? Is that so? And where am I?

— In the prison hospital. You've got typhus. Drink water, it is very good for you. Drink, — the roommate said, and he brought the cup to Alexander's lips.

After drinking the water, Alexander slid into unconsciousness again.

His fellow prisoner watched him in amazement. Alexander's face looked blissful and peaceful. He was so far away from that hospital cell. Alexander imagined he was in Kvasenina and mother Mindlya was hugging her son and saying words of love to him. Shmul saw himself as a child. He held his mother by the hand tightly and was very happy. Mindlya was stroking his head and saying,

— Don't be afraid, Shmul, I am with you. I will always be with you now. I won't leave you for a minute.

The next day Alexander opened his eyes again and, looking around the cell, said quietly,

— I am very hungry...

Medics would not enter the room — they were afraid to catch typhus. They passed food through a hole in the door.

The sick tended each other. When they brought lunch — liquid soup — his roommate ate Alexander's portion while he was unconscious. But now he had to give Alexander his soup.

It had been four days since Alexander had regained consciousness. He had no strength. He was not able to get up and get to the door to receive medication through the hole. The skin on his belly and his arms was flaking away. Alexander was aware that many people went straight to the cemetery from that hospital cell. His roommate had warned him that typhus is usually followed by severe diarrhea, which caused everybody to die. The roommate's words scared Alexander. He lost his hope of surviving. He lay there staring at the ceiling.

At that moment the door opened and a beautiful young woman in a white robe entered the room. Her blonde hair was smoothly brushed back and made into a tight knot. As she came up to Alexander she greeted him and asked him to pull up his shirt. Alexander obediently complied with the doctor's request.

— Why are you in the camp? — the woman asked.

Alexander told his story about the tobacco again, probably for the hundredth time.

After listening to the whole story attentively, the doctor said,

— I will look at your case. If everything you have told me is true, then I'll help you to get out of here. Otherwise you will die. Out of prison, everything depends only on you. I wish you happiness.

She turned and left the room.

Alexander silently followed her with his eyes. He no longer believed anything. The blond beauty seemed like a dream to him. Weakness overcame him and he fell asleep. Once again he was a young Shmul in his dream. He was sitting on his mom's knees. She was giving him sweet milk, and Grandma Hanna was breaking white bread and putting pieces into his cup. Alexander felt bliss in his dream, and he didn't want to wake up.

RELEASE

Three days passed after the appearance of the strange woman in the white robe. Alexander was constantly thinking about her.

When he had lost all hope, the door to the room opened noisily and a warden appeared in the doorway.

— Alexander Leventhal, come out!

Alexander didn't understand anything at first, but when the warden barked out the second time, he got up with difficulty and dragged himself to the door.

The warden led him through long halls. Stopping in front of the big door, he said,

— Stay, — and taking out a big key, he unlocked the door.

There was a heap of clothes dumped in the middle of the room. They looked very similar to those that Alexander had to sort in the camp.

Entering the room the warden fished old boots with holes, pants with holes on the knees, a mended shirt, and a ragged cap out of the heap. He gave all of it to Alexander, and topped it off with a paper saying that inmate Alexander Leventhal was released early for health reasons and was supposed to go to the law enforcement authorities to get his passport.

Alexander couldn't believe his eyes.

— Where is my soldier uniform, the one I wore when I arrived?

— What kind of fool are you? You want your uniform! You should be grateful that you are being released alive and also given biscuits for the road! And you demand your soldier uniform? Go to the front, you will get one there.

— Where will I go now? I don't know where to go, — Alexander tried to find out.

— With the help of this paper you will get a ticket to where you need to go. It's about three miles from here to Tashkent. So off you go. Almost nobody gets out of here alive but you are released. This guy is so lucky. He doesn't even realize how fortunate he is, — the warden kept mumbling. — Well, a happy journey to you, man!

And with these words, Alexander left.

When he was out of the prison hospital, Alexander still couldn't believe that he was free. Dressed like a beggar, he sat on the side of the road and began to eat his biscuits. After he ate all of it to the last crumb, Alexander got up. He looked around trying to determine where to go. At that moment a man appeared on the road. When he noticed Alexander he backed away, frightened.

— My kind man, — Alexander addressed him, — Show me the road to Tashkent.

— It's over 2.5 miles to Tashkent. You need to go down that road, — the traveler said as he pointed him in the right direction.

Alexander thanked him for his help and stumbled in the indicated direction. The man stood there for a while watching the "beggar" walking along the road to Tashkent.

Alexander's strength was failing. Exhausted by hunger and sickness, he moved with extreme difficulty. It took almost the whole day to cover a distance just over 2.5 miles. The scorching rays of the sun were burning him. He suffered from ferocious thirst.

The first thing he did when he reached Tashkent was to look for water. Upon finding a water post, he began greedily licking cool drops off the tap. He had no strength to pump water. Seeing that, one of the passer-bys helped him and Alexander put his head and neck under the flow of clean and clear water. People gathered around him, but he took

no notice of anything. After he had cleaned up and satisfied his thirst, Alexander lowered himself next to the water post and leaned against the iron pole. People were still standing around looking at him.

His cap lay right there on the ground, and he saw a woman put a small piece of bread into it. Upon seeing the bread, Alexander looked at the woman with gratitude, grabbed the bread and put it in his mouth.

— Thank you! — he said, swallowing the bread in one gulp.

— God bless you, — replied the woman. — I've got a son somewhere out there. Hopefully someone will give him a slice of bread, too.

People around him began to give him whatever they could. Somebody put an apple into his cap, another put a piece of scone and a beet.

After he gathered the handouts, Alexander went to the railway station to get a ticket to Namangan, but there he saw a huge line by the booking office. The crowd was fighting loudly. Alexander knew that he had no strength to stand in the line. He spent the night by the railway station walls and ate his gifts of food. In the morning he tried to get a ticket again, but failed.

Not far from the railway station he noticed a heap of stock beets, and next to it — a heap of cake (waste from cotton seed which had been pressed for oil). Alexander first started eating the beets and then ate the cake, too.

Suffering from heat and hunger, Alexander realized that he would not be able to get a ticket, as he had no energy to stand in line. He decided to try to board the train without a ticket.

RETURN TO NAMANGAN

Alexander was going to Namangan in order to look for his acquaintances. He had to find at least one person who knew and remembered him.

When the Namangan train came to the platform, passengers started to crowd around to board it. Alexander had no strength to move, but the crowd caught him and carried him along. When he got to the footboard, Alexander was struck dumb: he was not able to get into the car by himself; he wasn't strong enough. Then somebody reached out a hand to him, helped him to mount the footboard and pushed him inside the train.

The car was packed with people.

Soon the train left. Nobody checked tickets. Leaning against the car's wall, a washed-out Alexander slipped into unconsciousness. Once again he turned into a young Shmul running around his yard at home in Kvasenina. He was gathering eggs from the chickens' nests, and mother Mindlya was cooking a tasty lunch and was calling him to come and eat.

He woke up with a keen hunger. At first Alexander didn't realize where he was. Instead of mother Mindlya, there were strangers around him. Then he reached into his coat, got out a beet and began nibbling it.

The train arrived in Namangan at night. Hungry and exhausted, Alexander barely made it to the cotton factory dormitory where he used to live. The front door was unlocked. Alexander found the room he had stayed in before and recognized only one person he knew. His former roommate, Ivan Shved from Kamenetsk-Podolsk near the Polish border, slept peacefully on his bed.

— Ivan, Ivan, wake up, — Alexander quietly called him.

Ivan opened his eyes. When he saw Alexander, he was so surprised that he woke up at once and sat up on his bed. He couldn't believe his eyes.

— Is it you, Leventhal? What's the matter with you? Where have you been? — he bombarded Alexander with questions.

Alexander sat down on Ivan's bed and started crying.

The first words that escaped from his chest along with sobs were,

— Ivan, I am very hungry. Have you got anything to eat?

— Sure, — Ivan responded and opened his bedside table getting out a slice of bread and an apple and giving them to his friend.

Gulping the bread down in a second, Alexander then ate the apple. Ivan waited until Alexander finished eating.

— Well, can you tell me now what has happened?

Alexander nodded and began his story. While listening to him, Ivan cried.

In the morning Ivan dressed Alexander in his shirt, pants and sandals and took him to breakfast at the works canteen. The cook remembered Alexander, and without asking any questions, she put some food on his plate.

Ten days later the chief engineer Rautkin, who was a Tartar by nationality, hired Alexander to his former position.

After he had arrived at Namangan, Alexander went to the police station to present his certificate of release and to get a passport. He was to return to the police station every two weeks.

Once, when another two week period had passed and it was time to report again to the police station, he ran into a man in police uniform, walking down the stairs.

— I am sorry, — Alexander apologized politely, addressing the police officer.

The officer nodded his head acknowledging the apology, and made a few steps down the stairs. Then he stopped and looked towards Alexander.

— Comrade, do I know you from somewhere? — he wondered.

Alexander looked back and immediately recognized the police chief who had sent him to the lock-up.

Tremor thrusted through his body. He lost his head and didn't know what to do. The first thing that came to his mind was to say,

— I don't know you, comrade policeman.

However, the chief wouldn't give up.

— Show me your passport!

Alexander gave him his brand new passport with shaking hands.

— I thought as much — the chief said with satisfaction. — Now I remember the idiots with tobacco. Alive and free. What a rarity! You were born lucky.

Alexander stood there more dead than alive.

— I've told you that our country is the most humane one in the world. If you are not guilty, they will clear it up, — the chief continued giving the passport back to Alexander.

— Yes comrade chief, I've already seen for myself how humane our country is. I witnessed its humanitarism with my own eyes, — Alexander said, thinking of the children's skulls being crushed. Taking the passport out of the chief's hands, he walked away.

MEETING BRICK

Several weeks later Alexander registered for service. His strength was coming back to him by the hour. His diet was not very nourishing but it was regular, and his young body was successfully recovering. In the morning before work Alexander jogged for a few miles, did exercises, and lifted heavy logs and rocks to strengthen his muscles. Everybody was amazed at his perseverance.

— Why are you doing all this? — his roommates wondered occasionally.

— I want to build up my body and my spirit. I must return home strong and healthy, — Alexander responded.

One day he was summoned to come to the military enlistment office. He put on Ivan Shved's clothes and went. There were lots of people crowded in the reception room. Alexander went to the secretary, gave her his name and sat on a vacant seat to wait his turn. All of a sudden his glance lingered on a group of people sitting in the right corner. He couldn't believe his eyes! Among these people there was a childhood friend and his sister's Rosa's fiancée, Brick Zusman! How did he get here?

Alexander jumped off his chair and rushed to Brick.

— Brick, my friend, I can't believe it! Is it really you?

Seeing Alexander standing next to him Brick looked somewhat embarrassed. He recognized Alexander, but his behavior was very strange: his face didn't reflect the slightest sign of joy.

— What's up with you, Brick? — Alexander couldn't understand.

— It's me, Shmul Leventhal. Don't you recognize me? I am your fellow villager!

Finally Brick began to smile, reached out with his hand for a handshake and forced a few words out,

— By God! I can't believe my eyes. What are you doing here?

Grabbing Brick by his hand, Alexander began to tell him why he had come there.

Brick was listening to him inattentively, glancing at the people next to him time and again.

Upon completing his story, Alexander asked,

— How about you? How did you get here? What are you doing here?

Brick turned his head towards the women sitting next to him and said,

— I would like you to meet my wife and my mother-in-law.

Alexander was struck dumb. How so? What was he saying? Could it be that he had misunderstood Brick?

But one of the women gave Alexander a pleasant smile.

Brick took her by the hand and said,

— This is my wife.

Then he turned to the older woman and continued,

— And this is my mother-in-law.

Alexander had lost his tongue. He was smiling sheepishly. His head was buzzing, and only one thought was clear in his mind: What about Rosa? What would happen to her? She was waiting for Brick, trusting and hoping. How could he do this to his sister?

Taking Alexander's arm, Brick walked him aside.

— You see, Shmul, it's the war. I met this family, and I think I have done the right thing. I saw a lot of grief and trouble before I got here. People are dying like flies. I'd like to be able to stay here, if it works out. Drop by tonight. We'll be glad to see you.

With those words he walked his friend to his mother-in-law and addressed her.

— Let me introduce my friend Alexander to you. I have invited him to dinner if you don't mind of course.

— No, of course not! We'll be happy to have you! We'll be looking forward to your visit! — the woman rejoiced.

After giving his address to Alexander, Brick warmly parted with his childhood friend.

When he finished his business in the military enlistment office, Alexander went back to the hostel. His meeting with Brick had made him very anxious. He was not sure whether he should have dinner with Brick. Finally, he decided it was sensible.

He was welcomed with open arms and very cordially. Brick's new family turned out to be very friendly and hospitable.

When everybody gathered and sat down at the table, Alexander heard a Jewish prayer said before the meal for the first time in a long while. He got a lump in his throat.

After dinner they got up from the table and struck up a conversation.

Brick's mother-in-law brought her oldest daughter up to him and said without theatrics,

— Alexander, I've got one more daughter here. Marry her, start a family. Why look for happiness? It's right here with us. We are Jews and live by Jewish laws. The girl is pretty. Stay with us.

Alexander was struck dumb. Yes, the girl was very lovely and they had a great house, comfort. But what would he tell his parents? What would he say to Rivka? No, he couldn't do it. He dreamt so much of going back home. Rivka was waiting for him. Mother and father would host their wedding. No, he couldn't give up. He had already endured so much. He would go through with his original plan.

— My dear, no offense to you or your daughter, — Alexander began, — but I am in love with a girl from our village. Her name is Rivka. And I am going to return home to her after the war. I want to go home to my family. I cannot go against my conscience and cannot lie. I have to be in love with the person I marry.

And with these words he parted, leaving Brick with his new family.

On the way to the hostel, Alexander kept thinking about Brick and what he had done. Bitterness for Rosa burned his soul. He tried to justify Brick's actions in his head, but failed. He could not forgive Brick's unfaithfulness.

Alexander would never tell a soul about that meeting and about Brick's marriage. He was unwilling to profane the memory of the love of a Jewish girl, who had believed in the faithfulness and devotion of her beloved to her last days.

Brick died in Berlin on the 8th of May in 1945. In the death notice that came to the village of Kvasenina it said that Brick Zusman died as a hero of the Great Patriotic War and was posthumously awarded a medal for Berlin's capture.

BACK TO THE FRONT

Alexander continued working at cotton factory number 127th in Namangan. Every day the female cooks asked him to split the fire wood and help them prepare kindling for the stove. For that they would give him a pot of soup. Alexander got into a routine. Two months later, Alexander received notice to come to the medical examining board to have a health assessment. A group of doctors sitting at a long table was thoroughly examining the recruits. When Alexander's turn came, he began to feel a little anxious. A female doctor examined him, and then asked him to close his eyes and stretch out his arms in front of him. Alexander did what he was asked to do, and a few seconds later he heard,

— Straighten the fingers on your right hand.

Alexander opened his eyes and looked at his right hand. He had completely forgotten that three fingers on his right hand, starting with the pinky, did not straighten.

— I can't, — he answered, — I was wounded and they don't straighten.

The doctors began to whisper among themselves.

A few moments later, when the discussion was over, one of the doctors asked Alexander,

— Do you want to go to the front?

Alexander looked at the doctor quizzically.

— You can say no. Your right hand is injured. Therefore, it's up to you. You decide.

Alexander got embarrassed. He was fed up with going to the police station every two weeks to report, feeling insulted and humiliated, and he responded with confidence.

— Yes, I want to go to the front. I was there from the first days of the war.

It got quiet, and the head doctor placed a familiar stamp on his personal record: "Fit for military service".

Returning from the medical examination board Alexander kept thinking about all the humiliation and insults that he had experienced. A voice, calling his name, brought him out of his painful thoughts. Alexander stopped and looked around. Seeing no one, he kept on walking thinking he was mistaken, but at that moment he saw a man running towards him.

— Wait, Leventhal! How did you get here?

It was a man from Leningrad, who had been in the lockup with him.

Alexander stopped in his tracks in amazement. He did not expect to see anyone he knew.

Approaching Alexander, the man hugged him, and after catching his breath blurted out,

— I know that you had been sentenced to five years in the camps. And hardly anyone ever gets out. How did you manage to get out?

Alexander was at a loss, but the man from Leningrad kept right on.

— Leventhal, I live nearby. Let's go to my place.

Grabbing Alexander's hand, he dragged him with him.

The guy's wife was very happy to meet Alexander. She treated him to a tasty dinner which Alexander would remember for a long while. Saying good-bye, his fellow inmate took out 300 rubles and gave it to him.

— It is for the road.

Alexander began to cry. He didn't expect such a cordial welcome from people he barely knew.

— I am not sure when I will be able to pay you back, — he finally managed to get out a few words.

— Don't worry about it, Leventhal. It's OK — we'll settle up one day.

A few weeks later Alexander received a notice requesting him to come to the front. On the appointed day the recruits gathered around the military enlistment office. There were lots of recruits there. They were all sent to Samarkand. Before they reached their destination, the recruits were taken to a field and were told to take their outer garments off. Then they were given a new uniform, put back in the vehicles and driven to Samarkand, where the recruits were to stay for combat training.

The days of training dragged on.

Once a week the soldiers were taken to the bath-house in formation. Bathing day was like a holiday for the soldiers. Alexander walked briskly, looking about.

Suddenly he looked at a group of passers-by and broke step, not believing his eyes. There was his uncle Wulf — his father Gersh's brother. Alexander left the rank without hesitation.

— Uncle! Uncle!

Wulf looked at the young man in surprise.

— Who are you? I don't know you.

— Uncle, I am Shmul, the oldest son of your brother Gersh. Remember, you taught me how to buy cattle? Please recognize me.

Then, finally, Wulf recognized his nephew. He rushed to hug and kiss him.

— Shmul! How did you get here?

— And how did you get here? Is there anybody else from our area here?

— Yes, there are some people from Dobromil here. Can they let you go for a while? — Wulf asked.

Alexander immediately ran to the commander to ask for permission to spend some time with his uncle and he was given a liberty pass.

There was no end to the questions. His uncle filled him with food, bought him some scones for the road, and introduced him to his friends. Shmul got to meet with his fellow villagers. It was a happy day.

Afterwards Uncle Wulf took him aside.

— Shmul, come in the evening and I'll hide you. I'll get you papers and we will leave for Palestine. What do you say to that?

— I am scared, uncle, — Shmul admitted honestly. — I have been through so much already. If they catch me, they will shoot me on the spot. I have already seen our "humane" system.

— It's up to you, dear, — old Wulf responded after some silence. — You are the one to choose your own road. You are right. Anything could happen, and I don't want to be blamed if anything bad happens to you.

— Uncle, do you happen to know anything about my family? Is there anyone who knows at least something about them? — Shmul asked hopefully.

— No, Shmul, no one knows anything, — Wulf replied.

Hugging each other stoutly, they parted.

Autumn, 1942

It was a late autumn, 1942. The train full of soldiers was racing along. Nobody knew where it was headed. Occasionally the train stopped, and the red shoulder-straps (that's what they called the agents of the "Special Department") brought some new soldiers into the cars. Many of the new-comers were just boys. Alexander looked at the young soldiers, dressed in military uniform, and thought with sadness that half of them, if not more, would be killed in the first battle.

The train proceeded further and further away from Samarkand. It was getting colder and colder. The food was lousy. They got a pot of boiled wheat and a slice of bread. Only then did Alexander realize what a mistake he had made when he had asked to go to the front. But, who knows what they might have done to him if he hadn't gone?

Finally, the train reached its destination. The locks squeaked, the doors slid aside and everybody saw special agents running around, yelling through mouthpieces. Soon everybody was rushed out of the cars and pushed and yelled into formation.

"Here we go, — Alexander thought, — only where? What territory is it? Where are we?" Nobody wanted to answer those questions. Explosions thundered somewhere close at hand.

As he had already been in the fight, Alexander suspected what would happen next, and he was right. The special agents gave the order "Ahead!" and yelling "Hurray!" and waving their guns, they charged ahead for a while pretending to attack. Alexander and the rest of the soldiers followed them. When they got to the enemy line, the special agents set up their machine guns.

The Germans met the assault with intense gun fire and almost all those running ahead died during the first minutes. Alexander fell down, pressing himself into the ground. But what was that? Did machine gun bursts come from behind? Could it be that they were surrounded? No, that couldn't be true. Then who was shooting? At that moment a young soldier's body, shot through, fell on him. Sticking his head out from under the body, he saw that the special agents were shooting from behind at their own retreating soldiers. Alexander could hardly believe his eyes. The battle field was covered with dead bodies. The agents were persistently chasing young boys in military coats towards death.

Only after almost all of them were shot, partly by the Germans, and partly by the guys from the Special Department, did the order to withdraw come. Nobody cared for the wounded.

Seeing that the special agents had begun to withdraw, Alexander pushed the dead body of the young soldier off of him. The body had saved him from certain death.

— Thanks, buddy, — he whispered, closing the dead guy's eyes, — sorry I couldn't help you.

His thoughts were in chaos. Alexander was crawling towards his own troops. He still had the image of the soldiers falling from the bullets of their own special agents.

ADVANCE

The Germans were retreating with violent fighting. Every inch of ground was drenched in blood. Men were dying but, as 1943 came to an end, the joy of victory was looming. Soldiers believed that the war would soon be over, and everybody who managed to survive would once again lead a happy and normal life.

The battle of Stalingrad decided the fate of the war. Alexander fought that battle with the First Ukrainian front. He had only positive thoughts: that there would be an end to the war one day, that there would be happiness on Earth, and that he would go back home to his family and his beloved Rivka.

During the battle, they took over Kharkov twice. The first time the Germans managed to take it back, but the second time they took it for good. What a battle it was, but they managed to win!

Alexander saw women kneeling on the ground, making the sign of the cross and then blessing the passing soldiers for further victories. He saw women come up to soldiers, hugging and kissing their liberators with tears in their eyes.

The town was in ruins. He felt a tug at his heartstrings when he saw children begging for bread. Soldiers gave them every last slice of bread, not thinking about themselves. They tried to warm the children up with a kind word. The war brought so much grief! Why? What for?

Lying in the trenches, Alexander thought about his home and his family. Only one thing brought him out of these dreams: "Ahead! For Motherland! Attack! Hurray!" Picking up his machine gun, he would rush ahead. It seemed to him that he was running closer and closer to home, and nothing could stop him.

Sometimes his great-coat froze to the ground in the trenches. But the cold, hunger and constant danger could not break the young soldier's faith in life. He knew that he would return home.

In 1944, Alexander was with the Soviet troops when they advanced into Lvov. It was his native land, home was close at hand! He heard Ukrainian and Polish speech. But the people meeting them did not have the same joy or sincerity as the residents of Eastern Ukraine. There were a lot of things Alexander couldn't understand. But it didn't worry him. He hoped that his troops would go through Dobromil and Kvasenina, and that he would finally meet his family and fellow villagers.

The order came to advance. There were rumors that another German-Ukrainian army had appeared — SS Galichina. That army fought even more violently than the army of General Vlasov, which had also

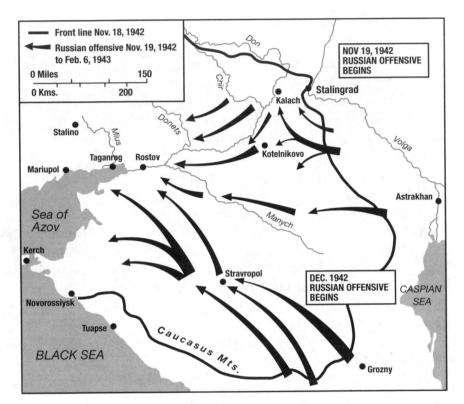

Legend

- — Front line Nov. 18, 1942
- ← Russian offensive Nov. 19, 1942 to Feb. 6, 1943

0 Miles 150
0 Kms. 200

NOV 19, 1942 RUSSIAN OFFENSIVE BEGINS

DEC. 1942 RUSSIAN OFFENSIVE BEGINS

Don

Chir

Donets

Mius

Manych

Volga

Stalingrad

Kalach

Kotelnikovo

Stalino

Taganrog

Rostov

Mariupol

Astrakhan

Sea of Azov

Kerch

Stravropol

CASPIAN SEA

Novorossiysk

Tuapse

Caucasus Mts.

BLACK SEA

Grozny

Soviet Advancement, 1942-1943
Alexander Leventhal is part of the Russian Offensive.

gone over to the German side. There were rumors about fierce fighting, but Alexander didn't take that to heart. He was almost home. Kvasenina was at hand.

Finally, the long awaited advance started. The front line was six miles from Peremyshl. And there, behind the mountain, was Dobromil and Kvasenina. If he was lucky, Alexander would get to free his native land. But the fighting went around Dobromil. They assaulted the Syan and Peremyshl rivers instead.

Peremyshl was taken with big losses. During the assault Alexander was wounded in his neck by a grenade fragment. The fragment cut off skin and penetrated into the muscle, but fortunately, vital arteries were not damaged. Everybody thought he was lucky. The medic patted him on the shoulder.

— You'll see, westerner, you will reach Berlin. You were born lucky.

Alexander was happy. He breathed his native Carpathian air and even rocks seemed to be talking to him, welcoming his return to his native land.

On one of the days in Peremyshl, Alexander was called to speak to the Chief of the Special Department.

— Leventhal, somebody has told me that you speak German.

— Yes sir, Comrade Commander!

— And where did you learn German?

— I was taught by the rabbi in my synagogue. I am a Jew, Comrade Commander. I was born six miles from Peremyshl. All the Jews speak Hebrew, which is very similar to German. During my childhood the rabbi taught me to read and write German.

— Do you think the rabbi is still alive?

— I don't know, Comrade Commander. I hope everybody is alive there.

— Many of them are already dead, Alexander. They have caught the chief of the Peremyshl prison. Come with me, we must talk with this jerk. We need an interpreter.

THE INTERROGATION OF FILUS

Crossing the bridge over the Syan river, they drove towards the Peremyshl prison. After the car entered through the wide gates, it stopped in the middle of the yard and everybody except for the driver got out of the car.

Alexander stopped to look at the yard.

— What have you stopped for, soldier? Let's go!

Alexander quickly walked to the building's entrance.

The prison was empty. There were several secret service agents and special agents sitting in the room which they entered.

— Well, young man, — the Chief of Secret Service addressed Alexander, — are you ready to meet these man-eaters?

Assuming that he was joking, Alexander replied with a smile,

— Yes sir, Comrade Commander.

Two German officers were brought in from the room next door.

— Well, Alexander, ask these jerks their names. Actually, we've got their papers here. We know who they are. Go ahead ask this one, — he pointed to a tall German proudly standing in front of them, — what he has been doing in Dobromil.

Alexander interpreted word for word and was impatiently waiting for the answer.

The German didn't move a single muscle in his face.

— Leventhal, tell this scum that we are aware that he was the Commandant of Dobromil, and that his name is Ludwig Filus.

Alexander translated that information, but the German obstinately continued to play the silent game.

— Leventhal, — continued the Chief of Secret Service, — tell him that I will be shooting at him until he starts speaking.

To Alexander's surprise, the German immediately responded.

— What would they like to know?

— What did you do in Dobromil while you were the Commandant?

The German looked at Alexander and asked with a curl of the lips,

— Are you a Jew?

— Yes, I am a Jew, — Alexander answered.

Staring Alexander up and down with a contemptuous look, the German said between his teeth,

— I don't speak with Jews. I kill them.

Alexander's throat got dry. He interpreted Filus's words to the Chief of Secret Service.

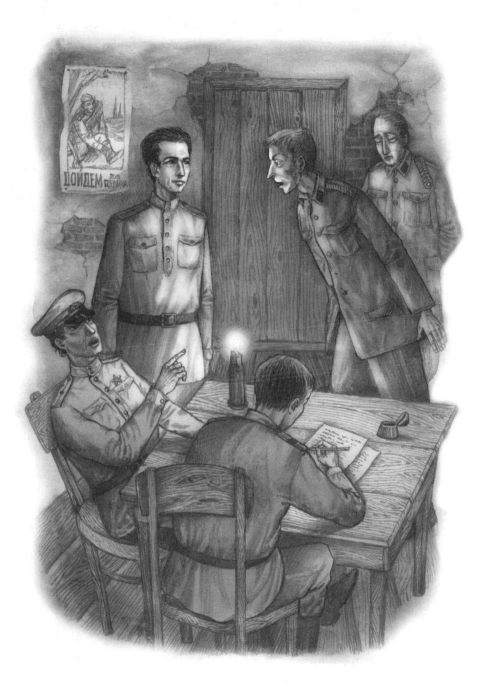

The chief got up from his chair, approached the German, put his gun to Filus' mouth and spoke to him in Russian.

— Scum, I know what you have done. I have live witnesses. Your dog was tearing your victims to pieces. But times have changed. Now it is our turn to tear you to pieces. And don't pretend that you don't know Russian. I know for a fact that you speak Russian as fluently as I do.

The German took a step back, but at that moment the Secret Service chief knocked him down with a heavy blow and, when the German fell, started to kick him.

Nobody interfered. Everybody stood and intently watched what was going on. The second German, the head of the Peremyshl prison, stood there as pale as a wall and trembled as if in fever.

After the Secret Service Chief had satisfied his hatred, he ordered Filus to get up. The bloody German could barely stand.

And then Alexander asked him,

— How do you feel now? You just traded places with your victims.

Filus gave Alexander a mean look and spit bloody saliva.

— Comrade Chief, — Alexander addressed the Secret Service Chief, — I am from Kvasenina. It is six miles from Dobromil. I'd like to ask him if he knows anything about my family. May I have your permission to ask a few personal questions?

— Go ahead and ask. We will listen to his answers.

— Do you happen to know anything about the Leventhals or the Flugers? — Alexander addressed Filus. — Are these names familiar to you?

The German looked at Alexander viciously and replied,

— I've told you already that I don't speak with Jews.

And the Secret Service Chief approached the German once again.

— So you are saying you don't speak with them? — and he hit him in the face with all his might.

The German reeled, barely managing to keep his balance.

— Are you willing to speak with me? Or don't you want to speak with me either? — He hit the German in the face again, putting all his power into the hatred-filled blow. Filus fell down.

— Get up, scum, get up! A Soviet Army Commander is speaking with you.

The German got up with extreme difficulty.

— Talk!

The German coughed blood.

— I don't remember the names. Names did not mean a thing to us. All the Jews were sent to work camps. In the fall of 1942 all the Jews from the nearest villages were gathered in Dobromil and sent to work camps.

— How about the old? — Alexander was almost screaming.

— No idea. I was only gathering and sending them to the work camps.

— You are lying, you scum, lying. You know everything. You are going to tell us everything, — the Secret Service Chief was hissing with hatred.

And then they heard the stammering voice of the other German, about whom at that point almost everybody had forgotten.

— I'll tell you everything. I will talk. It's true that we don't remember their first and last names. There were so many of them. But Ludwig personally shot them and his dog tore people to pieces. I will tell you everything you want to know. Everything I know.

Everybody was looking at the German, and Alexander was interpreting word for word.

— I want documentation. Is there any documentation left? — the Secret Service Chief asked.

— A lot was destroyed. There was an order to destroy all the evidence. But there is a lot that we haven't managed to destroy. I'll give you all I have got.

Filus gave his ex-colleague a mean look, clicked his heels together, threw up his arm and shouted,

— Heil, Hitler!

It was the last straw that broke the camel's back. Like a hawk the Secret Service Chief sprung upon the German. If the soldiers hadn't interfered, he would have killed him for sure.

The head of the Special Department said sternly,

— Don't. We will bring him to justice. He will be tried publicly as a war criminal. All the peoples of the world must know about their crimes, and the guilty must get the punishment they deserve.

Alexander did not know at the time that, following the orders of Commandant Filus, a young Jew by the name of Rivka had been beaten up and raped by Ukrainian police at the Dobromil market place; that she had gone to Dobromil from Kvasenina to buy food for her family and ended up being torn apart in public by Filus' dog. He did not know that Grandma Hanna had been shot in her bed by Ludwig Filus personally. He would learn about all that later.

Turning to the Secret Service Chief, Alexander said,

— Comrade Commander, my relatives lived in Peremyshl. It is not far from here. May I have permission to go there? They may know something about my family.

— You are saying it's not far? All right, let's go. They may be able to tell us interesting things.

Getting into the car, they all drove to find Alexander's relatives. Pulling up to the sought — for house, the car stopped and Alexander got out and went to the second floor. After knocking on the familiar door, he held his breath. He was waiting for the door to open and reveal familiar faces for him to see, but to his astonishment he saw a totally unfamiliar woman when the door opened.

— Excuse me, dear miss, — Leventhal said in Polish after greeting her, — but my relatives lived here before the war.

— Pardon me? — seeing a soldier in the Soviet uniform, the woman looked at him frightened.

— Don't be scared miss...

— Marysya, — she prompted.

— I am just looking for my relatives.

— Sure, sure... Excuse me, sir. Were your relatives Jews?

— Yes.

— Oh, my dear sir, everybody was taken away to the ghetto, and then to the concentration camps. And I don't know what happened after that. Almost no one is left in Peremyshl. Didn't you know that, sir?

Alexander did not hear anything else Marysya was saying to him. He ran down to the waiting car.

They could guess everything by the look on Alexander's face. No one said a word on the way back to their unit.

"I HAVE WALKED THROUGH HALF OF EUROPE..."

After taking Peremyshl, the Soviets took Rzeszow through fierce fighting, and forced the Germans to cross over the Vistula River. Alexander had seen a lot over the years. Men were constantly killed in the infantry. Alexander did not know where he got his strength. Bullets whistled around him; his friends and comrades were left dead on the battle fields, but it was as if he was under a spell.

Sometimes it would seem like the end had come, but then suddenly relief would come and strength would appear out of nowhere. Again the call would sound: "Ahead! Attack! For Motherland! Hurray!" and Alexander would get up once again and charge into attack. He would run to fight for life on Earth.

The Polish-German border was close at hand. He walked through all of Ukraine and Poland on foot. If someone had told Alexander that anything like that was possible, he would not have believed it.

The Poles gave soldiers bread, potatoes, milk, fruits and vegetables. They blessed the soldiers for fighting, helped to care for the wounded and dressed wounds. Alexander spoke Polish with local residents. Everybody asked where he had learned Polish. He willingly answered that had been born and raised in Poland. He was proud of his Polish heritage. When the Polish Army was created, he wanted to join it, but he was refused, so he stayed in the Russian Army.

They were getting closer and closer to Germany and eventually arrived in Elena Gura. His heart started to race when they were told how close they were to Hitler's lair.

And then the day came when they were all lined up.

— Comrades soldiers, sergeants and officers, we are at the German border now. The enemy will be crashed in its lair. Plenty of blood and tears has been shed on our land by the Nazis. Plenty of our best sons and daughters have been killed in unequal battles. Now we are going to enter their land. You are going to be judges and prosecutors. Retaliation will come for all our suffering and ordeals. After the victory, all those who survive — and you all will survive — will live happily and joyfully and recall the war like a nightmare. We were not the ones who started the war. We lived and built our country, and the enemy destroyed our life. But as they say, they that take the sword shall perish by the sword. Remember, you are judges! Ahead! Fight for our wives and children, for the fallen friends, for the ruined towns. Hurray, comrades!

And everybody yelled "Hurray!" believing everything the commander said. They believed they would all survive. They believed in victory and in a bright future. And Alexander already saw himself hugging his mother and father.

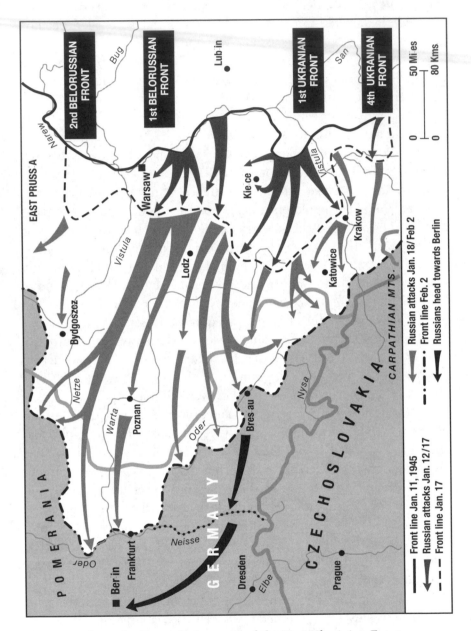

*Alexander Leventhal, as part of the First Ukrainian Front,
marches through Europe and fights in the battle for Berlin.*

The battles on German land were bloody. The Germans fought with fury. Alexander and his regiment forced a crossing over the river Neisse. The water in the river was red with blood. Every inch of land was showered with blood. The Germans were fighting hard for their native land, but it was impossible to stop the charge of the Russians.

The Russian troops moved through the German land slowly but persistently. The resentment that had built up over the past years assured it. Alexander believed he would survive and go home, and therefore attacked with no fear or doubts.

After another tough fight for some village, soldiers gathered in small groups to have a rest. Alexander stood among his fellow soldiers. His feet were soaked through. Looking around he saw a house nearby.

— I'll go see if there is anything that can be used as foot wraps, — he said to his friends, — because my feet got completely soaked through.

— Call us, Leventhal, if you find anything good there. You may find something to eat, — replied one of the soldiers.

— Sure. I'll be a moment.

The house was empty. Alexander went down to the basement. God Almighty! He was dumbfounded. The basement was packed with canned food. Seeing all that abundance of food shocked Alexander. He sat on the steps to calm down.

At that very moment he heard a shell explode nearby. But who cares about explosions? War is war.

When he found some clothes he wrapped his feet with them, put on his boots, smiled, and filled his bag with canned food.

"Boy, will the guys be happy about this! We will have a feast. It's not often that such a trophy falls into our hands" — he was thinking, getting out of the basement.

When he came out of the house, he was shocked: where his fellow soldiers stood just a few minutes before, there was now was a huge hole. All of them had been instantaneously killed by a direct hit of a shell.

Shortly after that Alexander was wounded in the leg. A shell fragment tore a piece of muscle out of his right leg. And again the medics tapped him on the shoulder, saying that he was born lucky.

Alexander was taken to a catholic church where there was a temporary medical aid post for the wounded. His leg was healing fast, and when he was back on his feet, he helped the medics any way he could.

Looking at the wounded soldiers he thought of the large number of infantry men who had caught bullets.

He grumbled to his friend Ivan Rashchupkin that they had already walked through half of Europe on foot, and it was high time to change their travel mode. One day they got lucky. A heavy mortar artillery unit under the command of Captain Gesin stopped by their medical aid post.

The guys were burying legs and arms of the wounded, which had been amputated during surgery, when the Captain's car stopped near them.

Alexander ran up to the car.

— Comrade Captain, take us with you. We want to go to the front.

— How long have you been fighting? — the Captain wondered.

— Since June 22nd, 1941.

— And what are you doing here?

— I was wounded in the leg, but it has almost healed now. Take us into your unit, you won't regret it.

The Captain looked around to check if anybody could hear them.

— Where is your great-coat? Go get your great-coat and get into the car, quick.

Alexander did not need to be asked twice. Everything was done in a moment. That's how he and Ivan Rashchupkin got into the heavy mortar artillery division of the CINCR — the Commander-in-Chief Reserve of Comrade Stalin.

The Machine Gunner's Heroic Deed

Bullets were singing in the air so that it was impossible to raise one's head. The Germans were charging. Just a few soldiers were still alive. All of a sudden Alexander heard the machine gun stop shooting. Without hesitation, he began to belly crawl towards the machine gunner. He was dead. In one jump Alexander reached the machine gun and pulled the trigger.

— Buggers! Scams! Take that! — he screamed.

As he shot he moved the machine gun from left to right.

— Take that, buggers, for us, Jews. You won't take me alive, you won't!

Bullets were hitting anyone who raised his head up.

The machine gun belt was finished. Alexander quickly inserted a new one, allowing the Germans to come closer. He began to shoot again, whispering again and again,

— Take that, buggers. It's for you from us. Take that!

He could not find other words. And then he heard something dear to his heart: "Hurray!" It was help coming. Soldiers were charging ahead, attacking the running Germans. Alexander's hands were still grasping the machine gun handle.

Somebody took him by the hands and whispered in his ear.

— Let go, soldier. Are you wounded?

It was a young nurse with a medical bag across her shoulder.

— No... I'm not sure. I don't think so, — he replied, putting his head on his arms, only then feeling how exhausted he was.

The battle was violent, but they won.

General Zhukov arrived on the battle field. Alexander stood next to him and listened attentively to every word he said. It turned out that they had been surrounded, but the Soviet troops had broken the noose.

— Is the machine gunner alive? — Zhukov asked. — The hero who stopped the German advance?

Alexander did not realize that they were talking about him. But the young nurse took Alexander by the hand and stepped forward.

— Yes, Comrade General, he is alive. Here he is.

— What's your name? — General Zhukov asked him.

— Alexander Grigoryevich Leventhal, Comrade General.

— I commend you for an award, Comrade Leventhal, for courage in action, for bravery, and for combat services.

— I serve to the Soviet Union! — Alexander saluted.

The medal "For Bravery" found Alexander many years later. It was handed to him in the Dobromil military enlistment office. Gratuity papers were signed by General Zhukov personally.

Alexander Leventhal was also awarded a medal "For Combat Services", had commendations from Comrade Stalin for forcing a crossing over the Neisse and Oder rivers, and for taking over German towns. The medal "For the capture of Berlin" had special value to him.

It was very difficult to capture Berlin. At every gate there were dead Germans lying next to dead Russians. Every house, every street

corner, every inch of land was washed with German and Russian blood; but the anger and pain for everything experienced and seen made the Russian soldiers inexorable.

THE LIBERATION OF A CONCENTRATION CAMP
NEAR BERLIN

The Soviet troops continued the advance. Although the Germans mounted a determined defense, the Red Army had become more powerful. The division in which Alexander was fighting took part in the liberation of a concentration camp located approximately thirty miles from Berlin.

Laying in trenches the soldiers heard loud shots, shell explosions, and voices of the German commanders barking orders. Shooting went on almost all night. At dawn they received an order to advance, and a few hours later the Russian Army took the camp. After the fighting was over, the liberators saw a vast area surrounded by high voltage barbed wire with watch towers. Alexander stopped in his tracks. Another camp sprang up in his memory, located many hundreds of miles from Germany — the camp in Tashkent, where he and Vasily had been sent,

There were dead bodies everywhere on the ground, now almost skeletons. Between them the survivors, shrunk to nothing, were moving any way they could, even crawling on all fours. They were leaving their shelters and crawling to the Russian soldiers, trying to touch them, as if still not believing that it was not a dream.

The soldiers stood there in shock barely believing their eyes.

The Secret Service Chief summoned Alexander. They had captured the Commandant of the camp and they had to clear up some circumstances. Alexander was to translate from German into Russian.

When Alexander approached, he saw a handsome blond man in a German uniform with a bandaged head and a bag behind his back. Russian soldiers with machine guns stood by, guarding the prisoner.

When he saw the Commandant of the camp, Alexander was shocked. He so resembled the head of the camp in Tashkent. A push in his side brought him out of his stupor.

— Are you deaf, Leventhal? — the soldier standing next to him pushed him again.

— What? I didn't get it. What do I need to do? — Alexander responded.

— You need to interpret, that's what! — the Secret Service Chief said. — You do know German, don't you? I need to talk with this bugger.

— All right, — Alexander replied, — I will interpret.

The questioning began.

— How long have you been in the SS party?

— Since 1933.

— Where is your Party card?

— At home.

— Where is your family?

— Back in Berlin, 15 miles away.

The Secret Service Chief ordered him to show him the camp and tell him what had happened there. The Commandant willingly led the "guest" to see his domain.

The camp was a death machine. The shots soldiers had heard the night before were made shooting the prisoners. The Commandant showed the barracks, the crematorium full of bodies, and the gas chambers, which looked like bath house with shower equipment through which the poisonous gas was let out. There were mountains of hair, clothes and footwear in the warehouses. Everything was painfully familiar to Alexander.

"The excursion" depressed everyone. But it was especially tough to see the children. The Secret Service Chief gave orders to feed the survivors and then send them to the hospital.

Alexander was as pale as a wall. Interpreting was really difficult for him. From time to time he had an irresistible wish to assault the Commandant and strangle him, but he could not let himself do it.

When the camp tour was over, the Secret Service Chief took his gun from the holster and, without saying a word, shot the Commandant.

After this shot, the other German raised his hands and screamed,

— I want to live!

But the Secret Service Chief didn't seem to hear him. He shot two more times and the German dropped dead.

He turned to Alexander and the other soldiers standing nearby and said sternly,

— Forget everything you've seen here. He deserved such a death. And now — all dismissed!

Soldiers began to leave, but Alexander could not bring himself to go away. He kept standing there, looking at the good-looking dead man.

— Why are you standing here, Leventhal? Haven't you heard the order? — he heard the voice of the Secret Service Chief.

Alexander turned his head to him and almost whispered,

— I have. I am leaving.

— Are you sorry I shot him? — the Secret Service Chief asked after a moment of silence.

— No, Comrade Commander, he deserved it. However, I think there are still plenty of people like him left in the world. And they all deserve punishment. But the problem is whether we'll get to the major offenders, to those who planned and arranged this.

— We will get to them, my friend, we will. We will slay the enemy in their lair. They all will get the punishment they deserve.

With those words the Secret Service Chief walked away.

Leventhal walked through the camp area in a fog. He could not shake off the feeling that he was back in the Navai camp in Tashkent. How similar the two camps were! The only difference was that in the Navai camp they did not shoot anyone. But both starved people, tortured them with back-breaking labor, and allowed typhus and tuberculosis to finish the task, taking the lives of innocent people. Who would answer for these crimes? Navai was built with the blood of the Soviet people. Who would be on trial there? And would there be any trial?

And would there be a memorial at the mass grave where they had tossed the dead bodies with smashed skulls? Would the names of the dead prisoners of the Navai camps be forgotten?

Those thoughts whirled inside Alexander's head. He often recalled his friend Vasily Krakhmalniy. How was he? Was he still alive? When he went home, he was going to look for him by all means. He had memorized his address for ever:

Vinnitskaya oblast,
Kopaigorodskiy region,
Village Shevchenko
Vasily Krakhmalniy

He would find him by all means!

With those thoughts Alexander left the liberated concentration camp in Germany.

VICTORY DAY

Berlin was taken at a high price, but the war was still not over. The unit Alexander served in was moved to Czechoslovakia. Fighting went on every day. One day, lying in the trenches about five miles outside of Prague, Alexander heard shooting, screams and laughter. It was the long-awaited Victory Day, May 9, 1945.

Happiness was endless. Tears rolled down the cheeks of the courageous, battle-toughened soldiers. The most violent fighting had not squeezed tears from their eyes. Everybody was hugging, kissing and congratulating each other. They all believed in life, happiness, and making it back home.

Alexander believed that he would go home and everything would be like it used to be; but not all the battles were over yet and still more blood was to be shed.

Alexander continued to serve. Captain Gesin was a decent and intelligent man and commander. He respected the soldiers and frequently talked with them. He appreciated Alexander enormously and one day summoned him.

— Leventhal, I've heard you are from Western Ukraine.

— Yes, Comrade Commander.

— I have an assignment for you. We are sending the old folks home. An escort is required. Are you ready to go on the road?

Alexander's heart began to race. That meant he would be able to visit home.

— I am ready, Comrade Captain. I am ready.

Captain Gesin tapped him on the shoulder.

— You will get all the papers tomorrow. Get ready. I hope that the way back will go though your home. Good luck.

— I serve the Soviet Union! — Alexander rejoined and added, — Thank you!

PART FOUR
A Soldier's Return

The freight train was pulling into the station. Alexander gazed at the trees flying by the window and his heart beat faster and faster. He recognized places dear to his heart. He recognized the city of Hirov! He was coming home to his beloved Kvasenina! His family and friends were waiting for him. He was on a long-awaited leave. Sweet home was so close. He couldn't wait to get there. He had been away for six long years and hadn't received any news from home whatsoever during the whole war.

Upbeat, he jumped off the train's footboard in Hirov. His maternal aunt lived there. Should he drop by her place? It was probably not a good idea, since it was getting dark and he still had a ways to go. His mom was waiting for him. How badly he had missed her! How often he had dreamt of her hugging and kissing him, her baby boy. How many tender loving words she said to him in his dreams while stroking his thick dark hair. "It will be all right, Shmul. Everything will be just fine", she was saying to him. And bliss filled Alexander's heart. He was going home and would become Shmul once again. Everything would be back to normal and they would live happily.

The young soldier walked quickly and steadily. The wind was flapping his great-coat's tails. He had a heavy backpack. There were small gifts in it. He got a little something for everyone.

He had been waiting for this blessed reunion for so long and now it was just six miles to his home — close at hand. He had walked across all of Europe, even as far as Berlin. He had a medal on his chest "For the

The road from Hirov to Dobromil, 2004
Alexander Leventhal walked down this road to get home,
not knowing his home was no longer standing.

capture of Berlin". He had so much to tell and share with his mother and father. He could almost see his sister Rosa rushing to hug him, mother Mindlya crying happy tears, and father Gersh rejoicing. As for Moisha, that madcap had probably grown up completely and might even be taller than his brother.

Alexander's steps were steady and long. He was slim in the army great-coat, with a garrison cap on his head. Deep in happy thoughts, he was oblivious of his surroundings. He came across lots of passer-byes, but for some reason they avoided him. Alexander took no notice of it. He knew the road well. So many times he had taken cattle to the market in Hirov. He recalled the unfortunate bull-calf that was as stubborn as a mule. Shmul and his cousin had big problems dragging it to market and then had sold it for peanuts. Alexander smiled recalling that incident.

He kept walking, and in his mind he saw his mother, father, Rosa, Moisha, and Grandma Hanna. He wondered whether she was still alive. After all, she was 94 years old when he left home. His brother Moisha was 14 at the time. And his beloved Rivka! He often had dreams about her bright dark eyes and her soft hands. He was going to ask his mother to go and match Rivka. He had an engagement ring ready for her.

When he was drafted into the Red Army, mother Mindlya had cried bitterly. She hugged Shmul and tears streamed down her cheeks. "I will never see you again, son", she said. "I won't. Who will be my strong support? Who will help me through the difficult times?"

Alexander remembered how tough it was to part with his family. He had hugged his mom and tried to comfort her, "I will be back, mom. I know I will. Don't cry, mom." He remembered getting into the truck, Rivka waving good-bye, and his father standing there sadly looking at the truck rushing forward to take their son to a strange country with weird customs and traditions, and with a strange language.

And now he was almost home. He was only on a leave to visit his family, but he had kept his word, he came back. Yes, he came back alive. Thinking about it Shmul walked faster and faster.

It was dawn by the time he approached Dobromil. A church stood on the right side of the road. And there was the bridge. But wait a minute — he no longer recognized the area. Where was he? The river and the bridge were the same as he remembered, but all the houses were in ruins, and so were the streets. Shmul was happy to see the memorial for

The site of the burnt-down synagogue, 2004

Mitskevich still standing. There was the city hall with the clock, still standing. Where is the synagogue? There were just ruins all around.

He stopped in front of the ruins. He did not know which road to take. Horror stricken, he walked past destroyed houses and stores with not a soul in sight. Apprehension crept into his heart like a snake. He had been away for six long war years. He had not received a single bit of news or any word about his family. He picked up his pace.

— Leventhal!

Alexander turned his head towards the voice: a man behind the fence was calling his name.

— Come over here, Leventhal, what's the hurry?

Alexander recognized the man. It was a neighbor of theirs. Sometimes they bought cattle together and took them to the market place.

— Leventhal, it's me, Marushchak. Don't you remember me? Take a good look!

Then Marushchak's wife came out to the porch of the house. Seeing Alexander she rushed to him, grabbed him by the arm, still not believing he was alive.

— God, Shmul, you are alive! Leventhal is alive! — She was grabbing him and tears rolled down her cheeks.

— Come on in, Leventhal! Let's eat! — She was pulling him into the house still in disbelief that he had returned home.

Alexander entered the house and took off his garrison cap.

— Only for a minute. I have to go home.

Marushchak stood there with his head down.

— You don't have to go there, Shmul.

— Where? — Alexander wondered.

— Home, — Marushchak's wife said.

— What do you mean? — the soldier was puzzled.

— Leventhal, all your family is gone. The Germans killed them.

It seemed to Alexander that it was not him they were talking to. There was a throbbing in his temples; blood rushed to his head. He heard their voices but not as clearly any more. He dropped to the bench. The backpack fell to the floor. He had been through a lot and had seen a lot, but could not believe in the death of his family — he just had no strength to do so.

The hostess put hot potatoes and some milk on the table. But Alexander didn't touch the food. There was a lump in his throat. How could that be — he is alive and they are dead? Tears kept rolling down the soldier's face which in an instant had turned to stone.

The hosts quietly sat down on the bench, weary of talking.

— How did it happen? — Alexander asked in a strained voice.

— They were taken to the ghetto in Dobromil. The older ones were taken to the railway station and pushed into freight cars and the young ones were shot at the saw mill, — Marushchak forced the words out. — Haven't you heard what they did to the Jews?

— I have. It is just hard to believe. After all, they were simple peasants and never did anybody any harm.

— Look, Leventhal, we saw the Germans torture the Jews with our own eyes. We were unable to help them — or we would have been killed with them.

The soldier had seen many deaths in his life, and a lot of grief, but life had sent him a new test. He was left alone. The damned war had ruined everything — all his hopes, all his dreams. Where to now? Where?

THE MEETING OF THE LEVENTHAL BROTHERS

Alexander left Marushchak's house and sat on a bench with his head lowered. After he had learned the fate of his family everything lost its meaning.

He had been so looking forward to coming home. He had been moving towards it for six difficult years. Sitting in the trenches in the front line under the bullets he dreamed about meeting his mother and father, dreamed about Rivka, about their happy life after the war. Life was so unfair and cruel. Where to go? The damn war had destroyed everything.

A man's voice next to him on the bench broke his thoughts.

— What are you thinking about, young man? — the stranger asked him.

Barely conscious, Alexander looked at the elderly man, trying to understand what the man was asking.

— What are you so deep in thought about, soldier? — the stranger repeated his question.

— I have come home on leave and just found out that my whole family was killed. No one survived. I am all alone, — Alexander said through frozen lips. — I am all alone now.

— What is your name, sir? — the old man asked again taking a real interest.

— Leventhal, — Alexander said quietly.

The man looked at him attentively.

— There is a Leventhal here working in the police department. Would you like to go there and inquire, young man? You must be a Jew, right?

— Yes, I am, — Alexander acknowledged.

— You need to look for your own, for those Jews who survived, — the man continued. — Have you been at the front?

— Yes, — Alexander nodded, — I was at the front from the first days of the war. I come from Kvasenina. I was told that all Kvasenina's Jews have been killed. How did that happen? Why were they killed? It just doesn't make any sense to kill everyone — the old, the children. Why?

— Because they were Jews, soldier, — the man responded.

Alexander stared at him.

— I don't understand what is wrong about that. What's the reasoning behind killing them for that?

The stranger lowered his head and said quietly,

— Soldier, you have been away for years. Everything's changed. Everything is very different now. People have turned into wild animals. Be careful. Go and look for your own who have miraculously survived. Even now it's tough for them here. They are still in grave danger. And you, young man, need to be careful, too. Although I realize that you are already used to tough times and danger, still be careful. Watch out for locals. Look for your own. Some of the Jews have survived. I've got to go. Good luck.

Having said that he got up, leaned on his cane and limped away from the stunned Alexander.

After regaining his senses Alexander went to the police to look for his namesake.

When he arrived at the police department, he spoke to the officer on duty.

— I was told that a Leventhal works here. May I see him and speak with him?

— Sure, — the young police officer said, — Only he is not in at the moment. He is on a lunch break.

— I'll go to the park and sit on a bench, and when he comes, please tell him I am waiting for him, — Alexander asked the officer.

He left the police department and sat on a bench in a nearby park. He sat there for over an hour watching the passer-byes without recognizing anyone.

Suddenly he spotted a handsome young man with thick dark hair. The man was walking towards him crying.

Alexander wondered what kind of grief the man had if he was walking in the street not ashamed of crying in front of the passer-byes.

Approaching Alexander the man wiped his tears.

— What's going on? Why are you crying? — Alexander asked.

— Don't you recognize me, Shmul? — the man asked.

— No, I don't. Who are you?

— I am your brother, Moisha.

Alexander's eyes shadowed. Could that be true? Had he really found his brother, all grown up from the child he remembered?

The brothers rushed to hug each other. They were crying happy tears. After so many years of wandering they finally felt happy. Moisha, who was now called Mikhail Grigoryevich Leventhal, began to share the events of the last six years with his brother.

After a serious head wound Moisha had been sent home. Actually, "home" was just a word, because there was no home to go to. He was well aware that the neighbors had stolen everything in the house little by little during the long war years.

Moisha went to Dobromil to decide what to do next. There was no place to go. Nobody was waiting for him. He had no idea how to start his new life.

It was getting dark. Moisha realized that he had to look for shelter, but where? Who with? He remembered that there were Bandera gangs around who called themselves militants. A Jew had better not cross their path or they would tear him to pieces. But what could he do?

At that moment he saw a building in front of him with a sign "Police".

An idea struck him. He knocked on the door of the police department.

— Who's there? — asked a man's voice from behind the door.

— I am a discharged soldier on my way home and I am asking for help.

A small window in the door opened.

— Show your ID, — the man said sternly looking out of the window.

Moisha handed his papers over and five minutes later the door opened.

— Come in, — the officer said. — Where are you coming from?

— From the front, — Moisha replied, entering the police department.

— Well, sit at the table and let's talk, — the officer invited him. — Let's have some tea, soldier. I've got some bread and salt pork here. You must be hungry.

The officer looked at the visitor attentively. It was easy to determine his Jewish origin by both his name and his looks.

— Do you eat salt pork? — the officer wondered.

— Yes, I eat anything, — Moisha nodded in response. — The war taught me to eat anything, even worms. As to salt pork — by all means. Give me some tea, friend, my mouth is all dry.

While drinking tea Moisha told the officer about his experiences during the war, and then the officer gave him advice.

— Listen, Moisha, you need to look for your own kind. It's a very dangerous time now, you must know it yourself. Look for the Jews. Stick with them.

— Where am I going to find them if they have all been killed? — Moisha shrugged his shoulders in bewilderment. — Where should I be looking for them?

— I know that not all Jews have been killed. A certain Gleikh lives in Dobromil by the river. He was in hiding with his brother in Tarnava for the whole war.

Moisha almost choked on his tea. So the Gleikh brothers had survived. That was great news! After he met them on Bald Mountain they had probably gone to their neighbor, Mistress Guskova in Tarnava, and she hid them until the war was over.

— Where does he live? Please tell me exactly. He is my cousin, — Moisha blurted out unable to control his emotions.

— See, and you said they were all killed, — the officer smiled.

After he got the address, Moisha rushed out of the police department and ran to look for Gleikh.

When he reached the house where Gleikh lived, he stopped, caught his breath and knocked on the door confidently.

There was a rustling sound behind the door, but it didn't open. Moisha knocked again and heard a painfully familiar voice.

— Who's there?

— It's me, Gersh. Moisha Leventhal, your cousin. I have returned from the front. Open the door.

The door opened. Gersh Gleikh and his brother were standing in the doorway.

Moisha rushed to hug his cousins. Tears were rolling down their faces but the young men were not ashamed of them.

The night was spent talking about the past and the future. Moisha finally felt reborn after long years of wandering, of being scared and humiliated.

MISTRESS GUSKOVA

Before Gersh and Motek Gleikh left for the ghetto in Dobromil, Gersh made an agreement with Mistress Guskova. They would leave her all the things that they couldn't take with them, and she would help them in a difficult situation if she could. After seeing what the Germans did to Jews in the ghetto, Gersh and Motek decided to change their plans. They had just escaped from the ghetto when they encounter Moisha on Bald Mountain and tried to persuade him to go with them to Tarnava.

Gersh and Motek waited until dark and snuck into Mistress Guskova's vegetable garden, and then into the barn where she kept two cows, some pigs and chickens. Early in the morning Mistress Guskova went to the barn to milk the cows. When she saw the two brothers sleeping in the stall on a heap of hay, she got frightened. Her legs were shaking, she lost control of her arms, and the poor woman didn't know what to do. The Germans severely punished anyone who helped Jews in any way. Whole families had been shot or hung in front of the village. And Mistress Guskova had six young children.

The poor woman was at a loss. Being a devoted Christian and a kind person, it was unthinkable for her to report her former neighbors to the Gestapo. She had been living with these boys since she was a kid and never experienced anything but goodness from them.

She woke the brothers up. When they opened their eyes they jumped up and looked apprehensively at their former neighbor.

— Mistress Guskova, please help us. We have nowhere else to go, — Gersh said in a trembling voice.

The woman silently pushed away the floor boards in the pigsty and said,

— Here, dig a hole right there. It should be big enough to accommodate both of you. And don't come out of it unless I tell you to. I will carry out the soil in buckets to the vegetable garden. No one can know about you, not even my children or my husband.

The brothers began to work. Soon the hole was ready and the boys had themselves a shelter. They sat in the hole during the day scared to even breathe. The night seemed like heaven to them because they could go outside, get the boiled potatoes in skins that had been left for them in the corner with some bread, milk and water, and be in the open air. At dawn they would return to their shelter.

A few weeks later Mistress Guskova brought two more Jews, also former neighbors, to the shelter. That's how four people ended up in the hole.

Occasionally Mistress Guskova told the boys news about Dobromil and the surrounding villages. But nothing they heard brought any joy or hope of survival.

One night somebody came into Mistress Guskova's yard. The boys had just come outside to go for a walk. There was no time to hide. They all froze and silently watched what was going on. The man sneaked into the henhouse to steal the goose that was nearest the door. Skillfully grabbing the goose by the head the thief broke its neck. It was obvious that he was accustomed to it. Placing the dead goose under his arm the man was creeping towards the vegetable garden when he noticed the shadow of a person on the ground and stopped. It was the Moon that betrayed the boys.

Upon seeing the shadow the thief quickly ran away. Sensing trouble the boys also rushed to their shelter, got into the hole, put the boards back in place and kept quiet.

At dawn car engines roared and Germans yelled. The whole village was surrounded by the punitive forces. The Gestapo had been tipped off that some Jews were hiding in Guskova's house.

The Guskovs were dragged outside. The children stood naked and barefoot in the snow. Mr. and Mrs. Guskov were beaten with whips. They were all crying and begging for a stop to the torture, trying to convince the executioners that the denunciation was false and made by some slanderer. The dogs which were brought to pick up a trail ran around the house but failed to pick up the scent. The Gestapo men turned the house upside down, but were unable to find any evidence of sheltering Jews.

Finally, a priest came to the yard holding the Bible. Approaching Mr. and Mrs. Guskov he said,

— My children, I conjure you by God to tell the truth. Put your hand on the bible and swear that you are not at fault.

Mr. and Mrs. Guskov, who were standing barefoot on the snow, kneeled down. All six children did as their parents and kneeled.

Mrs. Guskova grabbed the priest by his knees and crying desperately began to kiss his long robe.

— Father, we are innocent. Please speak in our defense. They are destroying innocent souls. Have mercy on the children. How can I hide anyone if we ourselves are starving? We don't have any good food, just potatoes, and even that won't last until spring. Help us, Father.

The priest turned to the Gestapo officer and said,

— If anyone had been hiding here, the dogs would have picked up the scent. Let them go. It will be a good lesson for others.

The German officer listened to the priest and ordered the soldiers to leave.

The whole village, awakened by the noise, gathered to watch the spectacle. However, nobody believed that the Guskovs would hide Jews. They were considered poor people who were almost starving to death. Who could possibly say anything against those people?

After the Germans left the Guskovs yard the children crawled to the house. They were so cold they were unable to walk. Mrs. Guskova rubbed their white feet with her hands. Barely recovered from what had happened, Mr. Guskov said,

— What's going on? And who is this person that decided to inform on us? We haven't caused any harm to anyone. Why?

Mrs. Guskova was silent.

After that incident the boys almost never left the hole. They would only push the boards aside to breathe. Day by day, months passed.

One day Mrs. Guskova bent over the hole.

— The Germans are retreating, and the Russians will be here soon. Hang in there.

Their joy was overwhelming. The boys were crying happy tears. They couldn't wait for the Russians to come.

After the Gestapo's night raid Anna Guskova lived in great fear, constantly questioning her decision to give shelter to her former neighbors. But every time she wanted to deny shelter to the Jews she was hiding, something would stop her. It could have been her conscience or fear. After all, if any of the Jews were caught, they could have broken under torture and admitted who had given them shelter, and then the whole family would get shot. Nobody would be spared.

A JAR OF JAM

In the late fall of 1943, Anna brought her "tenants" terrible news: Ruhtsya Leventhal had been captured by the Germans in Kvasenina. She was Gersh and Motek Gleikh's cousin.

After escaping from the Dobromil ghetto Ruhtsya had hidden in the woods not far from Kvasenina where she had lived before the Germans came. When it got cold and snow fell the woman began using her former neighbors' stalls for a bed. Usually, after spending the night in the stalls she left before dawn, afraid that she would get caught. That was exactly what happened.

One especially cold night Ruhtsya sneaked into the stalls of her former neighbor, Ivan Motsey, hoping to warm up in the hay next to the cattle. With shaking hands she picked up the leftovers of potatoes in the pig feeder. After she had satisfied her hunger a bit, she buried herself in the hay, got warm and fell asleep. Her sleep was peaceful and sweet. She dreamed of her father and mother. Everybody was having fun. They held hands and danced a Jewish dance. Suddenly her family began to leave her. Ruhtsya tried to talk them into staying but it didn't help. All of a sudden a huge dog appeared from somewhere and attacked her biting her painfully on the leg.

Ruhtsya woke up. Her heart was racing from fear. She felt pain in her leg. Abruptly throwing off the hay, she raised her head and froze: her former neighbor Ivan Motsey was standing in front of her. He held her tightly by the leg.

— Got you, Jewish bitch, — he growled.

Pulling the woman strongly by the leg he dragged her outside.

Scared out of her wits, Ruhtsya was not even able to scream. The big man was dragging her with enormous force and rage to the center of the yard.

— Hey, everybody, get over here, I have caught a sheeny! — he yelled loudly. — People, come gather here. I've caught a sheeny.

Collecting herself a little, Ruhtsya began to cry and asked timidly,

— Mister Ivan, I just wanted to sleep until dawn, please forgive me. Please let me go. I will never come here again. After all, I haven't taken anything. I implore you by God to let me go.

— You say by God? I'll show you by God, — and he began beating the woman with refined maliciousness. — You killed our God, you crucified Him, and now it is payback time.

Ruhtsya curled in a ball as if trying to disappear.

Fellow villagers began to gather around Ivan's yard, but nobody went in. Everybody was watching the awful spectacle from afar. Someone said timidly,

— Come on Ivan, let her go. She hasn't done you any harm.

Ivan stopped, looked menacingly at the crowd and said,

— Who said that?

There was silence. The daredevil had already left the crowd fearing for his life.

At that moment the gate opened and headman Opryshko with his deputy Korostenskiy entered the yard.

— What is going on here? — inquired Opryshko with an air of importance.

— Here, Mr. Opryshko, I have apprehended a sheeny. She was sleeping in my stalls. She probably planned to leave at dawn but overslept. I went to feed the cattle and saw a human leg sticking out. I grabbed her by the leg, and she woke up and stared at me, — Ivan spluttered.

Ruhtsya lay rolled up in a ball in a pool of blood.

Opryshko walked around her with an air of importance.

— You are a good person, Mr. Motsey. You are dedicated to serving the new authorities and you follow their orders correctly. We will take her to Filus in Dobromil and he will decide what to do with her. As to you, you will get rewarded. Come with us to get your jar of jam.

Motsey smiled happily. At that moment everyone heard somebody say,

— Jesus was sold for thirty pieces of silver, whereas you sold this poor child for a jar of jam. Bargain, you may get more.

Opryshko looked menacingly at the crowd and said sternly,

— They will not give more, just one jar and that's it. Order is order. The Germans appreciate order. — With these words he kicked the severely beaten Ruhtsya. — Get up. Let's go to the authorities for a ruling.

— I haven't done anything wrong. Please let me go, — the woman implored again. — You have known me since childhood, Mr. Opryshko. Please let me go.

— Mr. Motsey, — she continued addressing Ivan, — you used to come to our house. You ate bread at the table with my parents. You always borrowed money when you were in need. What has happened to you now?

— Shut up, sheeny brat, — Ivan barked. — Power has changed hands. Now it is ours.

Happy to hear that response Opryshko patted Ivan on the shoulder and told Korostenskiy to bring the cart.

Ruhtsya knew that she would die. Anyone brought to Filus did not survive. Getting up with difficulty she slowly dragged herself to the cart. People stepped aside making way for her.

After the headman tied her hands to the cart, he sat in the front.

— Well, let's go, God help us, — he said and whipped the horse. The horse moved forward pulling the cart and taking the poor victim to the place of bloody execution.

The crowd stayed behind and watched the cart disappear down the road.

In Dobromil, Opryshko personally reported to Filus' secretary about the apprehended sheeny. A few minutes later the Commandant showed up. He asked in broken Russian,

— Where is your sheeny?

— On the cart, Herr Commandant. According to your order we brought her here, — Opryshko said.

Without even glancing at Opryshko, Filus whistled to his dog which never left its master's side, patted it on the neck and went out.

When he saw the poor woman tied to the cart, he gave an order.

— Untie her and bring her to the square.

Opryshko quickly untied Ruhtsya and dragged her to the square.

Filus was saying something to his subordinates and laughing loudly. The officers also laughed while listening to their superior.

Ruhtsya was dragged to the center of the square, where the market place was held on weekends, and she was left there alone.

She glanced around in fear and whispered a prayer. There was only one hope left — God — because people had turned away from her. But unfortunately, at that time, God had turned away from all Jews, too.

Ludwig Filus emerged from the Commandant's office. He took out a cigarette, lighted it and quietly told his dog,

— Get her!

Following his order, the dog rushed to the poor woman in big leaps. It pushed her down with one forceful blow and began to tear her apart with its teeth, trying to get to her throat.

The woman screamed wildly, yelling for help and trying to resist the attacks of the wild animal, but no one came to her rescue. Everybody just watched the terrible spectacle. The officers enjoyed watching the dog tear its victim to death.

Opryshko poked Motsey in his ribs.

— What are you staring at? It's just a sheeny. Let's go get the jam.

With a pale face — everything Ivan had seen went against the grain — he followed the headman.

MALKA FLUGER'S CURSE

In August 1944, Anna brought the Gleikh brothers one more horrible piece of news: their cousin Malka Fluger had been caught and torn to pieces by Ludwig Filus' dog. She had lived in Hirov before the war. Her family owned a store located on the main street of the town. After all the Jews were forced into the ghetto, Malka decided to escape. She had hidden in the woods by the village of Pyatnitsa for the whole war. Bomb explosions and heavy artillery from the Soviet troops could be heard there. Everyone knew the Russian troops were coming.

One night the hungry woman was looking for food. She sneaked to a potato field and began to dig the new potatoes out of the soil, happy to be able to satisfy her hunger.

Suddenly a heavy blow to her head threw her to the ground. When she regained consciousness she saw a huge man standing over her with a stick in his hands. She realized she was going to die.

Grabbing Malka by the hair the man dragged her across the field to the road. She made attempts to free herself but failed.

Dragging her to the place where he had tied his horse the man stopped and began to beat the poor girl violently. She lay on the ground barely breathing.

The man tied her hands with a rope, fastened it to the saddle and told her to get up.

Malka raised herself a bit and said,

— Merciful mister, please let me go. I will never come back here again. Please release me.

But he did not listen to her. The man mounted his horse and rode to the village dragging the poor girl behind him.

Onlookers gathered in the center of the village to see the captured sheeny. The poor thing looked terrible. Smeared in blood from head to toe she looked like a monster. The woman was begging for mercy and kissing her torturer's feet. But he just kicked her.

Finally, after satisfying his rage, he dragged Malka to the Commandant in Dobromil.

When she realized that nothing would help her, Malka gathered the last energy remaining in her thin body and shouted,

— Let my blood fall upon your heads and the heads of your children!

Three weeks after Malka Fluger's horrible death Russian troops entered the village of Pyatnitsa and the terrible curse that Malka threw into the faces of her executioners began to come true.

The Russian authorities sent over half the village to Siberia. The man who had captured Malka and handed her over to Filus was tried publicly and sent to the Siberian camps. Fifteen years later he came back to his village a sick man, just in time to watch Malka's curse come true. His three sons died one after another in different accidents three years after his return from the camps. During the burial of his last son he asked for forgiveness from the Jewish woman who he had tortured.

THE RUSSIANS HAVE COME!

Anna was waiting for the Russians. Finally, that long-anticipated day came. Russian troops entered the village of Tarnava.

Anna ran into the barn happily shouting,

— My darlings, my dears, come out. The Russian Army is here.

It was amazing for such an exhausted woman to have so much strength. In an instant, she threw aside the boards that covered the Jewish boys' shelter.

There was a puzzled look in the boys' eyes. They were unable to fully comprehend that Anna was telling the truth, that their torturous imprisonment had come to an end.

— Well, what's keeping you, come out! — Anna was shouting. — That's it, your grief is over, and you are free now.

The young boys (if they could be called that — at that moment they looked more like monsters) began to climb out of the hole. Their long dirty hair was smeared in farmyard droppings. Only their eyes sparkled.

When they finally got out of their shelter, Anna realized how tough it had been for them to spend over two years in that hole. In front of her stood ghosts of the people she had once known. Then it occurred to her.

— Stay here. I'll warm some water. We need to make you look human.

She quickly ran to the house and started to warm a bucket of water.

Mr. Guskov was very surprised.

— What are you doing, Anna? — he wondered, smiling. — Are you going to bathe in the middle of the day?

Anna approached her husband, kneeled in front of him, hugged his legs and said,

— Forgive me, my dearest. Forgive me for keeping this secret from you for such a long time. But I couldn't do it differently.

He stared at his wife in surprise, not understanding anything.

— What's up with you? What's going on? — he helped her get up from the floor. What are you saying?

— I have been hiding four Jews in our barn, — Anna forced these words out.

She saw her husband's expression change. She saw his cheekbones move and his face turn a bluish-white color.

— What did you say? — he asked.

— I was hiding our neighbors in the stalls. I could not do otherwise. The Germans would have killed them.

— How about us? — her husband asked her quietly. — We would have been killed too if they had been discovered.

— But they weren't found. Let's help them look human. Come, you'll see what they look like.

She took him by the hand and led him to the barn.

When the water was warm, Anna washed many months worth of old dirt off the boys. After that she gave them a haircut.

Fellow villagers were watching them over the fence and whispering.

When the boys once again resembled human beings, Anna took them into the house, sat them at the table and gave them something to eat.

The same day all four of them went to the Soviet village to meet with the new authorities.

A week later Motek Gleikh transferred the title of his house in the center of Tarnava that had survived the war to Mrs. Guskova. That house was much bigger and better than the Guskovs house.

When Anna asked Motek why he was doing it, he answered,

— Anna, my family is gone and I don't need this house. You on the other hand, have children, and you also deserve it. This is a reward for your kindness. I don't have anything else to repay you with.

With that, they parted. The Gleikh brothers went to live in Dobromil, dreaming of moving to Argentina.

RETURN OF THE COWS

Alexander and Moisha sat silently for a long time afraid to break the silence. After hearing Moisha's story the older brother was still struggling to come out of shock.

Everything he just heard about the events that had occurred in Kvasenina during the German occupation was hard to comprehend.

Yes, he had read in newspapers about the Nazi atrocities, but he thought his family would not be touched by that disaster. If only he had known about it, he would have searched for his family and friends in the concentration camp that he helped to liberate. Then an idea came to his head.

— Moisha, let's go to Opryshko and take our cow back. Let's visit Korostenskiy, also. You said that Leon had stored a chest with the priest. Let's visit him, too.

Moisha agreed and the brothers did as they planned.

The next morning, just like in the army, they quickly got ready and went to Kvasenina. First they went to their own house. The house itself was gone. Neighbors had taken it apart while searching for gold. But the garden and the well were still there as a reminder of the former owners.

Alexander teared up, but Moisha patted him on the shoulder saying,

— Don't. Let's show all our enemies that we are strong. And the most important thing is that we have survived.

They went to see Opryshko. Before going into the house they went to the barn and saw a cow and a calf there. Moisha recognized his cow. He approached it, hugged it by the neck and said,

— Do you recognize me, dear? Your master is gone. Follow me.

He untied the cow from the stalls and took it outside. The calf followed its mother.

Alexander stood in the yard waiting for Opryshko. However, nobody came out of the house. He saw somebody peek out the window, not daring to come out.

The same thing happened in Korostenskiy's house.

It turns out that Opryshko and Korostenskiy were tried, sentenced to fifteen years of camps and sent to Siberia. After they had done their time, they came back and lived in the barn. Their families would not take them back because they were afraid of repercussions from the Soviet authorities. Soon they both died of serious health conditions which they had gotten in the camps.

After they had taken the cows and calves, the brothers took them to the market in Dobromil. They sold them and Alexander gave his brother all the money.

— Moisha, I need to go back to the army. Regardless of whether I survive or die, you need to get your life going. If I survive, I will come to see you. Here also are eight gold trophy watches. I found them in abandoned houses in Germany. Take them just in case, for a rainy day. Now let's go to the priest to get Leon's chest back.

The brothers went to the house where Kvasenina's priest lived. They approached the door and knocked loudly, but nobody answered. After knocking again Alexander said loudly,

— Reverend father, I know you are at home. We have come to get the chest which Moisha and Leon left with you for safe keeping.

There was a rustling sound behind the door, but it didn't open.

— Reverend father, we are not going to do you any harm, we just want to get our things back.

Finally a voice came from behind the door. — I don't have anything left. Militants have taken everything.

— Reverend father, open the door, we just want to see you.

— Go away, bandits, — screamed the priest, — or I'll alarm the whole village. Looters have come. Rescue me!

Alexander and Moisha stiffened in astonishment, hardly being able to believe what was going on.

— Reverend father, we haven't come to rob you. We are here to get back what Leon and I left with you for safe keeping during the German occupation, — insisted Moisha.

But in response they heard an even louder scream.

— Help! People! I am being robbed!

The brothers looked at each other. Moisha responded.

— I told Leon that you were a liar and cheat, but he trusted you. I can tell you that you will be punished, just like the rest of them. You will have to pay for everything.

But the response was the same.

— Help! Help me! I am being robbed in broad daylight!

The Leventhal brothers left the priest's house very upset.

— I told Leon he was a cheat but there was no other option. Everybody was so angry with the Jews then, and I don't know why. Neighbors who used to come over to our house and were considered friends became enemies overnight. During the first days of the war they burst into our house searching for valuables. They took the last bit of food, a box of macaroni which Rosa had brought from the store. And they yelled in our faces that we didn't need anything anyway because we were going to be killed soon. — Moisha was angrily shouting everything that had built up in his heart.

Alexander walked next to his brother clenching his fists. Anger and resentment boiled in his chest.

— But we survived. We are going to live. And they will get the punishment they deserve, — he said.

— There is no punishment that will equal what they have done to us, — his brother retorted with despair.

And then they heard someone's scream.

— Shmul! Shmul! Stop!

There was an old man standing by a gate, leaning on a cane, screaming.

— Mr. Tokar! — Alexander said in recognition.

All their lives Mr. Tokar's sons were Shmul's and Moisha's good friends. They always helped each other out in tough times.

— Mr. Tokar, how are you?

— I am so glad to see you, boys! I am so glad to see you! Come into the house. — he opened the gate for the brothers.

The young men entered the house. Mr. Tokar had been the headman of the village under the Polish authorities. The Soviet authorities had removed him from that position. When the Germans came to the village, they offered to make him the headman again, but he declined the offer claiming to be old and sick.

The former headman seated the guests at the table and asked his daughter-in-law and his son to treat the welcome guests to whatever they had. The Tokars were a big family, but none of the sons had served in the police or the Nazi National Guard known as the SS Galichina. He pelted the brothers with questions and it was obvious that he was sincerely glad to see them.

After lunch at Mr. Tokar's place, the Leventhal brothers once again went to the yard where their famous eatery used to stand. Only the garden and the well they used for water hinted of their old life.

The young men were leaving their back yard with heavy hearts. Moisha cried and Alexander walked away with a stoic face.

After spending three days in his native village Alexander got ready to go back to his unit. He said good-bye to everyone, took his backpack, gave his brother a big hug and said,

— I will come back. We will survive. You will see. You take care of yourself, kid. You are the only one I've got in the whole world.

With that, he left, steadily walked along the Hirov road towards the railway station.

DEMOBILIZATION

Alexander returned to his unit and continued to serve in the army. It was March of 1946 and Alexander's unit was in Hungary, serving in the 48th heavy mortar brigade belonging to the Commander-in-Chief — Comrade Stalin.

One day he was summoned to the headquarters.

Captain Gesin was sitting at the table with his head full of thick grey hair pillowed on his hand.

Alexander stood at attention.

— Sergeant Leventhal reporting as ordered.

Glancing at Alexander the captain motioned to him with his hand: "As you were".

He got up from behind the table, approached Alexander and patted him on the shoulder.

— Well, sergeant, have you visited your homeland?

— Yes, Comrade Captain, I have.

— How are things there? Tell me what you have seen. I, for one, have not received a single bit of news from my family during the whole war.

Alexander was looking at the captain unable to say a word.

— Why are you silent, sergeant? Tell me.

— Comrade Captain, I haven't seen anything good there. My parents, my sister and many of my relatives were picked up, put into the railway cars and sent to a concentration camp, like the one you and I liberated in Berlin. There was no news from them whatsoever. All I know is this: almost no one survived there. Only those who were hiding in the woods survived, and even so only some of them survived. I was lucky to find my younger brother. A German soldier helped him to escape from the ghetto. He had been hiding in the woods for half the war with young boys like himself, and later he fought in the war. The Germans brought a lot of grief to our land. A lot of Jewish blood was shed there. Mostly they liquidated the Jews. Captain, I don't know everything, but I haven't seen anything good there. Not only that — gangs of nationalists have appeared. They have been formed from the local population.

Captain Gesin was listening to him with his head lowered. He came from Ukraine, and his whole family had lived in Kiev before the war began. He lived with the hope that his family had managed to evacuate in time. While in Hungary he inquired in Kiev and to the Red Cross, trying to find his family, but the responses were not encouraging.

After a moment's silence the Captain said thoughtfully,

— Look, Leventhal, apply for examination by the health board. You have been wounded multiple times. They may give you a medical discharge from the army. A new law has just been adopted. Here's some paper.

Alexander quickly wrote an application, handed it over to Captain Gesin and said,

— I will be forever grateful to you, Comrade Captain.

He saluted and left the room.

Three days later he was ordered to appear before the medical board.

The doctors gave him a certificate stating that his right arm was impaired and that Alexander Leventhal was fit for duty only during a war and only in combatant forces.

He was discharged. He was given 360 rubles, five meters of cloth for shirts (white cotton print with blue stripes), some dry ration and papers certifying his discharge from the army.

GOING HOME

Leventhal hurried home. He hitchhiked and traveled by train. When he reached Hirov he decided once again to walk to Dobromil on foot, but on his way a truck carrying border guards caught up with him. After they checked his papers they offered to give him a lift in the truck.

Alexander gladly accepted and very soon arrived in Dobromil.

When he arrived he started thinking about where to spend the night. Like his brother Moisha had once done, he decided to go see his cousin Gersh Gleikh and ask him to accommodate him for the night.

Gersh was very happy to see Shmul. He treated him to dinner and found him a place to sleep.

For the first time in a long time Alexander slept like a baby. He had a dream about his house in Kvasenina, the blossoming apple orchard, Grandma Hanna sitting on the chair by the window, and Rosa running around in the back yard with a sieve full of wheat. In his dream Alexander tried to get into the house, but the door was locked. He tried to open it, but the door resisted his efforts.

Alexander woke up. Upon opening his eyes he looked around in surprise trying to determine where he was. Regaining his senses, he got up, washed, dressed, and ate a slice of bread that he found on a plate in the kitchen. Washing the bread down with some boiled water he felt energized and decided to go and look for a job.

He put on his great-coat and his garrison cap and went out.

Spring wind caressed his face. When he approached the building of the district Party committee he stopped. He was not a member of the Communist Party. Would he get any help there? On the other hand, he was a front line soldier, had gone through the war, fought at the front — they ought to help him!

He confidently went to the door. In the reception room he went to the secretary and asked to see the first secretary of the district Party committee, Mr. Okhota.

Upon entering the office of the first secretary, Alexander sprang to attention, saluted and reported.

— Discharged sergeant Alexander Grigoryevich Leventhal has come home for permanent residence. I am looking for a job and asking for your help.

The secretary got up from behind the table.

— Welcome, sergeant. We need people like you. Have a seat. Tell me about your war experiences. We will get you a job.

Alexander took off his garrison cap, sat at the table and began his story. Of course it was not possible to cover everything, but he said that he had walked across half the Earth on foot. He told the secretary how they had retreated and advanced. And then about how he came back home and didn't find anyone — the Germans had killed his whole family.

The secretary was listening to him attentively.

— Alexander, — he said suddenly, — the war is not over for us. Bendera gangs are operating here. They hide in the woods and occasionally attack the peaceful populace. They kill teachers, military men, members of the Party. These bands are formed out of the operatives of the SS Galichina Ukrainian National division. It's very difficult for us to fight them. Many local people support them, others are scared of them. It's a very dangerous time. Where did you work before the war?

— At the logging company, — Leventhal replied.

— In that case go back there. The will give you a job. If there are no jobs available, they still have to pay you your salary — that's the law.

Alexander felt relieved. He got up, shook the first secretary's hand firmly, thanked him and went out.

His thoughts were all jumbled together. He ought to go to the logging enterprise to ask for a job, but it was so dangerous. The Bendera operatives were killing Jews — he had already heard about it. Many of the Jews who had been hiding in the woods for the entire war met their death at the hands of nationalists after the war. So the question was what to do.

— I shall go there anyway and have a look, — Alexander finally decided. — I'll see and I'll listen to what they say.

He briskly walked towards the logging company.

When he entered the office he asked to meet the director.

A few minutes later he was invited into the office.

There was an old and very unpleasant man of Polish origin there.

Seeing a visitor in front of him the man sneered wryly and said,

— What can I do for you, comrade?

— I am looking for a job. I used to work here before the war.

— There is no job available for you, comrade, — the director said still smiling.

— But I was told that you must hire me, — Leventhal insisted. — If you don't hire me, you will still have to pay me my salary.

— I'd rather they pay your salary than tolerate you here, — the old Pole hissed no longer hiding his malice.

Alexander turned to leave when he heard,

— Young man, I've got a job for you.

He turned around and saw a balding man sitting in the corner. How had he missed him in the first place?

— I am glad, — Alexander smiled. — I will take it. Tell me what I will be doing.

— Let me introduce myself. My name is Andrey Nikitovich Studenok. And what is your name?

— Alexander Grigoryevich Leventhal, — Alexander reported in military style.

— Great. I am appointing you to be a deputy manager of the whole-sale/retail system — WRS. You will start working tomorrow.

— Tomorrow? And such a position right away?

— So, do you think you will fail at it?

— Why, no. I'll manage. I will work day and night, but I'll manage.

— Very good, my dear. Come tomorrow to the WRS. You'll find Comrade Bruce there. He is the WRS manager, an old guerilla fighter. He fought the Germans all through the war. You two will pull together.

He shook Alexander's hand cordially and patted him on the shoulder.

At that moment Alexander didn't know that Andrey Nikitovich Studenok would become his good friend, and many years later he would refer to him as a jewel of a man.

MOM'S OVERCOAT

That day he walked along the main street of Dobromil full of hope, in a hurry to bring his cousin Gleikh the good news.

Suddenly his glance fell on a woman who was turning the corner. What was that? Alexander could hardly believe his eyes! A woman was wearing a familiar overcoat. Mother Mindlya's overcoat.

His heart began to pound, and blood throbbed in his temples. He rushed after the woman, but she had already disappeared around the corner. Alexander didn't notice that he was almost running, and his lips were repeating the same word over and over: "Mom, Mom..." With each step the whisper was getting louder and louder, and finally it turned into a scream.

As he screamed "mom", Alexander caught up with the woman and grabbed her by the arm.

The woman looked at the soldier with surprise, but Alexander was unable to utter a single word. It was a strange woman wearing his mom's overcoat.

— What can I do for you, mister? — she asked.

— I... I, — Alexander stuttered. I thought you were my mom. Where did you get this overcoat?

— I bought it. Do you think I stole it? — the woman got nervous.

— Oh, no, I am sure you bought it. But could you please tell me who you bought it from? My whole family perished. And this is my mom's overcoat.

The woman got even more nervous. Her hands were shaking.

— What is your name? — she asked in a trembling voice.

— Leventhal. My name is Leventhal. Have you seen my family? Do you know anything about them?

— Mr. Leventhal, my name is Pogranichnaya. Your parents stayed at my place before they were sent to the freight cars. They sold me this overcoat.

The woman began to tell him how it had all happened. Alexander was crying. There was virtually no hope left that his parents had survived.

— Mrs. Pogranichnaya, as of tomorrow I am staring a new job. I will make some money and will buy this overcoat from you.

— Mr. Leventhal, it will not be cheap. I paid three hundred rubles for it. I would like to get my money back.

It was obvious that Mrs. Pogranichnaya was not telling the truth, but Alexander didn't care. He was willing to pay any amount of money to get that overcoat. He had a feeling that he was buying his family.

Alexander was upset and bewildered on his way home. Mom's overcoat and Mrs. Pogranichnaya's story troubled him. He entered the apartment, sat down on a chair, lowered his head and covered his eyes with his hands.

At that moment the door opened and Gersh entered the room.

— What are you thinking about, Shmul? — he wondered.

Alexander raised his head and looked at him with sadness.

— What has happened? Tell me, — his cousin repeated.

— I met Mrs. Pogranichnaya. She was wearing my mom's overcoat. That got me extremely upset. She told me that before being sent to the freight cars my family had lived with her for a few days. She said she had bought the overcoat from mom for three hundred rubles.

— I think she lied. Most likely she gave them a little food for this overcoat. I have met Peter Petrovich, you must remember him. As a boy he was friends with your brother.

— That's right, I remember. Where is he?

— He is here. After you warm up a bit you'll meet everybody who survived and talk with them. You will learn a lot of things. Don't get sad. Tell me what's new with your job.

— I am going to work tomorrow at WRS, — Alexander sounded much happier.

— Oh, this is great news. What will you be doing there?

— I will be the deputy manager of the WRS, the wholesale/retail system.

— Really? It's a good position, but very dangerous. Bendera operatives are out of control. Every day we hear news of somebody getting killed, but we have no other option. We've got to live, we've got to work.

— I've got news too, — Gleikh added after a pause. — I am leaving for Palestine next week. First I'll go to Poland and from there — to Palestine. I have already got all the papers. I am leaving you this room and everything in it. Of course it's not great riches, but at least something to give you a start. Don't get upset, you should be happy for me. As soon as I get to Palestine, I'll write a book on all my misfortunes, experiences and everything I have seen. You'll see, reporters will come to see me some day.

Alexander smiled.

— And we've got something now. Look, I have brought some potatoes. Let's boil them. And I also got a slice of salt pork. We'll saut some onions on it and we'll have a tasty meal.

— Unless you are going to be kosher again, Gersh smiled slyly. — Are you?

Alexander laughed heartily.

The young men began to cook dinner together. Alexander was finely cubing the salt pork and telling his cousin how he had treated Moisha to some salt pork. They laughed happily and at that moment everything tough and terrible seemed to be put behind them.

Gersh suddenly asked Alexander a serious question.

— Could you help me move the remains of my relatives to the Jewish cemetery and bury them according to Jewish traditions?

— Sure! I am willing to help you with anything, — Alexander responded anxiously. — I am so grateful to you for taking me in and letting me stay. It's my duty to help you.

The next day the boys went to the place near Lihtman's sawmill where thousands of Jews were shot and buried in a trench. Witnesses who had observed the execution showed Gleikh the place where his uncle and his family had stood before they died.

Gersh began to dig. At first it was just soil, but soon bones and pieces of half decomposed clothes appeared. Alexander was shaking. But his cousin went on digging skulls and bones out of the soil. Suddenly he had a tiny skull with little teeth in his hands. He lifted those remains carefully, cleaned them meticulously and put them next to the other bones with care.

It was the first time that Alexander saw his cousin cry. Gleikh wept over the mass grave of his uncle's family, who had been shot with his wife and children, the youngest of which had been just two years old.

The deeper the boys dug, the more bones they saw. After gathering the remains, Gleikh put them into a box he had prepared in advance, and they took that improvised coffin to the Jewish cemetery where their grandfather and great grandfather were buried.

When they came to the cemetery the young people discovered that the gravestones from the memorials had been removed and it was impossible to determine which grave was whose. So, in accordance with Jewish tradition, they decided to dig a grave and bury the box with the bones while reading a prayer.

They put a big stone on the grave which they had brought from the trench. They carved the names of the dead on the stone with a knife.

The cousins returned home heavy hearted. Gersh told Alexander what he had heard about the mass execution of Jews on that spot. The stories shocked Alexander, but most of all he was shocked by the cruelty of the local residents — those people who had been neighbors and friends with the Jewish families, but betrayed them during the war.

EVERYDAY WORK

Alexander went to work the day after he was hired.

When he arrived at the WRS office, he saw a man sitting at the table trying to write something, but he was barely able to accomplish the task. He was scribbling some incomprehensible squiggles on a sheet of paper. Alexander realized the man was either sick, or very drunk.

Alexander coughed to attract his attention. "The writer" raised his head and stared at the visitor, trying to focus but failing to do so. It then became clear the man was dead drunk. The man fumbled for the right words.

— Who are you? What brought you here?

— I have come to work. My name is Alexander Grigoryevich Leventhal. And who am I speaking with?

— Nikolay Bruce, former guerilla fighter, a reconnaissance scout, — the man tried to report in a military manner.

— Nice to meet you, — responded Leventhal. — I am a discharged sergeant.

— Come on in, friend. Let's work together, — the boss warmed up. — I've got a snack as well as a warmer-upper. Let's celebrate.

— No, dear Comrade Bruce, I do not drink or smoke, — Alexander replied smiling.

— How so? I don't know anyone like this. Did you fight during the war?

— Yes, Comrade Bruce, I did.

— In that case you must drink. Will you drink to the Motherland?

— To the Motherland? — Alexander was confused. It was a loaded question.

— I can toast to the Motherland. But just one sip. I am allergic.

— Everybody's allergic, — Bruce grumbled. — And yet we drink. Come over here, take a seat. Here's a glass and some rye bread for you. You drink first as a guest, and I will drink after you.

Pretending to pour a drink, Alexander covered the glass, raised it and pretended to be drinking.

The manager was so happy that he clapped his hands.

— There you go!

He generously poured a drink into the glass for himself.

That's how work at WRS started for Alexander. He saw that his boss was a sad drunkard unable to do business, so Alexander got to work with great zealousness.

At first he studied all the papers lying around. Then he inspected everything connected to the WRS and came to the discouraging conclusion that it was necessary to start from scratch. The enterprise had been greatly neglected.

When he got home he told Gersh Gleikh everything he had seen there and shared his plans.

— Shmul, I beg you, — his cousin responded, — do not go to the logging sites after 4 pm. When it gets dark Bendera operatives crawl out of their holes and they are merciless towards us.

— I understand, Gersh. I'll try to be careful.

— Shmul, I need to go to the shoemaker. You can cook the duck. Be careful and don't leave the door open. Have you met my neighbors yet? Sara and Peter Ashkinadze live next door. They are Jewish, but they are so nasty I can't even describe them to you.

— Sara? Does she by any chance come from Tarnava? — Alexander wondered.

— Yes, the one that worked as a secretary for the KGB before the war. She married Peter Ashkinadze. He works in a special squad of border guards. I've told her, "Sara, so many great and beautiful Jewish girls were killed, but you survived. It's not fair." She is a thief and a mean person, and as to him... I don't even know what to tell you. Well, in time you'll see for yourself. I'm leaving. I'll be back in about an hour and a half.

Gersh Gleikh left, locking the door behind him.

Alexander began to cook the duck. He was in high spirits. They were going to have a feast that night. Where in the world had Gersh gotten that duck? Alexander had no idea, but he knew that Gersh was a great guy, and that soon he would go to Palestine.

FAREWELL, GERSH

Alexander looked out of the window waiting for his cousin. It was high time for him to return from the shoemaker. It was dark and the goose was completely cooked, but Gleikh still had not gotten home.

259

Alexander was anxious, but there was nothing he could do. He cut a slice of meat for himself, poured some broth and quickly ate his dinner. After dinner he went to bed, but he had trouble sleeping. The night seemed endless.

At dawn Alexander went to see Gleikh's friend, Shpreher. Shpreher had a horse, which he harnessed to a cart, and together with Alexander they went to the shoemaker to find out about Gersh. When they approached the river, they saw an object lying in the water. Looking closer, the young men couldn't believe their eyes. Gersh Gleikh's body lay in the water.

Alexander sat on the bridge hugging his head in desperation. He knew this wasn't a dream — this nightmare was real.

The boys took their friend's body out of the water. A bullet had been shot through the back of his head from a very close range. Gersh's hands were squeezed into fists as if prepared to fight.

— Look, Shmul, nothing was taken from him. He was already on the way home from the shoemaker. His shoes are over there, and here is his pocket watch and some money. Why do you think he was killed? — Shpreher asked Alexander.

Alexander examined the site where the bullet went in.

— They fired point-blank. These were not Bendera operatives. They would have undressed him and taken everything they could. Look, he was prepared to fight, but the bullet was shot into the back of his head. Someone familiar killed him. But why?

Heart broken, the boys placed Gleikh's body on the cart and took it home.

On the way to the apartment, Alexander knocked on the door where Sara and Peter Ashkinadze lived.

Sara opened the door.

— What do you want?

— Gleikh has been killed, — Alexander said.

Sara didn't say anything; she just shrugged her shoulders indifferently.

He walked away, paying no attention to her. He found his key to the apartment and started to insert it in the keyhole, but to his surprise the door was open. He remembered very well that he had locked it when leaving. Anxiously he entered the room and froze: the apartment had been robbed.

Alexander turned abruptly and left the apartment. Sara was still standing in her doorway.

— Sara, who was in the apartment? — he snapped.

— I have no idea. I haven't seen anything. You know what, give me all the tableware. You don't need it, after all you are single. Otherwise some stranger will take it anyway.

Alexander was in shock. And Sara, without waiting for his response, went into Gleikh's apartment and began to pick up the dinner set which Gersh had found in his aunt's apartment after the war was over. This was the last memory of their family. Alexander ran out of the room.

The funeral procession was moving along the main street of Dobromil. Gersh Gleikh's coffin, made of poorly hewn boards, was on the cart. The horse moved slowly and unwillingly as if wishing to show its displeasure with what was going on.

Alexander, Misha, and Motik Shpreher followed the coffin with their heads lowered. Not one of the onlookers joined them. Some were whispering back and forth. Then the boys heard someone yell.

— You are being finished, sheenies!

Alexander raised his head, trying to see the person who screamed, but to his astonishment he saw a whole group of young people standing by a tree and smiling wickedly.

Alexander made fists, but Motik grabbed him by the sleeve.

— Don't, Shmul. It's not worth it. It will lead no where good.

Finally, they reached the cemetery. They took the coffin off the cart, dug a grave, lowered the coffin into it with the ropes, and the two older boys began to say a prayer. Misha stood there silently and looked at the coffin. Motik pressed him in the ribs.

— What are you waiting for? Go ahead and pray.

— I have forgotten the prayer, — Moisha replied.

— He never knew it, — Alexander said quietly. — Unfortunately, we didn't pay much attention to this. We thought the rabbi would live forever and that the Jewish community would always be the same as it used to be. Who would have thought it would turn out this way? Why do they hate us so? I have walked on foot through all of Europe, captured Berlin, fought in the war for so long, slept in the trenches for so many years, frozen to the ground dreaming of coming back home. And what should I dream about now? I'd like to know what I have fought for.

Addressing the coffin in the grave he said,

— I have come home, but home is no longer here. I wanted to hug my mom, dad, sister, Grandma Hanna, but fate had other plans for me. I thought I had found a brother and a friend, but enemies took him away. When will there be an end to it? So much blood has been shed. So many tears have been cried! Farewell, my dear cousin, a man of noble soul. You wanted to write a book about what happened here, you wanted to tell mankind about all the barbaric crimes committed on this land, but as it turned out our war is not over yet, and it is not known when there will be an end to it. Farewell, and rest in peace.

The boys began to bury the coffin. They planted a weeping willow on the grave so that it would weep with them for Gersh Gleikh. Several weeks later when Alexander went to visit Gersh's grave, the willow was uprooted and thrown into a trench. Once again someone showed hatred for the Jews.

NADYA

Alexander buried himself in his work. The loggers needed lunch brought to them, but nobody wanted to take the risk. It wasn't easy to hire loggers, either. Alexander was able to form teams of loggers from local residents, promising them whatever he could. He tried to recall everything his father and his uncle Leon had taught him. He needed all their knowledge and experience, combined with his own, in order to raise the district up from ruins.

Alexander moved to a different apartment after Gleikh was killed. Many times when he came home he noticed that somebody had gone through his things. Alexander had no idea why anyone would do that. What could be found there? Gold?

Shortly after Alexander returned from the war, he had gone to Kvasenina and visited Yarinka. The woman was crying with happiness, and didn't know where to sit the dear guest or what treats she could put in front of him. But Alexander had spoken to her angrily.

— Why didn't you hide Grandma Hanna? After all, you called her mother.

Choking with tears she had responded,

263

— I would have hid them all if I could, Shmul. But you can't even imagine what was going on here at the time. We would have all been killed. Believe me, Shmul. I grieve for Grandma Hanna every single day.

Alexander left Yarinka's house holding his head down, full of anger.

Eventually the residents of Kvasenina, including Yarinka and her family, were moved to Dobromil because the territory where the village stood was given to Poland. Kvasenina was no more.

By this time, Alexander better understood the situation Yarinka had been in and helped his "sister". He hired her husband, Michael, to work as a packer at a slaughter house and shared a good relationship with the Bats, who lived together in harmony and peace until old age.

One day Alexander met a beautiful girl downtown. She smiled at him. Alexander's heart began to race. Smiling back, he said hello. The girl responded to the greeting coquettishly. He learned that her name was Nadya.

A few days later he met her again and she approached him.

— Hello, Mr. Leventhal. How are you?

— I am fine, thank you. And you?

— I am fine, too. Would you like to go to the dance tonight?

— I'd like to, but I don't know how to dance.

— I will teach you.

— All right, then I will come at nine o'clock, — Alexander agreed.
— See you tonight.

That evening as Alexander was getting ready to go to the dance he realized he had a problem. He had nothing to wear other than his military uniform. What could he do? She expected him to come and he could not break his word. So he put on his army uniform and went to the dance at the Cultural Center.

Moisha was playing the accordion at the dance. The talent for music was in his blood — after all, both his grandfather and Uncle Leon were talented musicians.

When Nadya saw Alexander, she ran to him.

— You have come, Alexander. I am very glad.

— Yes, Nadya, how could I not come? After all, you promised to teach me how to dance.

— Great, — the girl said, — let's go and dance then!

Time flew that night.

After the dance Alexander took Nadya to her home.

On his way home, he saw his neighbor, Mr. Motsyak standing outside.

— How was your night, Mr. Leventhal?

— It was great, Mr. Motsyak, thank you. I met a very beautiful girl named Nadya. I think she will be my girlfriend.

— Nadya, you say, — Mr. Motsyak repeated thoughtfully. — You are forgetting, Mr. Leventhal, that you are of sheeny nationality, whereas Nadya is a Ukrainian.

Alexander was stunned.

— What do you mean, Mr. Motsyak? Are you trying to insult me?

— No, Mr. Leventhal. I would just like to point out to you that during the occupation Nadya used to be one of Ludwig Filus' girlfriends. She dated someone who killed people of sheeny nationality, and now she will be a sheeny's girlfriend? — Mr. Motsyak squinted slyly.

Alexander could not breathe. He could barely restrain himself from attacking Mr. Motsyak. Without responding, Alexander walked around Mr. Motsyak and went into his room.

He had trouble sleeping that night. No matter how hard he tried, he was not able to get to sleep. In his mind he kept seeing his mother, wiping her tears, Grandma Hanna, Rosa, and his father. How everything had changed! Where did this inhuman hatred towards Jewish people come from? It used to be different. What had happened over those years? And Nadya...she was so beautiful. How could she have lived with that slaughterer? Could something have forced her to do it? Maybe he ought to talk with her? No, there was no need to offend the girl. It was none of his business to meddle in another person's life. He would just forget about her.

He thought he would have a better life in Poland and asked Moisha to go there many times, but he would flatly refuse. Moisha had a girlfriend — a beautiful girl named Yana. She had a mother, father, and a sister who loved and respected Moisha. He was happy. He was going to have a family. What else could he wish for? Alexander was very happy for his brother. He wished he could also find a girl and start a family.

OLGA

One morning Alexander went on a trip to Drogobych to get merchandise. It was not easy to find things because there was a shortage of just about everything. Nevertheless, he managed to fill the truck with goods. Having finished their business, he and his driver went to a cafeteria where they enjoyed some tea with buns and then returned to the truck.

Their truck was surrounded by people. What was happening? Could they have been robbed? There was an enraged police officer standing in the middle of the crowd who was loudly yelling something and waving his gun.

Alexander approached the truck. He asked a man standing nearby what happened.

— I don't know. He is looking for his wife. He wants to kill her.

— Look at him. He is crazy, — Alexander responded.

— He can't find her.

Alexander and the man laughed.

— Things happen, — Alexander said as he nodded his head, winked to the driver and got into the cabin of the truck.

They soon left the scene of the incident.

At the entrance to Dobromil a military patrol met them. The soldiers checked their papers, inspected the truck's body and let the truck through.

When they reached the WRS store they stopped to unload the merchandise. The salesmen were waiting.

Unloading went at full speed. The driver got into the body of the truck and began to pass out the merchandise. Suddenly he heard a suspicious sound. What was that? Could it be a mouse that got into the body? He listened closely. The noise reoccurred.

— Mr. Leventhal, something is scratching in here, — the driver shouted.

Alexander got into the truck's body.

— Where?

— I think it's in this barrel.

Alexander went to the barrel and knocked on its wooden side.

Everything was quiet. Alexander smiled at the driver.

— Well, friend, you are starting to imagine things.

At that moment he heard either a whisper or a squeak.

— Help!

Alexander was stunned. Jumping to the barrel in one leap he lifted it. The barrel had been placed upside down, and there was a blonde girl sitting under it tense with fear and cold.

Alexander just about fell off the truck in surprise.

— Who are you? — he asked.

— I am the woman who ran away from her husband. If I hadn't hidden here, he would have killed me.

— That's true, — Alexander agreed. — He was in such a state he would have done it for sure. What is your name?

— Olga. Olga Agureyeva. I got married and went to Drogobych with my husband. But he was drinking vodka heavily and beating me. I decided to go home, but he threatened to kill me if I left him.

The girl looked scared and miserable. Alexander's heart softened. He could not possibly leave that poor creature in the street in a strange town.

— Feed her and warm her up, — he told the salesmen. — And after the unloading I will handle everything.

Alexander was thinking where to take her for the night. He decided to let her stay in his room, and he would go to his brother's place for the night. Everything would be all right in the morning. And that's exactly what he did.

When he came home the next morning to talk to Olga about her accommodation, he discovered that the room had been cleaned and his shirt had been washed and was drying outside. His heart started to race. At that moment Mr. Motsyak came out of his room.

— I can see you have gotten yourself a mistress.

Alexander didn't know what to say.

Olga stood in the middle of the room with a guilty look.

— Olga, I have come to discuss your accommodation with you.

— Yes, yes, thank you so much, — the girl responded.

— But I have just had an idea. Would you like to stay at my place?

Olga timidly lowered her head.

— But I don't know you at all...

— So what? You will get to know me. I am single. Do stay, please.

Olga froze, perplexed. Her beautiful face blushed.

And that's how Alexander found his family. Olga and Alexander were married soon afterward.

WRS Manager

At the beginning of May 1947, Alexander sat in his office preparing for a meeting. He was supposed to make a speech to the workers explaining what they had to do in order to improve the service at the logging company.

His thoughts were interrupted by a telephone call.

— Hello, Leventhal speaking, — he said, picking up the receiver.

To his great surprise he heard the voice of a telephone operator.

— Poland is on the line. You are going to speak with Peremyshl, Poland.

A few moments later a female voice spoke at the other end of the line.

— I apologize, Mr. Leventhal, for bothering you, — she spoke faultless Polish, — but I am looking for my relatives. My name is Golda Brodgaim. I live in Peremyshl. I had family in Kvasenina and Dobromil. People from Dobromil told me that there are two people named Leventhal living there. Could you be so kind as to tell me which Leventhal you are?

Listening to that monologue Alexander lost his tongue. What was going on? Could it be that another live family member existed for him in this world? He wanted to shout into the receiver but there was a lump in his throat and he was not able to utter a word.

Meanwhile the woman on the other end was almost yelling.

— Hello... Hello! Mr. Leventhal, can you hear me?

— Yes, Golda, yes, — Alexander finally managed to say in almost a whisper. — Yes, Golda! It's me, Shmul Leventhal, your cousin. And Moisha lives here with me, also. We are the only ones who survived out of the whole family.

— How did you manage to survive? Where are all the relatives? Has anyone else survived? — Alexander was now screaming into the receiver.

He heard the woman cry on the other end of the line.

— My dear Shmul, I am so glad to have found you. Our neighbor, Yuzek Gromadskiy, saved me. He became my husband, and now I am

269

not Golda any more, but Genya Gromadskaya. It was necessary in order to survive. And how are you, my dear cousin?

— I have changed my name, too, — he replied. — I am now Alexander Leventhal, and Moisha is Mikhail Leventhal. And we have both gotten married. My wife is expecting a baby now, the next generation. And Moisha's wife is pregnant, too.

Alexander didn't notice that there were tears rolling down his cheeks. He was extremely excited by Golda's call.

— Shmul, I am going to have a baby, too. I will try to come to visit and see you when I can. It is very difficult to do, but it is still possible. Kisses and hugs. I'll write to you about everything in a letter. Write to me, too. The voice broke off and then there was only a dial tone.

Alexander put the receiver on the hook, wiped his tears, got up and went to the window. From his window on the second floor he could see the street and the passer-byes walking along it.

Dobromil... it had changed so much after the war! The town used to be famous for its stores and was known for its culture. Everything had been destroyed. How could this town be raised to its former level?

A knock on the door brought Alexander out of his reverie.

— Come in, — he said.

About ten men entered the room followed by the secretary.

— Take your seats, please, — he said. — And you, dear, please sit over here and take the minutes of our meeting.

They all sat around a long table and gave the boss a chance to speak.

— I have gathered you here today to announce my plan. I have been developing it for several weeks and now it's time to reveal it to the team. The first goal is to develop our economy. In order to achieve this, it is necessary to set up self-sufficient canteens. We will use waste food, of which we have plenty, to feed pigs, chickens, geese, and rabbits. It will enable us to have our own cash income. By doing so, we will not use state funds. Moreover, we will be able to double the portions in the canteens for our employees.

Goal number two — to build a bread-making plant. There are probably still some people left who know how to bake bread. So we will set up a bakery.

Goal number three — to open a sausage manufacturing room.

The fourth goal — a brewery and a soda water department.

The fifth goal — a dairy plant.

It simply cannot be true that all the competent people have been killed. It is necessary to search for specialists among the local residents.

We will open the Lihtman sawmill and attach a shop for manufacturing furniture. There must be some cabinet makers left somewhere; we just need to find them. The old will teach the young. That's how there will be new jobs for people. Men will be coming to us from all the other villages. The economy will improve.

Leventhal was speaking with deep emotion. In his mind's eye he already saw all these facilities open, people going to work in the morning, women buying pretty clothes and Dobromil becoming the same solid and respectable town it used to be.

Everybody sat there and listened to their boss with open mouths. Some believed Alexander's words, others didn't. After all, he was so young, he was just twenty nine years old, and he was already appointed to be the manager of WRS. To some, he was just a dreamer, that's all there was to it.

But at this point he surprised them all.

— I have already chosen the right people. And I have chosen the building sites.

And he read the names of the people who were going to carry out the plans. The town was buzzing like a beehive for several days with gossip and idle conversations. Soon they all found out that the young WRS manager meant everything he had said. Mr. Leventhal's plans started to become reality.

He spent most of his time at work. During the implementation phase of his plans he went to the district to make agreements with the authorities there; he frequently went to ministries in Moscow or Kiev to get approval for his ideas. When the ministers saw a young enthusiastic man who sincerely wished to make his dreams come true, they often got on his side and helped him implement his plans. It took less than a year to open all the facilities he had talked about in Dobromil.

Alexander was consumed by the work of trying to master all the sales outlets and to improve the service of the workers. The abundance of food products surprised people. Dobromil had become the top supplier in the Drogobych region.

Leventhal began preparing consignments of apples to be sent to Pechora. The crop was picked up and sent by railroad to the North.

After a while Alexander received thanks from the Minister of Forest Industry of the USSR for giving the children in Pechora a chance to eat juicy ripe apples.

People started to treat Leventhal with great respect.

The door to his office was almost never closed. People came to him for advice and to ask for help. Alexander helped everyone in any way he could. He listened to every visitor with rapt attention. The town started to prosper just like during the prewar years, and under his leadership the WRS was awarded first place in the development of the district.

He wrote to his cousin Golda in Poland about the many things that were happening in Dobromil, and she told her story to Shmul and Moisha in several long letters.

GOLDA

Golda Brodgeim was the daughter of one of Gersh and Leon's cousins. The Brodgeims were known to be exceptionally kind. When Rosa got sick and required treatment in Peremyshl, Mindlya and her daughter stayed at the Brodgeims' place for months. Golda's mother, Faiga, tried to help Mindlya any way she could and Mindlya always made flattering remarks about their wonderful family.

As children, Golda and her brother Genyk would go to Kvasenina to visit the Leventhals for a few weeks every summer. Golda was a real beauty, a blonde with blue eyes. Not even slight plumpness tainted her — all the boys tried to court her. Genyk was a kind boy and the two Brodgeims' got along very well with the Leventhal children.

In Kvasenina, fresh air, milk right from the cow and a farm diet made Golda and Genyk healthy and energetic. The children all played together on the lawn and went to the forest to pick mushrooms and berries. At the end of every visit, the children did not want to leave. One thing made it OK — they would be back again next summer. Golda always parted warmly with Rosa, Shmul and Moisha.

The war caught the Brodgeims in Peremyshl. The Germans began to shoot Jews on their first days there. Life was getting more and more dangerous for them. Golda almost never left the house. The family was frightened by the atrocities going on in the town.

Once there was a knock on the door. Golda's mother was afraid to open it, but the knock continued and so Genyk opened the door. Yuzek Gromadskiy, a young man from next door, stood in the doorway. Genyk gave him a questioning look.

— May I speak with Golda, please? — the neighbor asked quietly.

— Sure, come on in, Yuzek, — Genyk nodded his head and went away from the door.

Golda looked at Yuzek with fear.

— I haven't seen you for a while, Golda, — he mumbled fidgeting, — and I wondered if something had happened to you. That's why I decided to drop by.

— I am all right, Yuzek. I am just afraid to go out, — the girl replied.

Her mother and father stood by and watched with surprise. Before that day they had no idea the boy next door, Yuzek Gromadskiy, was interested in their daughter.

— I have brought something for you, Golda, — Yuzek said as he got a loaf of bread and some jam out of his bosom.

Seeing the food the girl approached her neighbor and said quietly,

— Thank you, Yuzek, but you are risking your life. Don't do it again.

The young man was silent.

— If the Germans see you take food to the Jews, they will shoot you, — the girl added with fear in her voice.

— Golda, next week they will begin to force Jews to live in one area. Don't go there. They will kill you all there. An acquaintance of mine, Yanush, told me this. He serves in the police. He knows everything. He saw Germans shoot Jews. There were women, children and the old among them. They don't spare anyone. Jews are not human beings to them.

When Golda's mother heard that she began to cry. Her husband embraced her shoulders and hugged her silently.

— Genyk, don't go there either. You are young. You need to hide somewhere.

Genyk was silent, lowering his head.

— I will drop by again in a few days, — with those words Yuzek made for the door, and Genyk followed him whispering something in the guest's ear.

After their neighbor left the family sat down to dinner. They were all happy to have the bread and jam. While they were still sitting at the table, Genyk announced that he wanted to leave and hide in a safe place. If everything went fine, he would take all of them to that place. Without a word his father got up and gave his son his last savings, hoping that he would find a place for them all.

A few days later the German authorities announced that all the Jews would be moved to one area of Peremyshl. The Brodgeims took the news with fear. There was no news from Genyk. Yuzek didn't show up either. There was no other option, they had to pack and move to the ghetto. And then a boy next door brought news about Genyk: Germans had killed him in downtown Peremyshl.

Rumors were that he went to his lover to get help — a Pole by the name of Helena. The woman welcomed him with love, tricked him out of his money and talked him into taking a hot bath to relax. Unsuspicious, Genyk got into the aromatic salt bath prepared for him, relaxed and snoozed. After a while he heard engines roar and soldiers yell in German. The boots were stamping somewhere close. Genyk grew suspicious. He called his girlfriend, but she was not in the apartment. The sound of running boots was closing in on him and a few seconds later the bathroom door was knocked out by a gun-butt. Genyk realized he was trapped. His beloved had betrayed him. The blood was pounding in his temples. He had to make an attempt to escape. He jumped out of the window on the second floor and ran naked and wet, but a machine gun burst hit him by the porch of the house.

When the family got that news, they were all terrified. The mother was crying. Golda was silent. They knew they were going to die.

Things were put together and tied into big bundles. But who would be able to carry them? Golda's father was old, and so was her mother. It was up to Golda. The girl lifted a bundle and slowly went to the door. Her father was whispering a prayer while leaving the apartment. They walked slowly as if hoping that something would change any minute, that someone would come up to them and say, "Go back home, there has been a big mistake".

But nobody came up to them, and nobody said anything. There were just Germans and policemen standing at every corner watching an endless flow of people with babies in their arms, and with old men barely walking. People walked in the middle of the road, and the local residents stood on the sidewalks. Some of them did not hide their malevolence. Some picked up lumps of dirt and threw them at the passing people shouting,

— Get out of here, sheenies!

But there were some who watched that sad procession with sympathy and compassion.

Upon arriving at the ghetto the Brodgeims stopped near the porch of one house wondering what to do. At that moment a policeman approached them and grabbed Golda by the hair and dragged her to the gates. Her old mother threw herself at his feet trying to protect her daughter, but she was kicked back by a severe boot blow to her face. Her father rushed after the policeman in desperation, but a blow to his head with a club knocked him down. Golda tried to wriggle away from the violator, but he held her hair tightly in his fist. A strong blow with the club silenced the beautiful girl.

The policeman dragged her to the gates. His face was twisted with hatred and anger. Golda lost her tongue when she saw Yuzek standing around the corner.

Yuzek got something out of his pocket and slipped it into the policeman's hand.

— Yanush, I'll just play with her a little, no longer than a couple of hours, and then I will bring her back.

— No, Yuzek, I'll come to your place. I, too, want to have fun with this sheeny. They will all be killed anyway. We'll kill her there. I'll just finish working my shift and will come over then. Just be careful, don't let her escape.

— Where will she run, Yanush? Just look at her. She will be caught at once. Also, after what I do to her, there is not much chance she will be able to run.

The young men laughed heartily.

Still laughing, Yuzek grabbed Golda by the hand and dragged her with him.

When they turned the corner, Yuzek pushed Golda inside a house, pushed her against the wall and began to tear the hexagram off her sleeve.

Golda, still in shock, was shaking with fear.

— Golda, — Yuzek whispered in her ear, — we've got to escape. We need to escape right now. There is a small closet under the stairs.

Get into it and stay there quietly. I will come back for you in half an hour and will bring you some clothes and we will do your hair. And I am telling you once again. Sit here quietly so as not to attract attention. We've got to get out of Peremyshl today.

Golda could hardly believe what she was hearing.

— What about my parents? How can I leave them there? — she whispered.

— You saw for yourself what was going on there. We will not be able to help them. Save yourself. We don't have time.

With those words the young man helped Golda get inside the small closet where she was to wait for him.

Half an hour seemed like an eternity to the girl. Finally, Yuzek came back. He brought a dress, a raincoat and a head scarf. Golda quickly changed, tied the scarf around her head and taking the young man's arm went out of the house trying to walk calmly.

— Remember that you are no longer Golda, but Genya, — Yuzek whispered, — you are Genya Gromadskaya, my wife and you don't have anything to do with Jews. I got all the papers and an ID for you over the last few days. Just behave with dignity, don't be afraid. We will go to the catholic church now, I have a bicycle there. We are leaving Peremyshl.

— And where are we heading? — Golda asked, also in whisper.

— I don't know, but we need to get out of Peremyshl. We will go to the West where nobody knows us.

They entered into the church, sat on the bench and pretended to pray while looking around. Golda was kneeling and looking at the faces of Catholic saints and praying her own prayer in her mind. Meanwhile Yuzek got everything he had prepared for the long journey. His love for Golda made the young man take enormous risks, but he didn't think about it. His only dream was to save the girl and be by her side, to live or to die with his beloved, the one who was destined to become his wife and his son's mother. But at that moment in the catholic church, they had no idea what was going to happen. Golda also didn't know that she and Yuzek would be getting married in that same church after the war was over and she would find out a big secret that Yuzek had so carefully hidden from her — that he was six years younger than her.

Alexander Levental with his children, 1955
Photo from the author's archive

GENNADIY AND LUDMILA

In 1947, Alexander and Olga had a son who was named Gersh after his grandfather, but he was officially registered as Gennadiy. Three years later, a daughter was born whom they named Ludmila. Alexander loved his children more than life itself.

Alexander moved most of Olga's family from the Kharkov region so that they could all be together and Olga could have some help with the children. He especially loved Aunt Dasha, who was the twin sister of Olga's mother. She was a simple Russian woman, not able to read or write, but she was a smart and wise person who had had a tough life.

She had survived the revolution but became a widow at the age of 27. She never attempted to marry again. Besides, men were scarce after the Second World War was over. She decided to move to the Western Ukraine to escape famine and help her goddaughter, Olga.

She took care of the toddlers with the love and tenderness of a mother and a grandmother. To her, they seemed to be the most beautiful and smart children in the whole world. Alexander loved Aunt Dasha very much and appreciated her devotion to his family.

Gennadiy's birth was a very important event for Alexander. A new life began for him. He was a father. He had his own family. He was not alone. His son's first steps gave him tremendous happiness.

For the first time in many years Alexander was truly happy. Dasha helped around the house and taught Olga to take care of the baby. Although she didn't have any children of her own, Dasha had had experience helping her sister Matryona raise Olga and her three siblings. Now, Dasha dedicated her life to Olga's young kids, who she loved with all her heart.

Alexander dreamed of raising his son well and giving him a good education. He already envisioned him grown up and smart. He perceived every word out of the baby's mouth as a miracle. In fact, the baby really was quite gifted. He learned to walk at the age of nine months and at three could count to ten and write his name.

Stroking Gennadiy's blonde hair Dasha would say,

— Look, his head looks like a hammer. That's wit. He's got Daddy's head, a Jewish head.

And she kissed the back of his head.

— When you grow up you will be like your Daddy — big, strong and kind. You will support everybody. Learn from him. You are my dear Jewish head.

And she kissed the boy all over.

When he was barely through the door Alexander would take his beloved son in his arms, sit him on his shoulders and run around the room. Little Gersh laughed loudly, making everybody around happy.

At that time, Alexander's apartment was tiny — one room and a kitchen. But everybody lived happily and harmoniously.

One night Aunt Dasha woke up from a knock on the window. She came to the window and asked,

— Who's there?

— Friends, open up. We want Mr. Leventhal, — she heard the reply.

Aunt Dasha's heart stopped. It occurred to her that it was Bendera men.

— He is not in, — she said in a strange voice. — He went to Drogobych. I'll give him a message.

— We'll leave him a note. He needs to read it. And he needs to think carefully. We will be back.

— All right. Where will you leave it?

— We will push it under the door. Remember to pass our words on to him.

— Don't worry, I will, — Aunt Dasha said, but she was shaking anxiously, mostly scared that Sasha, as she called Alexander, would wake up and go outside. That would mean trouble.

Something rustled under the door and the night guests disappeared.

Aunt Dasha sat on the chair completely drained of energy. Why did they come to Sasha? Would it mean trouble? What should she do?

— What is going to happen? — Aunt Dasha thought. — Should I wake him now or wait until morning?

She decided to wait until morning. She could not sleep that night. The night seemed endless.

When dawn broke Dasha got the stove burning, the kettle boiling, and was ready to make breakfast. Then she thought for a while, went to the front door and opened it. There was a letter there folded into a triangle.

With trembling hands she picked up the letter and placed it on the table. She couldn't read but her heart felt it was trouble. At that moment the door to the kitchen opened and Alexander appeared in the doorway. His thick hair was all tangled and he wasn't fully awake yet.

— Sasha, — Aunt Dasha said quietly, — Bendera men came for you last night.

— What? Why didn't you wake me up? — he wondered.

— Sasha, they would have killed you. I was praying to God you wouldn't hear them, because you would have run out and that would have been it. It's trouble, Sasha, trouble. They left you a letter, — and she pointed to the table.

Alexander grabbed the letter and read it. Then he sat down on the chair wearily.

— What is it, Sasha? What are they writing? — Aunt Dasha asked.

— They want me to bring them some flour and wheat.

— How much and where?

— Oh, Aunt Dasha, Aunt Dasha, — Alexander was only able to say.

— Sasha, if the KGB finds out, they will put you in jail; and if you don't do it, then the Bendera men will kill you! — She grabbed her head in despair.

There was no choice. He had to do what the night guests wrote in their letter.

RESTORATION OF DOBROMIL

Alexander stood by the office window and looked at the street full of people. Crowds of people were in a hurry to get somewhere. Many of them had bags of food. The abundance of food products made people happy. Alexander smiled. Yes, he had raised Dobromil's economy almost up to the level of the "Polish" times. Trade was lively. People had jobs. They had started to build their own houses. And that meant people were well off. They had restored Dobromil from ruins.

At the moment they were building a movie theatre at the place of the burnt synagogue. Alexander tried to get authorization to put up a memorial there for the murdered Jews, but it was denied. The response was that a memorial should be put for Comrade Stalin — he destroyed the Germans and liberated Western Ukraine from Nazis and nationalists.

So, in the center of the park where Ludwig Filus' dog tore its victims to death, opposite the burnt synagogue, they built a big memorial to Stalin with an arm reaching forward.

Somebody advised Alexander to join the Communist Party. Alexander replied,

— I am not worthy yet to be a member of the Communist Party. I will study some more, will understand politics better and then will call myself a communist. But right now I am not yet ready.

Some people didn't like it. If Alexander had been a Ukrainian he would have been sent to Siberia that very day. But because he was a Jew, a veteran with multiple war injuries, decorated personally by Comrade Stalin for war services, and fought in the war from the first to its last day, they could not dispose of him that fast. But they didn't leave him alone either. There was a secret order made to "watch this Jew".

Alexander had no idea that clouds were gathering over his head. He continued to work creatively giving it all his heart and soul.

Once while he was working in his office he heard a knock on the door.

— Come in! — Leventhal said loudly.

The door opened and his two young blonde kids ran into the office and hung on his neck screaming "Daddy, daddy!" The children were followed by Alexander's wife Olga, a blonde Russian beauty.

— Are you coming to lunch? — she asked smiling.

— Yes. What has Dasha made for lunch? — Alexander smiled back at her.

— Chops and potatoes and chicken broth.

— Well, even the tsar wouldn't refuse to eat such a lunch.

While Alexander and his family were walking down the street, Mrs. Vishnevskaya, the wife of the post office manager, came running up to him.

— Mr. Leventhal, Mr. Leventhal, — she called. — Alexander Grigorycvich, wait, I need to tell you something.

Alexander stopped,

— Oh, hi there. How are you doing? — he greeted her smiling.

— I am fine, Mr. Leventhal. Alexander Grigoryevich, I've got very important business with you, — the woman was barely able to catch her breath, and her voice trembled.

— What's going on? — Leventhal wondered.

— It's a big secret. I need to talk to you in private.

— Oh, Sasha, what about the lunch? After all, Aunt Dasha tried so hard, — Olga pleaded.

— Sure, I will come right away. Go home, and I will catch up with you in five minutes.

Alexander kissed his children, tenderly hugged his wife and approached the woman to listen to her secret.

— Alexander Grigoryevich, you are under surveillance, — she whispered into his ear. — I was given an order by the Police department's chief Tereshchenko to connect all your telephone calls with his telephone. They are listening to everything. What is going to happen now? Mr. Leventhal, you are in danger.

Alexander turned pale, but tried to stay calm.

— Mrs. Vishnevskaya, thank you for being so kind, but I don't have any secrets and I am not doing anything illegal. So let him listen if it makes him happy.

— Alexander Grigoryevich, believe me. You are in great danger. Leave Dobromil. You are young and full of energy, you will be OK anywhere. Here you will be in trouble. They have destroyed a lot of people and nobody knows what for.

— Calm down, I'll think about it. Don't worry, Mrs. Vishnevskaya. Just don't talk about it with anyone or you will get into trouble. Thank you for the warning.

He shook the woman's hand and quickly walked towards his house.

Thoughts were tumbling around in his mind. He didn't remember how he got home.

— What's going on with you, Sasha? — Aunt Dasha wondered, casting an attentive glance at him. — Are you sick?

— No, no, Aunt Dasha, but I need to be alone for a while and collect my thoughts.

— What about lunch?

— Oh, yes. Sure, let's eat together.

They all sat at the table. Alexander looked at his children. He loved them so much! His children were his happiness, his life. Family was everything for him. He had dreamt of having his own family. If only mother Mindlya and father Gersh could see their grandchildren! And now Aunt Dasha was trying to be a mother to him. That smart and kind Russian woman with all her warmth was a good mother.

Mrs. Vishnevskaya had said run away. Run where? And what about the family? Run from whom? No, he was not guilty of anything. He would not run anywhere. Everything would work out. It was some kind of mistake. Fate could not be that cruel.

They all sat at the table and looked at Alexander.

— What's wrong, Sasha?

Alexander startled. Only then did he notice that he hadn't even touched his food.

— What's with you? — Aunt Dasha repeated.

— Nothing, nothing, I am just tired.

After lunch he went back to work. He sat at the table in his office, put his head in his arms, closed his eyes and began to think. What happened? Who did he upset?

Suddenly the phone rang. Alexander picked up the receiver and almost fell off the chair from surprise. It was the police chief himself.

— Hello, Alexander Grigoryevich, it is Tereshchenko speaking. What's new with you?

— Well, hello, hello. Same old, same old, nothing new. How are you? — Alexander replied barely concealing his surprise.

— Well, I am fine, but I am calling you about some business. I need to urgently borrow a thousand rubles. Can you lend it to me?

Alexander lost his tongue. So that's what it was. Tereshchenko wanted money.

— Well, Alexander Grigoryevich, I can't hear you. My dear, why are you silent?

— Hmm... Hmm... Sure, Comrade Tereshchenko, not a problem. If necessary, I'll do it.

— Then come to my office and bring it.

— No, I will go to your home and give it to your wife.

— No, that's out of the question. I'd better come to your office today.

— What time? Can we do it tomorrow?

— No, my dear, I need to have it today before 6 pm. Got it?

— Yes, I got it, comrade chief.

— That's better, — barked Tereshchenko. He hung up without saying good bye.

Alexander sat there in shock. Where could he get such an amount of money? He needed to borrow it from somebody. He ran to his brother Moisha, but he didn't have that much money either.

Finally, after borrowing the required amount from a number of friends, Alexander went to his office to wait for Tereshchenko.

At six pm sharp the door opened and the chief of police showed up in the doorway.

— Hello, Alexander Grigoryevich!

— Hello, hello, — Alexander replied with a strained smile. — Have a seat.

— No, Alexander Grigoryevich, I haven't got time. I came to see you on personal business. Well, is it ready? — Tereshchenko looked impudently into Alexander's eyes.

— Yes, it's ready!

— I thought it would be. Where is it?

Alexander got an envelope out of the safe and gave it to Tereshchenko.

The man put the envelope into his pocket.

— Thank you, Alexander Grigoryevich. I have another favor to ask.

— I am listening, — Leventhal said with a blank face.

— My wife needs a good length of fabric for a coat. Please take care of it, dear. And hurry up. Well, thanks a lot.

He left the office.

Alexander remained standing. That was why Tereshchenko had ordered him put under surveillance — he was looking for an excuse to take bribes. Alexander felt trapped. Thoughts were tumbling in his mind. He also needed to get money to pay back the money he had borrowed from people. His salary would not be enough to do it, plus he had to support his family. How could he escape this situation? That vampire would not leave him alone easily.

A LENGTH OF FABRIC FOR A COAT

After Mrs. Vishnevskaya's warning, Alexander tried to talk as little as he could over the phone.

Once he ran into a strange woman while leaving his office.

— Hello, Alexander Grigoryevich, — she said quietly and continued never giving him a chance to respond. — Alexander Grigoryevich, please help me get a length of fabric for a coat. I work as a teacher at a school, and would like to dress better, but I am not able to get myself a good coat. Please help me.

— Excuse me, who are you?

— My last name is Bychok. You got my husband a position at the distribution center. And I am a teacher of the Ukrainian language and Literature at the school.

— Why don't you ask your husband since he works at the distribution center? — Alexander wondered again.

— He is new there. Besides, he is not good for anything. Everybody in Dobromil says, "Go and ask Mr. Leventhal. He won't reject anyone. He can even get pigeon's milk". That's how I decided to ask you for this favor.

It was true that out of the kindness of his heart Alexander helped everyone who came to him. The fame about "almighty" Leventhal was spreading in the area. Well, the woman needed help and he nodded.

— All right, I will try to help you and will talk with the goods managers.

— And when can I come? — the woman asked immediately.

— Well, come next week, — Leventhal said and she left.

A few days later the woman was waiting for him by the doors of his office.

— Alexander Grigoryevich, you promised to get some fabric for a coat for me.

— Yes, yes, I remember. I haven't gotten it yet, but I have already requested it. It will come next week.

Alexander tried to quickly get rid of the nagging woman; communicating with her was unpleasant. He thought he had better get the fabric for a coat as soon as possible, otherwise she would not leave him alone.

He immediately went to the store manager and asked him to get him a length of coffee color coat fabric at the Drogobychskiy distribution center and to bring it to him personally. A few days later the fabric was brought to Leventhal.

As Alexander had anticipated, the woman was waiting for him by the entrance to remind him about the fabric.

Without waiting for the annoying woman to ask a question, Alexander said,

— I know, I know. I've got it. Come into my office.

He quickly ran up the stairs to the second floor. The woman was right behind him.

Alexander entered his office, quickly opened the safe and got out a package.

— Here is your length of fabric. Here's the price.

The woman grabbed the package, looked at the price without unwrapping it, got out the money and gave it to Leventhal.

Alexander put the money into the safe and closed it. When he turned around the woman was gone. She disappeared without even saying thank you.

Alexander sat at the table thinking about what had just happened.

What kind of person behaves like that? She didn't even thank me, and what's more amazing is she didn't even un-wrap the package. What if there was something wrong with it?

But it was no longer his problem. He did what he was asked to and got rid of the annoying woman. Alexander sighed with relief, but as it soon turned out — not for long.

The next day Tereshchenko, the chief of the police, summoned him to come to see him.

When he entered his office he was very much surprised to see that same woman by the name of Bychok sitting at the table with the police chief.

— Hey, Alexander Grigoryevich, — Tereshchenko greeted him, — come in, come in.

Alexander entered the room and sat opposite the woman.

— Alexander Grigoryevich, I've got a question to you. Do you recognize this woman?

— Yes, I have seen her several times, — Alexander replied.

— Good. And here is another question. Do you know what's in this package?

And he got the package from under the table which Alexander had given the woman the day before.

— Do you know what it is?

— Yes, — Alexander replied.

He was trapped. He realized that the woman was a decoy and he had fallen into a trap.

— So what can you say about it? — Tereshchenko continued to say.

— Nothing, really, — Alexander said more confidently, trying to think how to get out of the trap.

— This, my dear, is the fabric which you stole and sold to this woman here, — Tereshchenko blurted out.

— Well, comrade chief, you are going too far. You are insulting me calling me a thief. I have not stolen this fabric. I brought it from Germany as a trophy. I fought in the war in Germany and found this fabric in one of the empty houses. And this woman was following me and begging me to get her some fabric for a coat. So I decided to give her my trophy fabric in order to get rid of her, — Alexander said energetically.

Tereshchenko didn't believe it.

— So, you are saying it's a length of trophy fabric? Why did you keep it for so long and not make anything out of it for yourself?

— I just didn't like it, that's all, — Alexander replied.

Thoughts were tumbling in his mind. Trophy fabric. That's what he would stick to. The important thing was not to say too much. He ought not to involve other people — those who had bought the fabric for cash, those who work at the distribution center. There was no proof that the fabric was bought at the distribution center, therefore, he would stick to his version that he got it from Germany.

— I don't believe you, Leventhal, — Tereshchenko said openly.

— I can't do anything about that. — Alexander shrugged his shoulders and turned to the woman. — I already told you that I've only got this piece. I didn't choose it, I took what there was.

— Well, Leventhal, you can go now, we'll deal with you later. We will conduct an audit and will find out. We'll discover everything.

Alexander said good-bye and left Tereshchenko's office. His feet were moving by themselves. His thoughts raced.

— They wanted to uncover something, but what? I need to be more careful, but how? And this woman — what a damned wretch. I got her husband a job, and she did such a mean thing to me. It's a good thing that the fabric was bought for cash. There is no paper trail at the distribution center or at the store. What is going on? What's going to happen?

The next day an audit was started at the WRS. The auditors worked there for three months, but were not able to find anything illegal.

SEARCHES

A few days after the completion of the audit Alexander was on his way to work. When he approached the porch of his office building, he ran into a man who blocked his way. Alexander stopped.

— Excuse me, — Leventhal said politely and tried to go through.

But the man kept standing there, brazenly looking at Alexander.

— Excuse me, please, — Leventhal repeated and tried to go around the "obstacle", but the man blocked his way again and said,

— Turn out your pockets.

— What? — Alexander didn't get it.

— I am telling you, turn out your pockets, — the man rapped out.

— I am sorry, you don't look like a bandit. Why are you demanding that I turn out my pockets? — Alexander asked beginning to realize who it was.

— Don't play dumb, — the man hissed showing a KGB ID.

Alexander glanced at the ID and said with dignity,

— Comrade Gruzinov, that's not enough. The ID of an officer of national security doesn't give you the right to make people in the street turn out their pockets.

— You turn out to be a smart Jew. Then tell me what else do I need? — Gruzinov hissed.

— A search warrant, Comrade Gruzinov.

— Well, in that case, let's go to the department and I will show you the search warrant, — and he pushed Alexander in the shoulder.

— Behave yourself, Comrade Gruzinov, — Leventhal got angry, — I am not under arrest yet.

— That's OK, you will be arrested soon. Go! March to the department. — He pushed Alexander in the shoulder again.

In the KGB department Gruzinov opened the safe and got out a blank search warrant and placed it in front of Alexander.

— Well, see, Jew? I told you there wouldn't be any problem with a search warrant. Look, it has already got a seal and the appropriate official's signature. All that is left to do is to write in the name of the person that needs to be searched, — and Gruzinov roared with laughter. — And I will put your name here, Jew. Well, are you going to turn your pockets out voluntarily or do you need help to do it?

With that, he wrote Alexander's first name, last name and patronymic on the search warrant.

Alexander watched Gruzinov fill in the form.

— You know my name, Comrade Gruzinov, but you call me by nationality. Why?

— Don't stall me. Get everything out of your pockets and let's go to your home to do the search there, — the KGB man angrily hissed.

Alexander took out the contents of his pockets: a gold watch, a hundred dollars in small bills, and a few peanuts that he always carried along for his daughter Ludmila. She loved to put her hand into his pocket and take out the nuts which she would then nibble on like a squirrel.

— Aha! — rejoiced Gruzinov, — You carry a gold watch, you bastard. I'm confiscating it!

— What right do you have to confiscate it? — Alexander protested.

— Shut up, I am telling you, — Gruzinov growled, still eyeing the trophy. — Let's go and do the search of your house.

He swept the nuts on the floor, and put the watch and the money into the safe.

The search lasted for eight hours. Alexander stood there pale, hugging the kids. The children had never seen anything like that before and looked at the strangers with wide open eyes full of fear. They didn't know how to behave and that's why they tightly clung to their father seeking protection from him.

Policemen in uniform and several men in leather coats were turning everything in the house upside down. Newspapers and books were all mixed up. Pillows and blankets were felt through.

Aunt Dasha was praying in the kitchen, and frightened Olga, with an expressionless face, stood by her husband holding his hand tightly.

Finally the search was over.

Gruzinov, who was upset by the lack of results, slammed his fist on the table.

— Well, Jew, you're in luck today. We found 800 rubles in your house, which we are confiscating along with the gold watch found in your pocket. But remember, we'll be back. We may trash your lair to pieces, but we will find what we are looking for.

— Excuse me, Comrade Gruzinov, but what exactly are you looking for? — Alexander asked. — Maybe I can be of help to you?

— Stolen government money — that's what we are looking for.

— I don't have any. I've got honestly earned money. For your information, the 800 rubles that you want to confiscate — it's my monthly salary that I received yesterday. As for the gold watch, I brought it from Germany. It's my trophy watch.

— We know about you Jews. You've got an answer for everything. Well let's go, — he addressed his men and the whole group left the house leaving complete chaos behind.

Aunt Dasha rushed to clean. Olga looked at Alexander and tears were rolling down her cheeks.

— Sasha, what's going to happen? — she whispered. — Sasha, why are they doing this to us?

Alexander stroked her blonde hair saying over and over,

— It's a mistake. All of it is a mistake. You'll see. I am now going to call the KGB Director Lobadenko and everything will be all right. They will give me back both the money and the watch. You'll see.

He went to the phone and dialed the KGB Director's number.

They all heard a man pick up at the other end of the line.

— KGB Director Comrade Lobadenko speaking.

— Hello, Comrade Lobadenko. This is Leventhal bothering you. We've had a mix-up here. Your men came to my place led by Comrade Gruzinov, searched my place, and took my monthly salary and the trophy watch which I brought from Germany. I don't know what's going on because Comrade Gruzinov spoke to me very rudely and didn't want to explain anything. Can you clarify this, please?

The man on the other end of the line said that he would check into the matter and call back.

— See, I told you it was a mistake. Lobadenko will straighten it out and everything will be back to normal. There is no need to worry. I am not guilty of anything. You'll see. Everything will be fine. — With these words he kissed his wife's blonde head and stroked the blonde heads of the kids.

Aunt Dasha stood by the wall still saying prayers.

The next day Alexander was summoned to the KGB department, where they gave back his money and watch.

When he came home he showed everybody the returned items. They all calmed down at once, but it was too soon to relax.

A few weeks later a second search occurred. Then another one, and another one, and one more. These searches were conducted not by the KGB, but by Dobromil police with interrogator Melnikova in charge.

Nobody was able to explain the reason for the searches. Melnikova was the Drogobychskiy Region prosecutor and had a reputation of being a merciless wretch who bullied everybody. She had taken Leventhal's case in order to receive brownie points from her boss. Searches were done twice a month. Sometimes "auditors" would barge into the Leventhal's home at night.

After one of the searches, when everything was once again turned upside down, Aunt Dasha approached Alexander and began to beg with tears in her eyes.

— Sasha, please, go somewhere. Get out of their sight. They will put you in jail, and that will be it.

— Where should I go? I've got kids, family. Where could I hide? If I leave, they will think I am guilty of something. They will make you all suffer.

— Listen, Sasha, we've already been through something like this. Olga's father hid a sack of grain in order to feed his children in 1933. If Olga's mother and I hadn't hidden him, he would have been shot. He was in hiding for seven years, and he came home only after that. If he had come home sooner, he would have been killed. For God's sake, leave. Get out of their sight. Somebody wants to take away your life.

— Aunt Dasha, dear Aunt Dasha, I am not hiding anything from them. How can I abandon you all? How can I abandon my kids? Look at them. I will not be able to live without them. They are my happiness. I love them so much. I dreamed of having a family. I've wandered for so long! I have dreamed of sleeping in my own bed, dreamed of having my own house. The war took away everything I had, but now I have everything again. And now I have to abandon it all just because somebody wants it? No, no, my dear Aunt Dasha, I will fight. I won't go to the scaffold the same way my parents did.

— Sasha, it's impossible to fight them, they are unbeatable. They have destroyed many people. It is an infernal death machine. If it grabs you, you are finished.

But Alexander was stubborn. Almost seven long years of war wandering had made him tough. And there were the children... how would they manage without him? He had worked as the manager of WRS for ten years, and it had been two years already since he became the head of the Regional Consumer's Association. He worked his fingers to the bone. He made WRS and then the Regional Consumer's Association the best in the district. So much had been accomplished! After all, he had built the town out of ashes. And what now? No, he couldn't run away like a thief.

The searches continued. There had already been 18 raids on Leventhal's house, but nothing suspicious was ever found. Melnikova racked her brains trying to find something that would give her grounds for Alexander's arrest, and suddenly a "brilliant" idea flashed upon her: Did she really need any grounds? No, not at all.

THE ARREST

Alexander stood by the window in his office and watched a man who was guarding the front door. Alexander knew that the man was following him. His house had been searched numerous times. He did not understand what they could find there. Books? He was not into politics. Money? Gold? He did not have any of that.

Alexander knew that his family was in big trouble. The last search was the most terrible one: they looked and felt through everything — even pillows and comforters. But the worst thing for Alexander was to see the reactions of his kids. Little Ludmila was sick with the measles. With a rash all over, she stood in the corner and watched them tear up her house with her huge blue eyes.

Alexander's heart sank. What would happen to his wife and kids if they put him in jail? Was there any guarantee that those monsters wouldn't touch his family? He worked so hard and selflessly. He did his best for the welfare of the people. He accomplished so many good deeds for the residents of Dobromil. Was this the reward for his hard work?

Alexander turned away from the window. Heavy thoughts wouldn't leave him. His wife Olga had not worked for ten years. What would

happen to her? What kind of job would she be able to get if he got arrested?

— Maybe, everything will work out, — Alexander began to calm himself down. –Maybe, they will finally leave him alone. After all, he is not guilty of anything. And what kind of authorities are those, anyway? You never know what they will do to you tomorrow. Tomorrow... there may be no tomorrow. He knew Soviet power only too well.

After walking around his office Alexander approached the window again. The man was no longer there. Alexander smiled.

— Tired? Right — where else can I go except home.

There was a knock on the door. Alexander didn't even manage to say "Come in" when the door swung open. There was interrogator Melnikova in the doorway surrounded by three policemen.

— Hello, Alexander Grigoryevich, — she almost sang. Her hawk nose was quivering in pleasurable anticipation.

— Hello, — Alexander replied trying to stay calm.

— We have come to arrest you. Here is the sanction for your arrest, — continued Melnikova in the same songful voice eyeing Alexander with her wolfish eyes.

Alexander turned pale.

— What for? What are the grounds for my arrest? — he asked trying to talk in a steady voice.

— You are interfering with my investigation. You will be more harmless for society behind bars, — the investigator replied smiling.

— Is there such a law that allows you to arrest innocent people? — Alexander asked again.

— Don't kid around with me, Leventhal! Where have you seen innocent Jews working in a position like yours? You better sign this paper, — and she pointed at the sanction.

— I am not going to sign anything. I consider your action illegal.

— Really? Well, we'll see. — she turned to the police officer. — Arrest him and place him in the lock-up ward.

One of the policemen said,

— I need to arrest you, Alexander Grigoryevich.

The policemen seemed apologetic for what he had to do. He was red and sweaty and it was obvious that what was going on was not to his liking.

Melnikova looked at them with angry eyes.

— Well, Alexander Grigoryevich, put your arms behind your back and follow this policeman, — she hissed.

— And you, young man, — she addressed the policeman, — learn how to behave with the arrested.

— Yes, madam, — the policemen responded.

— Let's go, please — he said, addressing Leventhal.

Alexander left the office. All the workers in the reception room froze watching the policemen take away their boss. Nobody was able to say a word.

People in the street stopped upon seeing that scene, watching them go.

— Let me call my wife, — Alexander asked.

— Why? She will be told. Get into the police car. Your family will be taken care of.

Alexander caught his breath.

— Leave them alone. I am not guilty of anything.

— And that, my dear, will soon be figured out. After all, you know that our country is the most humane in the world. We do not put innocent people in jail.

Alexander was startled. He had already heard those words once. Was this a dream or did fate decided to play with him again?

On Remand

Two days later, Alexander was taken to the Drogobych prison "Brigitky" and placed into solitary confinement. They fed him once a day. They gave him thin soup and a slice of bread. They called him to questioning once every two days. Alexander flatly refused to answer the investigator's questions alleging that the investigator was talking nonsense. By the questions he was asked, Alexander determined that they had neither evidence, nor specific charges. Melnikova was looking for grounds to put him behind bars. Obviously, somebody on top had given the order. He had displeased somebody at the top, but who? Why? He did not find an answer.

After a month in prison, Alexander had not gotten any news from home.

During yet another questioning he asked Melnikova,

— I request explanation of why you are keeping me here. I also know that you can keep me in prison under remand for only one month because this sanction is for just one month.

Melnikova grinned maliciously in response and placed a new sanction for arrest in front of Alexander — for another month.

— What's a sanction, Alexander Grigoryevich? — she smirked. — We can do it. Your wife came and went to her knees in front of me. She promised to give me a sack of money if I release you.

— I think you are lying. My wife could get on her knees, but she could not have promised you a sack of money because she doesn't have it.

— I don't believe it, Alexander Grigoryevich. I am starting to check the harvesting of apples in 1954 and 1955 and their shipment to the North. Have you got anything to say about that?

— You can check all you want. I was the manager of WRS, not a packer. I did not harvest the apples myself. Other people did it.

— But you signed bills of lading for them which were used by the banks to give them money.

— Yes, but, I did not give them any money, the banks did. I gave the state one million three hundred thousand rubles of profit over three months. And for your information I received acknowledgement from the Minister of Forestry Department for getting apples to the children of Pechora, which they had never had there before.

Melnikova smiled viciously.

— You bought your house for a big price, but registered it as a smaller amount. What for? Tell me please.

— I have no idea what you are talking about and I am just amazed at your stupidity.

Melnikova blushed to the roots of hair, but soon she recovered.

— Go to your cell and think carefully. I am going to send you to a penal colony, sly Jew.

Alexander realized that he would not be able to get out of prison. His attorney Fris was smart, but not strong enough to fight the authorities. Who was able to fight the power which gave an order from the very top "to restrain Jews"? Many had already been execute. Others were in prison awaiting trial.

One day when Alexander was being taken to the investigator's office on the fourth floor for questioning, a rather respectable man stepped into the hall.

— Are you Leventhal? — he asked.

— Yes, that's me, — Alexander nodded.

— Come into my office.

Alexander went in. The guards stayed outside.

— Sit down, Leventhal. I am a chief investigator of the Drogobych regional prosecutor's office. I was offered to prosecute your case, but I refused. I was not able to find anything. Anyone can be charged with abuse of office. Don't get me wrong, Melnikova is a good prosecutor. She took your case for a reason. There is an order to put you in prison. Don't get upset, but they will charge you with something and will put you in prison.

Alexander listened to him with his head down. Yes, you can't escape fate.

— Please tell me if you know anything about my family. I haven't had a bit of news in three months.

— How they are? They are living. It's tough for them. But they manage. You know how it is here.

— Please help me to see them. I am begging you. If only for five minutes.

— I'll give it a try. Well, good luck, — the investigator ended the conversation.

Alexander left his office and went to Melnikova's office accompanied by the guards.

A few days later Alexander was called to a questioning. He was taken to the fourth floor again where he was to meet investigator Melnikova.

On the way there he was told to stop by the door of another office. The door opened and he saw Melnikova smiling.

— Alexander Grigoryevich, you asked to see your wife. We have granted you this favor. Your wife is waiting for you.

Alexander caught his breath. Could it be true? What happiness! He was going to see Olga, and maybe the kids, too. God, he missed them so much!

He quickly entered the office and was shocked. His wife was sitting on a chair but what was wrong with her? Her hair was messed up, her white blouse was wrinkled and unbuttoned in the front, lipstick was smeared all over her face, and her eyes were half closed. Could she be... drunk?

Alexander rushed to his wife, but a man in civilian clothes blocked his way.

Alexander stopped and called quietly,

— Olga, what's the matter with you?

— Nothing, I am tired. I am tired of waiting for you.

Her tongue faltered, and Alexander confirmed that she was drunk.

His heart started racing.

— Olga, where are the kids? How are they?

— The kids are with Aunt Dasha. They are fine.

— Why haven't you brought the kids?

— They wouldn't let me bring the kids, — Olga said with a thick faltering tongue.

— Who are they? — Alexander almost screamed.

— Take it easy, — the man in civilian clothes said. — Take it easy.

— Who got you drunk? — Alexander asked in a calmer voice.

— They did. I am tired. I am very tired.

— Olga, how are the children? How do they do at school?

Olga didn't reply. She sat with her eyes closed, slightly swaying on the chair.

After seeing Olga, Alexander went to his cell with his head down. They did it on purpose in order to break me, he thought. But Olga... they will play with her life. They are capable of anything, — his thoughts changed quickly. — Will she manage to bear it? And the kids? How my heart aches for the kids! But Aunt Dasha will not abandon the kids. All my hope is with Aunt Dasha..."

Alexander was not mistaken. Aunt Dasha took full responsibility for the survival of the Leventhal family. She became a mother, a father and a grandmother to the children. She protected them by trying to seclude them from the "bad world".

Questionings continued. Melnikova regularly called Alexander "for negotiations". But the "case" was advancing badly, in spite of the fact that all the usual techniques were utilized.

At first they put people into his cell, who were supposed to pump information out of Alexander in order to pass it later to the appropriate person. But Alexander kept saying that he had nothing to say, and that he was innocent.

Then the tortures began. When the days were warm, the heating system would kick on full blast. Almost losing consciousness from the heat, Alexander hammered on the door asking them to lower the temperature. But nobody listened to him. The doors which brought coolness would not be open until he lost consciousness. Only after all sounds coming from Leventhal's cell stopped would the guards open the door and pour water on the prisoner from a special bucket, which was specifically prepared to revive him.

THE CHILDREN'S VISIT

Alexander's nightmare continued for a year and a half. With not a bit of news from home and exhausted by numerous questionings and tortures, Alexander stopped answering the investigator's questions. Ignoring those who surrounded him, he remembered just one thing — the most sacred for him — the faces of his blonde children looking like angels. He often talked to them in his dreams and when awake imagined the children were by his side. As usual, he called his daughter little baby and asked her if she still liked peanuts.

The wardens who peeped into his cell window thought inmate Leventhal had gone crazy. But it wasn't true. All those imaginary conversations with the children made his spirit stronger and helped him survive and get through those tough times.

One day Melnikova decided to play with her "fosterling". She brought Alexander's wife and children to Drogobych, but she did not allow Olga to come to the visiting room — only the children. Olga begged Melnikova to let her stay with the children, but two policemen dragged her to another room, tightly holding her by the elbows. Looking at their mother the kids began to cry loudly, too, and tried to run after their mother. But at that moment the doors opened and an unsuspecting Alexander entered the room.

When he saw his children crying hysterically he rushed to them, but he was stopped by a man in civilian clothes who blocked his way.

— Let me through, bastard, — Alexander hissed. — I am going to hug my kids. Get out of my way.

Seeing Alexander's eyes full of anger the man stepped aside.

Alexander rushed to the children.

— Daddy, daddy! — the children ran up to their father. — They dragged mom somewhere. She was crying very much. Daddy, help mom.

Hugging the kids, Alexander turned to Melnikova who was in the same room and looked at her menacingly.

— Where is Olga?

— We took her out to calm down. She was making a hysterical scene here.

— You are scumbags. You are torturing my family.

— No, Alexander Grigoryevich, it's you who is torturing your family. You don't want to help us investigate your case. In Lvov the Konchiky brothers were more talkative. We have already executed them and now their family lives peacefully. Help us and we won't touch your family. Your wife has been sleeping around for a long time. She is not waiting for you. So it's up to you.

— You are lying. You have chosen Nazi tactics. I can't tell you anything because I don't know anything. I don't know any Konchikov brothers. And leave me alone for a few minutes. I need to calm down the kids.

— Well, go ahead and calm them down. I'll give you half an hour. — With that, Melnikova left the room.

Alexander tightly hugged his son and daughter. The children, who hadn't seen their father for a long time, couldn't get enough of him.

— I love you very much. Whatever happens to me, remember that I love you very much. I want you to grow into strong and healthy people. Listen to Grandma Dasha and mom. Study at school. And I will be back. Just wait for me. Do you hear me? Wait for me.

The children looked at their father with their eyes wide open and whispered,

— All right, daddy... All right, daddy...

He turned to Gennadiy.

— Treat your mother and sister well. You are now the only man in the house. Take my place and wait for me.

The boy nodded his head.

— Remember: I love you all and I will be back. Take care of mom. She is going through a very difficult time now.

— All right, daddy.

The children hugged their father clinging to him with all their might. At that moment it seemed that no strength could tear them apart.

But half an hour passed. Melnikova appeared in the doorway.

— Leventhal, your time is up, — she said. — Go, children. Your mother is waiting for you.

— No, I want to stay with daddy, — Ludmila cried.

— Baby girl, my beloved baby girl, go to mom, — Alexander whispered in her ear, — Hug her for me and kiss her. Tell her that I love her very much. She just needs to trust me and wait for me. Go and tell her my words. I will come home soon.

Once again he hugged the children, waived his hand to them and headed for the door.

— Go, your mom is waiting for you. Give my regards to Grandma Dasha. Go on, run quickly.

Looking back at their father, the children ran out of the room.

— Well, Leventhal, are you going to give sincere answers? — Melnikova asked when the door closed behind the children.

— I don't know what I should give you, — Alexander shrugged his shoulders.

— Motsey and Podolyak have already told us.

— And what did they tell you?

— They said that in 1954–55 you gathered many more apples than were documented.

— Really? And what did we do with them? Did we eat them without sharing with you?

— Don't be sarcastic, Leventhal. You sold them and pocketed the money. And this is embezzlement of State property.

— You have gone crazy, comrade investigator. You have gone crazy...

— No, I'll arrange it so that you will go crazy. Sign this testimony.

— No, I cannot give such testimony. And I am not going to sign anything.

— Stubborn Jew! You are finished anyway. Have pity on your children.

— I won't sign. I will not sign! — Leventhal was now screaming. — Do what you want, but I am not going to sign anything and will not give any testimony.

— Don't. We will try you in court anyway, — Melnikova responded harshly and left the room.

TRIAL

Legal proceedings regarding Leventhal were held in Dobromil, so Alexander was transferred to the Nizhenkovich prison. Alexander was thrown into a one-man cell. The only window's glass was broken. There was no heating. Snow blown in by the wind was building on the cell's floor, which was where Alexander sat and slept. Dressed in light clothes, Leventhal was cold on the snowy cement floor. Cold cut him to the bone.

He began to bang on the door with his fist.

The warden opened the window.

— What do you need?

— Listen, my good man, give me something to cover myself with, or I could freeze to death by morning and there will be no one to put on trial.

After considering it for a moment the warden said,

— I will bring you a wool blanket. But you need to give it back to me before 6 am. There is an order not to be in contact with inmates. I may be severely punished for giving you the blanket.

— Thanks. I will give it back.

In the morning, Alexander was taken to the Dobromil court house frozen to the bone. When Alexander was brought in the people crowding by the door began to whisper. The courtroom was full of people. Alexander was looking around trying to find familiar faces, but mostly he was hoping to see his wife and the kids. But for some reason they were not there.

Suddenly he heard,

— Sasha, Sasha!

Abruptly turning his head to the scream, he saw Aunt Dasha.

— Sasha, they locked the kids and Olga in a different room. They didn't want the children to be here.

Then her voice faded and Alexander saw a man in civilian clothes grab her by the elbow and lead her to the exit.

Alexander's soul rebelled. Suddenly he got the strength he needed. He steadily stepped to the prisoner's dock. His attorney, Fris, was already seated. Upon seeing the defendant, he got up and approached him.

— Hello, Alexander Grigoryevich, — he said.

Without any greeting Alexander blurted out,

— What are they doing to my family? Please help my family. Do something, I beg you.

— What can I do? Olga's behavior is not smart, and they are using it.

— You have to understand. I was not given a single normal visit with my wife. How can she behave? She wants the children to see their father at least once in eighteen months. They harass both me and my family. If I stay in the same cell I was in last night, I'll freeze to death.

Fris lowered his head. It was obvious that he was not really able to help; but Fris did get Alexander transferred to the Dobromil lock-up ward, where he stayed for the remainder of the trial.

Testimonies in favor of Leventhal were not taken into account. The key witness for the prosecution was an agriculturist who gave his opinion that four years ago more apples were supposed to grow than Leventhal recorded in the bills of lading.

The attorney objected to that testimony on the basis of the opinion of the Moscow Agricultural Institute which said that in order for that statement to hold true and have scientific value, it would be necessary to cut down all the apple trees and conduct research on each cut trunk, which was impossible to do.

There were two more witnesses — Podolyak and Motsey. They testified against Leventhal to avoid getting themselves into the prisoner's dock. They said everything to please the investigator and the judge.

Periodically the trial would turn into a market place. Associated judges didn't know what to do. Fris, not able to bear the "testimonies", almost screamed,

— Nikita Sergeyevich Khrushchev said that the field was supposed to give a certain crop of corn, but there was no crop. But he was not on trial for this. It's clear even to a horse that it is impossible to predict how big a crop will be!

But nobody listened to him.

The associated judges quarreled among themselves and investigator Melnikova sat behind the screen and listened to everything that was going on in the courtroom.

After thirty three days of court sessions regarding Leventhal's case, the associated judges deliberated for another six days.

The originally amount of embezzled State property was calculated to be 676,000 rubles (about $170,000 U.S.). This figure went down to 270,000 rubles ($67,500 U.S.), then to 120,000 ($30,000 U.S.) until finally, Leventhal was charged with the embezzlement of State property in the amount of 90,000 rubles (about $22,500 U.S.). Both the investigator and the judge knew that if Leventhal applied for a reversal of judgment, even that charge would be dismissed since the court didn't have any proof of his guilt whatsoever.

But Melnikova was not going to give up. She invited the judge and the prosecutor to dinner. The restaurant she took them to was located on the second floor of a building next to the Gorkiy movie theatre. For important guests like these, a special area was available. In the small private room where the three important guests sat, the windows and doors were decorated with beautiful curtains. The best dishes and drinks were served. The "dear guests" were almost always treated free of charge. After a substantial meal and free drinks on the house, the guests usually left the restaurant without even remembering to ask for a bill. Nobody dared to approach them to ask them to pay for dinner. Everybody was afraid of getting out of favor.

During dinner, Melnikova presented the prosecutor and judge with an ultimatum. The ninth volume of Leventhal's case, in which his innocence was proven, needed to be lost. Leventhal must be sent to a maximum security camp.

Barmaid Nina Ivanovna, a simple Russian woman-veteran, the wife of a major who was a border guard, accidentally overheard their conversation. What Melnikova said amazed and shocked her tremendously. Investigator Melnikova was insisting on the judge sentencing Leventhal to capital punishment. But the judge was refusing to do it. Finally, even the prosecutor could not take it any longer.

— Listen, why do you hate him so much?

— He is a Jew. That's all that needs to be said. Jews should be eliminated.

— Please understand that I cannot sentence him to capital punishment, — the judge said. — I have no proof of embezzlement whatsoever. Not a single agriculturist wants to give the kind of testimony you require.

— There is such an agriculturist, — Melnikova responded. — I have found one. He owes me one. He murdered his wife.

— Really?! How did he get away with it? — the prosecutor wondered.

— He just did, — Melnikova smiled slyly. — He will give any testimony we need. And Motsey with Podolyak will, too. You don't need anything else. That's your proof. Embezzlement of State property needs to be severely punished, so that others won't do it.

— And who are Podolyak and Motsey? — the judge wondered.

— Just Ukrainian scum, the lowest kind, — Melnikova said. — We threw the Siberia scare at them and they immediately fell on their knees. They won't give their life for a Jew. They will both say and sign everything we need.

— This sly Jew holds up very well, — she added. — Another in his place would have broken already, but he hasn't signed a single paper. The dummy doesn't get it — that it doesn't really matter.

— All the same, I cannot sentence him to capital punishment, — the judge persisted. — I can't. My conscience won't let me.

— Well, my dear, now you are talking about conscience? — Melnikova hissed. — Do you want to acquit him?

— If it were up to me, I would acquit him, — the judge muttered, being fairly drunk.

— Don't joke like that, — Melnikova got mad. — You will not get a pat on the back for such words. Don't play with fire.

With those words, she abruptly got up from the table and headed to the exit. The judge and the prosecutor followed her.

All that time, Nina Ivanovna stood behind the curtains barely breathing. As soon as the guests left she sat on the floor breathing heavily. Her heart was pounding.

— What a bitch this Melnikova is, — Nina Ivanovna thought angrily. — The man will be destroyed for nothing. I need to tell Leventhal everything, to warn him. Only how do I do it? Maybe I should bring him a package? Yes, I need to put together a package. Bread and sausage. And a bottle of vodka for the warden.

She took off her white robe, put on her coat, broke off a piece of sausage, grabbed a loaf of bread from the counter and ran out of the restaurant. When she approached the lock-up ward she remembered that she had forgotten vodka for the warden.

It's all right, — she decided, — I'll ask him to come after work to the restaurant and I'll settle with him there.

With those thoughts she entered the lock-up building.

The warden was snoozing on the bench. He heard the noise, opened his eyes and recognized the barmaid from the restaurant.

— What has happened, Nina Ivanovna? — he asked.

— I want to see Leventhal, — she answered.

— What are you talking about? It's forbidden to talk to him.

— Have you gone nuts, Pavlo? — the woman started to attack him. — Have you lost all human emotions? You are keeping a man cold and hungry. Come to see me after work, and I will feed you, pour you a drink and will wrap something to take home. Don't be a fool. You know well that Alexander Grigoryevich has not done any harm to anyone. Let me talk with him for a minute and give him some food. Look — all I have is a slice of bread and sausage. Well, what do you say?

— All right, go. I will look the other way, — the warden agreed. — Just remember your promise.

— Sure, Pavlo, sure. After work come to me right away. — She ran to Alexander's cell.

— Alexander Grigoryevich, it's me, Nechayeva.

— Nina Ivanovna? How did you get in here?

— I don't have time to explain, Alexander Grigoryevich. Here, I have brought you some food. Take it and eat. — She paused. — I have overheard Melnikova's conversation with the judge and the prosecutor. It's bad, Alexander Grigoryevich, it's bad. You are in very big trouble. She is a serpent. It's all her doing. You won't be able to get out of it easily. They have found some agriculturist who killed his wife, and Melnikova saved him from the death penalty. So now he will come to testify. Besides, Motsey and Podolyak will testify against you, too. I don't even know what to advise you or how to help you...

— My dear kind Nina Ivanovna, I have known for a while that I shouldn't expect anything good. They will put me in jail. Yes, I know about it. Please, help my family. Get Olga a job. Feed the kids occasionally. And when I come back — I will repay your kindness. Well, if

I don't come back... good deeds will always be repaid. God will repay you if people don't.

Nina Ivanovna stood there with her head down. She didn't want to upset Alexander even more by telling him that Melnikova was pressuring the judge to sentence Leventhal to death.

Nina Ivanovna was leaving the lock-up ward with a broken heart. Tears were rolling down her cheeks. It seemed to her at that moment that Leventhal would never again walk the streets of Dobromil. She was bitterly crying about the fate of that kind man who had always tried to help everybody.

One of the associate judges was a woman by the name of Salamaha. Having a good knowledge of the law, she courageously defended Alexander's rights, pointing out the mistakes and flaws in the investigation. Realizing what was going on, she tried to prove that the investigation was conducted in violation of the rules. Finally, she was asked directly who Leventhal was to her.

The question perplexed the woman.

— What do you mean?

— I mean who is Leventhal to you — a relative, a friend or a lover? Why else would you be defending him so fiercely?

Salamaha blushed all over.

— He is nobody to me personally, but he is a human being. And in our country, all people are equal before the law.

— Yes, our country is the most humane one, and no innocent person in our country is convicted.

— That's true, — Salamaha rejoiced. — It means that Leventhal has nothing to be convicted for, he is innocent.

— You must have gone crazy, Comrade Salamaha, — the prosecutor said. — Don't you know that he is a Jew?

— I do. But that doesn't mean that he is outside the law, — the woman persisted.

— Stop talking nonsense, — the prosecutor said angrily, — the sentence will be given. And you, as a communist, need to reconsider your views if you don't want to find yourself in the same situation.

The threat was effective. Salamaha did not voice any protest on behalf of the defendant any more.

The court was ready to make a decision. The prosecutor delivered the final address for the prosecution. He asked for 25 years of maximum security camps for the defendant.

During the delivery of the speech, Aunt Dasha lost it. She jumped off her chair and yelled with a pain in her heart,

— I wish twenty five sores would pop up on your lousy tongue, scum bag. You are all bastards! Animals!

Aunt Dasha was taken out of the courtroom. Sentencing was postponed to the next day.

At last the final sentence was read. Considering that the defendant, Alexander Grigoryevich Leventhal, was a participant in World War II and had numerous decorations, he was "only" sentenced to twelve years of maximum security camps.

There was noise and yelling in the courtroom, but the police quickly dispersed all the protestors and the convict was put into a police car and taken to Drogobych.

CONVICTED

Three months later, Alexander was transferred to the Lvov prison which was located on Shevchenko Street. During the German occupation there was a Jewish ghetto there. Along with the other inmates, Alexander spent his time there hammering boxes together.

Alexander was amazed at the diversity of the people he met on the prison plank beds. He was especially surprised by how many people were from the older generation. Many of them were well over seventy. Some were blind or disabled. All of them were convicted for long terms which meant for the rest of their lives.

One day there was an order to send several trains of inmates to the Rovenskiy camp. Construction of a big plant in Rovno required a lot of man power. The head of the Lvov prison was ordered to select and send all the disabled men and those over seventy to the Rovenskiy Labor camp.

When the train with the "reinforcements" arrived in Rovno and the local authorities saw the labor force, there was a big scandal. The train with the inmates was sent back to Lvov. Many old men did not survive the trip, and those left alive were so weak when they returned that they were not able to move without each other's help. It was a terrible scene. Feeble, weakened old men leaned on each other to walk, barely able to drag their feet. Those who were stronger helped the weaker ones.

Young men with wide shoulders and machine guns, who guarded the convoy, silently watched the wretched men. The inmates who were present when the unclaimed "work force" returned wanted to help the poor people, but the guards did not let them.

Then everybody heard loud screams from one of the prisoners. It was a former hero of the Soviet Union, a fighter pilot who had fought all through the war, but he had displeased the authorities during the postwar years. He was convicted and stripped of all his awards and decorations.

— Nazis, bastards, — he yelled, — what are you doing to people? Where is your bright future? You have destroyed and continue to destroy people. You are Nazis. Damn you.

Everybody in the prison yard heard those curses resonate from the prison walls. But it only lasted a minute. There was an immediate order to grab the speaker and strong young men jumped at the veteran. He had walked across Europe liberating the world from Nazi evil, unsuspecting that the same evil ruled his own country.

Nobody ever saw the fighter pilot again.

EVERYDAY LIFE AT THE CAMP

After six months in Lvov Prison, Alexander was sent to the Zhitomirskiy camp to serve his sentence. To Alexander's great surprise, a man named Teslyar came to see him before he left. Teslyar used to live on the same street as the Leventhals before the war.

Teslyar held a package in his hands and smiled.

After greeting each other they sat at the table.

Teslyar unwrapped the package in front of Alexander. There was a piece of sausage and a loaf of bread.

— Help yourself, Sasha, — Teslyar said.

Alexander broke off a piece of sausage, swallowed it greedily and wrapped up the rest of the food.

— I will take it with me on the trip. I am being transferred to the camp in Zhitomir. I'll take it with me.

Teslyar nodded and after he recounted the latest Dobromil news, said good-bye and left.

The next day Alexander and the other prisoners were taken in covered trucks to the railway station where freight cars awaited them. The cars were very filthy and there was barbed wire on the windows. A water barrel was in one corner with a cup on a chain that could be used for drinking. In another corner there was a small hole in the floor. It was encircled by two boards and served as a toilet.

Each "traveler" was given one and a half day rations — one loaf of stale bread.

After everybody was forced into the cars, they attempted to settle comfortably, but it was not easy. They had packed 80 people into each car. Alexander got into a corner trying to find some peace.

The trip from Lvov to Zhitomir was supposed to take a day and a half.

The train started moving and all the "passengers" calmed down.

Night came. A voice called in the quiet,

— Bros, has anyone got an extra slice of bread? For God's sake, please give me some.

One of the people next to the man took a piece from his loaf and gave it to the hungry man.

When morning came, the train was still going. According to Alexander's calculations they ought to be approaching Zhitomir.

When the train stopped Alexander looked out of the window and read the name of the railway station: "Rovno".

What was going on? He was assigned to the Zhitomirskiy camp.

He quietly sat at his place. Thoughts tumbled in his mind. One could expect anything from those bastards. But how could he find out where they were going? Nobody talked to them. They locked them into freight cars like cattle and were taking them to slaughter. How painfully familiar it all was! How unfair fate was! His years of youth were spent in the trenches under bullets, the years of maturity — in prisons and camps. What had he gained by fighting? After all, their commanders had told them, "As soon as we defeat fascism we will live happily. We will build and restore the country out of ashes."

Hadn't he restored Dobromil out of ashes? Hadn't he returned the town to pre-war prosperity? Hadn't he given people the life they dreamt about? Why were they doing this to him? Why?!

Who could answer this question for him? He answered it himself: because he was a Jew. Out of fifteen hundred Jewish families in Dobromil, only two were left alive — his brother's family and his own. And somebody wanted to destroy them, too. What was the reason for that? Envy? It's unknown. What is known for sure, it's anti-Semitism.

A song interrupted his train of thought. Somebody began to sing about cranes.

Alexander's heart ached. He pushed himself deeper into the corner forgetting about hunger. And the wheels kept clattering mile after mile.

It had been two days since they started the trip. The bread given for the trip was gone. Now and then there were requests to share some food. Nobody knew any longer where they were being taken and when they would arrive at their destination.

They arrived at Zhitomir in seven days, half dead. It turned out that the train was sent through Sarny and Rovno in order to pick up more prisoners for the Zhitomirskiy camp.

When the car's door was opened, people, exhausted to a frazzle, were not able to get out by themselves. The stronger ones helped the weaker. The arrival of the "reinforcements" at the Zhitomirskiy camp was terrifying.

All the newly arrived were lined up. Each of them was to come up to three KGB officials, who sat at a table covered with a red table cloth, and announce his name, his sentence and put his signature down.

Nobody planned to feed the "new recruits" that day. Everybody was forced into the barracks.

That was how Alexander's life in the Zhitomirskiy camp started.

UNCLE PETER

Inside the barrack the new arrivals began to ask the people living there for some food to satisfy their hunger a bit. The prisoners shared everything they had. They asked for news and wondered what was going on in the country, but nobody knew anything. They were all out of touch.

Zhitomir was a maximum security camp with hard labor. Murderers and criminals could be sentenced to light work, but those who embezzled State property had to purge their guilt with hard labor. There was just 10 rubles (about $2 U.S.) spent each day on the prisoner's food. That meant they would be on short rations for many years.

Alexander was assigned to work at the saw mill. He was to saw boards and make pressed sawdust boards. Only extraordinary stamina and his endurance from the war years helped Alexander survive. News from his wife didn't bring any joy either. The exhausted, downhearted woman wrote angry, irritated letters. Alexander didn't blame her. He knew how difficult it was for her. She, a pure Russian, was called a sheeny and mocked, and so were the children.

They warned Alexander on the very first day that the head of the camp was a real beast. If he didn't like someone, that "lucky guy" would be at once sent to the punishment cell for ten days. He had a special attitude towards Jews, so he better not get in his way.

One day the head of the camp came to the shop where Alexander worked. Looking around his kingdom he saw Alexander lifting a board, trying to avoid looking at the head of the camp.

— What are you here for? — he asked, coming closer.

Alexander put the board down and sprang to attention.

— I am asking you why you are here.

— I don't know, citizen chief warden, — Alexander said clearly.

— How so?

— They haven't explained it to me, citizen chief warden.

The camp's director twisted his lips into a wry smile.

— During the war you must have been in the rear, right? Were you engaged in speculation?

— Not at all, citizen chief warden. I spent the whole war at the front, from 1939 until 1946. I captured Berlin.

— You are saying you captured Berlin? Were you wounded?

— Yes, I was. Four times.

— Were you decorated?

— Three citations signed personally by Comrade Stalin. Medals "For bravery under fire", "For courage", "For the capture of Berlin", and "the Order of the Red Star", citizen chief warden. I have walked across all of Europe.

The camp's head turned abruptly and left the shop without saying a word. He never approached Alexander again.

One day Alexander got a letter from Maks Abramovich Kuchenberg. After reading it he sat in the corner of his plank-bed and cried with his eyes closed. The passing prisoners looked at him in astonishment. Alexander's face was expressionless, but tears kept rolling down his face. The open letter was on his lap.

The past emerged again. After many years the fate of Moisha Lihtman, the former owner of the Dobromil sawmill, became known.

One night, three months after Paraska took Lhitman's baby grandson to her house in Nizhenkivichy, somebody knocked on the window. Alarmed, Paraska's father grabbed the baby and quickly went up the ladder to the attic. Shaking all over, Paraska approached the window.

— Who's there?

— It's me, Paraska, open up.

Upon hearing the familiar voice, Paraska rushed to the door.

When the man came into the house, Paraska was shocked. It was very difficult to recognize Mr. Lihtman in the dirty, unshaven man standing before her. He used to dress elegantly and was always clean shaven and smelled of good cologne. Now he was standing helplessly in the doorway shaking from cold and bent over.

The woman quickly pulled him inside the house, and ran into the yard to see if anyone was there. When she came into the house she caught her breath.

— Thank God, nobody saw you. Take off your outer clothes, Mr. Lihtman.

— Paraska, I came to find out how my grandson is doing.

— Do sit down, please. The boy is growing. Everybody believes that he is my son. They call him a "foundling", but it's better than sheeny.

Somewhere close the ladder squeaked. Mr. Lihtman got worried, but Paraska made him relax.

— It's my father and your grandson coming down from the attic.

Mr. Lihtman got up and reached with his shaking hands towards the squeak.

Paraska's father appeared out of the dark with the baby in his arms.

The old Jew kneeled down in front of him and embraced his feet. His shoulders were shaking with sobs.

Shocked by the scene, Paraska rushed to get Mr. Lihtman up.

— Calm down, Mr. Lihtman. Everything will be all right. Please calm down.

She seated the guest on the chair. The old man was wiping tears with his hands smearing them all over his dirty face.

— Mr. Lihtman, take your clothes off. Get washed. Eat. You are hungry, — the woman offered.

— Paraska, I am afraid to get you into trouble. You realize, if somebody finds out I came to you, you will be killed. And I don't want that. My grandson must live. I'll go away from you and everything will be fine. I am asking only one thing: save my grandson.

— No, Mr. Lihtman, I am not letting you go anywhere. You don't have anywhere to go. For now you will stay in the attic and later I will give you Uncle Peter's papers. He died a week ago. And then we will see how it goes.

Old Lihtman cried and kissed Paraska's hands. His fear for his grandson was very deep. He wanted to sacrifice himself in order to save the baby, but Paraska insisted on her offer.

The clothes Mr. Lihtman arrived in were burned. But when they were removing the clothes, they discovered the Torah tied to Mr. Lihtman's body.

— What's this, Mr. Lihtman? — Paraska's father asked.

— It's the Torah.

— I can see it's the Torah. We need to burn it to be out of harm's way.

— No, no, we can't... it's a Holy Scripture.

— This holy scripture can take us all to the gallows.

— We will bury the Torah in the basement, — Paraska suggested.

And they did. They placed the Torah at the bottom of a barrel and poured wheat on top of it.

That's how they began to live. "Uncle Peter" almost never left the house. He took care of the baby, fed him and babysat him. The little boy brought him great joy.

A few months later Paraska's family decided to move to an outlying village in the mountains. It gave old Lihtman, now only called Uncle Peter, a bit more freedom. As time passed, he began to take the growing boy to school. And in the evenings he would take out the Torah and secretly teach his grandson the Jewish laws and religion. He taught him to read Hebrew and Yiddish. Eventually, Peter's grandson was drafted into the Soviet Army.

After his grandson left, Peter kept busying doing the household chores. Sometimes he even went to gather firewood in the forest; but Peter was getting old and frequently grabbed his chest. His age and a tough past showed. And he missed his grandson.

One day his neighbor Ivan invited Peter to go to the forest with him to gather firewood. The neighbor's offer made him happy. It was more fun to go to the forest with someone else. Besides, the neighbor's horse, although old, would help carry the wood.

When they were done gathering dry sticks the neighbors sat on the edge of the cliff to have a rest and a snack. They unwrapped their food and began to eat bread with milk. They started talking.

Ivan began to recall what tasty sausage they used to sell in Dobromil before the war. Everything was incredibly tasty then. Bread was baked in such a way that it melted in your mouth.

Glancing at his neighbor, Ivan made a suggestion.

— Peter, how about going to Dobromil and having a look at what's going on now?

Peter was silent, but Ivan persisted.

— Let's get in the cart. Although my horse is old, it will make it there and back.

Peter kept silent.

— Why are you silent, friend? Have you ever been to Dobromil?

— Yes, I have. But it was a long time ago, before the war. They say everybody was killed there during the war.

— Yes, yes. I was there. I saw everything. What a mistake it was! Why did we do it?

— What do you mean "we"? — Peter asked.

— We — policemen. At that time I served in the police. We caught poor Jews and turned them over to be tortured by that slaughterer Filus. He executed them mercilessly.

Peter started coughing, and Ivan went on,

— Even children were not spared. Dogs tore them apart. I have nightmares to this day. What time is it Peter? You have a watch, haven't you?

— Yes, but it shows the wrong time. Could you get it to the watch-maker when you go to Dobromil?

Ivan took the watch and put it in his pocket.

— You know, Peter, the old watchmaker was thrown into the salt mines.

Peter was shaking as if from cold.

— And what happened to those who were at the saw mill? — he finally squeezed out.

— They were all shot and buried in a trench. Some of them were still alive and we put soil on top on them. The Germans didn't want to waste the bullets needed to finish them off. The children cried so loudly we couldn't bear it, so we pushed soil on top of them. I still hear those screams. Tell me, friend, who can I beg for forgiveness and peace of mind?

Ivan looked at Peter and got scared. He sat there with blue lips holding the left part of his chest. Ivan grabbed Peter by the hand to comfort him, but Peter pulled it away with all his might. His body, unable to keep its balance, fell off the cliff and smashed against the rocks.

Ivan was terrified. He screamed and began to call for help. But who could hear him in the forest? The old man jumped into the cart in shock and rushed the old horse to the village, but on the way he lost consciousness. When he was found and revived, he began to call Peter's name, and everybody realized that something bad had happened to Peter. The whole village ran to search.

Peter's smashed body was found at the bottom of the cliff. When they brought it home to Paraska, she got hysterical, calling Ivan a murderer.

Although Ivan swore on his knees that he wasn't guilty, he was arrested. When he was searched they found the engraved gold watch which had been given to Mr. Lihtman by his wife on his fiftieth birthday. When Ivan was asked where he got the watch, he openly said that he got it from Peter.

The trial was held in Dobromil.

To everybody's surprise, Paraska brought something wrapped in dark cloth to the trial and put it in front of the judge. It was the Torah which Mr. Lihtman had brought with him to her house in Nizhenkovi-chy. She also brought the grandson's letters to his beloved grandfather. There was so much love and tenderness in them! The young man knew what his grandfather had done for him. He gave up his name and his life in order to save his grandson's life. He did not want anyone to insult or hurt his grandson and decided to keep his secret to the very end. All he wanted for his last offspring was peace and happiness.

Ivan sat on the prisoner dock in shock and started to yell.

— If only I had known that it was Mr. Lihtman! If only I had known... I would have fallen at his feet and begged for forgiveness for everything and everybody. I would have asked forgiveness from all the victims who died at our hands. But I didn't know... I couldn't even imagine who was with me.

For the past evil deeds which were discovered during the trial, Ivan was sentenced to death.

Alexander read this news and sat on the plank-bed and cried. If only he had known! Occasionally, Paraska had come to him for help. He even gave an order to the packers to buy apples from her orchard at the highest price. If only he had known that the old man who stood aside and watched him carefully, was the same Mr. Lihtman who owned the saw mill where he once worked.

Days passed. Gradually Alexander was gaining prestige among the prisoners and the wardens.

Once a prisoner climbed the highest smoke stack and began to scream from there.

— Down with communism! Down with the tormentors of the people!

One of the prisoners came up to Alexander and asked,

— Why do you think he climbed the smoke stack and is yelling up there?

— He wants to talk to the government at the top level, — Alexander answered. — So that he is heard.

The prisoner stared at Alexander in disbelief.

— What, you don't believe me? — he smiled.

— Well, that may be right, — replied the man.

Alexander watched the guards run around the smoke— stack at a loss for what to do. He saw the brass hats arrive.

The man sat on his platform the whole day right up until dark.

Passing tourists stopped and took pictures, but policemen dispersed them right away.

When the "speaker" got off the smoke stack, he was immediately taken away and nobody ever saw him again.

The head of the Zhitomirskiy camp sent Alexander, along with some other prisoners, to the saw mill to get wood scrap which was intended for heating the houses and the camp's kitchen. When the prisoners arrived at the saw mill, the chief warden gave an order to load construction boards on the bottom of the truck. Silently the prisoners began to load. They put good building materials on the bottom of the truck, and covered them up with fire wood.

From the saw mill the truck headed to the house of the camp's director. There the prisoners were told to take out the boards and place them in the corner of the yard. It wasn't easy to pull the boards out with the firewood lying on top of them. Fairly exhausted, the prisoners nevertheless tackled the task. After they finished stacking the boards in the prison head's yard, the prisoners got into the truck wiping off sweat. The youngest of them said,

— What dopes! Why did they tell us to put the boards on the bottom? It was so hard to pull them out. We could have put them on the very top.

Another prisoner looked at him and agreed,

— You know what, you are right. What dopes. They exhausted us.

Alexander sat there with his head down not participating in the conversation. And then he felt a poke in his side.

— What do you think, grandpa?

At first Alexander didn't realize that he was the one being called "grandpa". He looked around. Could it be they were addressing him? Could he have grown so old? He wasn't even forty yet.

The young prisoner stared at Alexander and asked again.

— Why aren't you saying anything, grandpa?

— What can I say? The boards were stolen, that's why they were placed on the bottom of the truck. And we helped get them out of the timber mill's territory.

The man opened his mouth in surprise.

— What do you mean they were stolen?

— They did not have authorization to take those boards.

— I can't believe it. — Another prisoner had a hard time understanding. — So we just helped them steal? Let's keep our mouths shut, otherwise they can add to our sentence and we will never get out of prison.

The young man wouldn't quit.

— It's so unfair!

— What's unfair? — Alexander asked.

— That we have been put in a camp and treated like cattle for stealing, and they are thieves themselves!

Alexander looked at him.

— Don't get excited, friend. Take it easy. You have been put in prison because you are not good at stealing. Here you will go through a very good school and then they will let you out. After that, it's up to you.

The young prisoner wanted to say something, but this time Alexander spoke seriously.

— Forget about it and never recall what you have seen. Otherwise they will destroy your young life.

The man sat in the corner quietly thinking about Alexander's words.

They were sent to the saw mill many times, and every time the same thing happened. But none of the prisoners ever said a word about it.

Trakhtarchuk's case

Alexander had been in prison for six long years — six tough years of painful contemplation. Suddenly he was sent to the Ivano-Frankovskiy prison without any explanation. Alexander had no clue what was going on. Nobody answered his questions. He was thrown into a one-man cell. He was fed once a day. They gave him some thin soup. Two days later Alexander was called for questioning.

Having once again been brought to an inquiry cell, Alexander was puzzled and unsure of what was going on.

There was a nice young man sitting at the table. It was an investigator for particularly important cases. Raising his head from some papers, he looked at Alexander and said thoughtfully,

— Do you know why I am here?

— No.

— Any guesses?

— No.

— Did you know the manager of the Drogobych WRS, citizen Trakhtarchuk?

Alexander was silent, unsure what was behind that question.

— Your wife got involved in a "business" case. You must confirm everything she said. Trakhtarchuk has been already imprisoned regarding another case.

— I don't understand what you are saying, — Alexander said.

— You must confirm your wife's words or we will put her in prison and will place your children into an orphanage to be raised there.

Those words made Alexander tremble. He looked at the investigator with haunted eyes.

— I don't know what you are talking about.

— Did you give Trakhtarchuk a bribe?

— No.

— Tell the truth. Think about your children.

— I am thinking, but I can't say anything. I cannot tell a lie about a person.

— When was the last time you saw your children?

Alexander was silent.

— Why are you silent?

— Because you are blackmailing me. You are trying to push my buttons. But you won't be able to do it.

— But your wife has told us...

— I don't believe it. She couldn't have said anything like that.

— You don't believe it? In that case we'll arrange for a confrontation with your wife.

The investigator kept his word. A few days later Olga was brought into the office of the investigator. She was pale and frightened.

Alexander got up from his chair and extended his arms to his wife, but the abrupt order "Freeze!" paralyzed them both. Olga was then seated in one corner and Alexander in the other. The questioning started.

— Dear citizen Leventhal, — the investigator began politely, — you have testified that your husband gave a bribe.

Olga shuddered.

— That wasn't me testifying. It was you who told me that my husband stole money from you by giving bribes.

— Citizen Leventhal, don't forget where you are. You have signed an important document. If you husband doesn't confirm everything you have signed, you will be put in prison and we will place your children in an orphanage.

Upon hearing that, Olga drooped.

— Citizen investigator, — Alexander said, — this is blackmail. You have maligned me in my wife's eyes. If you charged me with the theft of money, and I didn't bring it home, anyone could think I had given it away to people. But where would you find fools who would steal money to give money it away?

— You are very sly. Justly a Jew, — the investigator muttered. — But we will look into the matter.

— In that case I will not say another word. Go ahead and look into it, — Alexander said.

And he kept his word. He was taken to questionings for six months. But nobody was able to squeeze a word out of him. Alexander denied everything.

He was still kept in a one-man cell with some thin soup delivered once a day. One time a supervising prosecutor was inspecting the cells. Alexander asked him why he was being kept in the interrogative cell. After all, he was not under investigation.

This plea worked. The next day he was transferred into a mass cell.

Alexander was called as a witness at Trakhtarchuk's trial.

— Did you give a bribe to Trakhtarchuk? — he was asked when they brought him to the courtroom.

— I have not given anything to anyone and I don't know anything. I myself have been convicted falsely.

— Get him out, — the judge ordered.

A month after Trakhtarchuk's trial, Alexander was transferred to the Ivano-Frankovskiy labor camp.

AMNESTY

At 6:00 in the morning on January 17, 1966, when all the prisoners had been lined up at attention, the camp radio called Alexander Leventhal to come to the watch. Usually that "invitation" meant big trouble. Prisoners were called to the watch when they had done something wrong. Alexander didn't feel he was guilty of anything, but one could expect anything from "them". Catching his breath, he went to the watch.

Three soldiers from the Ministry of Internal Affairs (MIA) were already waiting for him with expressionless faces and machine guns in their hands. Alexander was ordered to get into a police car. What? Why? Where am I going? All the questions he tried to ask were stopped with an abrupt order: "Shut up!"

Leventhal obeyed. His heart beat loudly and anxiously because of the suspense.

The car drove for a long time. Finally, it stopped, the door was opened and he was ordered to get out. When he emerged from the car, he began to look around trying to determine where he was. He saw a sign on a building that said "Ivano-Frankovskiy District Court".

An order to move brought him out of thought.

Alexander was taken to the court building. On the third floor he was told to sit down in a chair and wait.

At eight thirty an MIA officer whom he had frequently seen in the camp passed him. The officer stopped, looked at Leventhal, and then looked at the guards holding him at gun point.

— Why are you pointing your guns at him like this? He is not going to escape, right Leventhal? — he addressed Alexander, smiling this time.

He nodded in agreement. The officer left.

Alexander followed him with his eyes. What's going on? Why was he brought here?

At exactly nine thirty, he was taken into the courtroom. There was a judge, two associated judges and the familiar MIA officer sitting at the table.

The officer started the proceedings.

— Alexander Leventhal was sentenced to twelve years for embezzlement of State property. During the eight years and three months of his time in the prison camps he has been at his best. He has behaved well and has worked hard. During the time spent in camp he has been completely reformed. He hasn't committed any violations. I suggest releasing the prisoner Leventhal early.

The judge looked through Leventhal's case and took off his glasses.

— I don't have anything against it.

— Neither do I, — the prosecutor said. — Where are you going to go, Leventhal?

— To my children, — Alexander blurted out, barely recovering.

— And where do they live?

— In Dobromil, on the border with Poland.

— And where are you going to work?

— Wherever. It's all the same to me where to work. I am not afraid to work.

— I think you deserve to be released, Leventhal. What do you think? Have you been reformed over these years?

Alexander looked at the prosecutor with his eyes wide open and thought: what the hell are you talking about? Did the guy really believe what he said? But Alexander knew better and answered with what they expected to hear.

— Absolutely, comrade prosecutor. I have been 100% reformed.

— That's great. Go. You are free. In the camp they will give you papers, cash assistance in the amount of 20 rubles and a ticket to get home. Have a good trip, Leventhal. Good luck!

Return Home

As promised, the next day Alexander got papers regarding his release, a train ticket and 20 rubles (worth about $20 U.S. after the currency reform of 1961).

Arriving at the railway station Alexander bought a loaf of bread and some fried fish at the buffet. He sat on a bench and started eating greedily.

People sitting next to him stared. His clothes and his shaved head made it obvious that the man had just been released from prison. But the side-long glances and whispers did not bother Alexander at all. The only thing he could think about was getting home as soon as possible. He already imagined his meeting with his wife and children.

He was on the train to Stryi all night. There he transferred to the train going to Sambor, and from Sambor to Hirov. He got off at the station in Hirov and was quite close to his native town. At an intersection he raised his hand to hitchhike to Dobromil.

A truck stopped.

— Get in the back of the truck. There is no space in the cabin, — the driver shouted.

Alexander jumped into the truck's body and settled in a corner.

Soon he was in Dobromil. The driver stopped the truck downtown, right at the place where Alexander had been arrested eight years before. He got out of the truck's body and went to the cabin holding money in his hand to pay for his ride, but he was greatly surprised with what he heard.

— Alexander Grigoryevich, I don't want your money. Welcome home, Alexander.

Alexander was taken aback. He didn't recognize the young man and was unable to guess how he knew Alexander.

— Do you remember me? — the driver asked. — I was very young when you hired me. I was eighteen. I am glad you are back.

— Well, thank you for giving me a ride.

Alexander walked along Krasnoarmcyskiy Street, formerly known as Koliyova Street. His family — his mother, father, sister Rosa and Uncle Leon — had once walked along that very same street on their way to their deaths. And now he was walking on that street to get home.

The snow crunched under his feet. Alexander looked around. Everything seemed different and strange. Houses looked grey and unfriendly. People passing by stopped when they saw him, recognizing him and not recognizing him at the same time.

There was the church. So many people around! Oh, yes, it's January 19th, the Epiphany. Alexander walked faster. The closer he came to his house, the louder his heart pounded.

Finally, he reached his house. God, it was such a ramshackle! Only the walnut trees had grown. There was the gate. The fence had almost fallen apart. The gate was tied with a rope. It was obvious that the man of the house had been away for a long while.

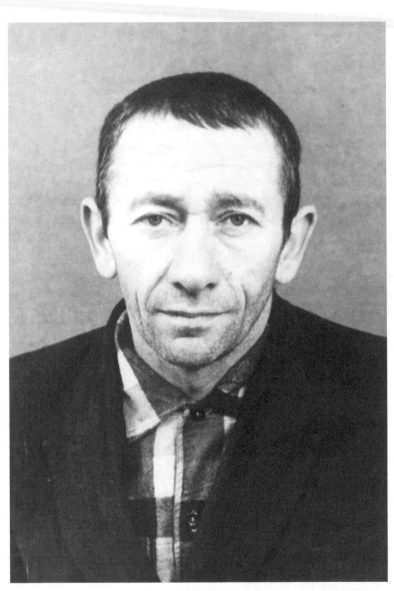

Alexander Leventhal upon returning home from prison, 1966
Photo from the author's archive

Who was going to open the door for him? How would the meeting go? Alexander was nervous.

Entering the yard he looked around. Where were the swings he had made for the kids before his arrest? And where were the benches he had put under the apple trees so they could admire the tree's blossoms? The yard was empty. It had become completely strange and unfriendly. Why even be surprised? It had been so many years.

Alexander went up the steps and opened the door. He didn't recognize the house. Everything inside was different. The stairs leading to the second floor were now in the former kitchen. Oh yes, Olga had written to him that the State had taken the house and divided it into two apartments. Now somebody else lived on the second floor.

Alexander knocked on the open door and heard Aunt Dasha's voice.

— Who's there?

Alexander entered the kitchen.

Aunt Dasha stood by the stove cooking dinner and stirring the soup in the pot. The spoon fell out of her hand.

— God Almighty! Sasha! — she cried. — Sasha! Sasha!

She could not find any other words. Nobody could ever squeeze a tear out of that woman's eyes, but at that moment her eyes were filled with tears. She had waited for her benefactor for so many years. She had tried to keep his family together and made many sacrifices to raise his kids. She had been waiting for Sasha for so many years and finally the day had come.

— Sasha! Sasha !Our benefactor. God bless you. Why are you standing there? Come on in! You must be hungry. I've just made soup. Come on in, my dear.

She was fussing around in the kitchen trying to seat the man so dear to her heart at the table and serve him.

Alexander took off his hat and, without taking off his coat, approached Aunt Dasha.

— Hi, Aunt Dasha. I am back. How have you been without me?

— Oh, God, — Aunt Dasha continued, — it was tough without you. It's tough without you, our supporter. But now that you are home, everything will be all right. The children are at school. Have a seat, please, have something to eat. We've got food. We have potatoes, cabbage, and bread. There is no meat — there hasn't been for a while — —but we don't go hungry. Have a seat. You must have forgotten what home made soup tastes like.

She began to take off his coat.

— Oh, Sasha, you are so thin, — she was upset again. — Have a seat. Here's some bread. Go ahead, eat some freshly made food. And I will run to the school and let the kids know their daddy is home.

Alexander began to eat the soup.

— And where is Olga?

— She is at work in the tea-house. She works with Nina Ivanovna Nechayeva. She is such a good woman. She always gives Olga some food for the kids. God bless her. I'll drop by there, too.

And without waiting for his response, she put on her coat and left the house. She ran to the school and approached the first person she saw — the cleaning lady.

— Could you please tell me what time the bell will ring?

— The classes have just begun. It's thirty five minutes until the break, — the woman answered. — Has something happened?

— I've got to pick up the Leventhal children. Their father is back from prison.

— What a joy, — the woman said happily. — God bless him. Go to the third floor, their classes are there.

Aunt Dasha went to the third floor. There was a door with the sign "Grade 9-A". It was Ludmila's classroom. She knocked on the door. A moment later the teacher, Natalya Kondratyevna, opened the door.

— What's going on, Darya Gavrilovna?

— My dear, — Aunt Dasha began, out of breath from running. — Ludmila's father is back from prison. I would like to take her home now.

— What good news!

Natalya Kondratyevna taught Russian language and literature, and loved Ludmila dearly. She tried to be a good friend and mentor to the young girl, whom she believed had sincerity and talent. She opened the door widely, so that Aunt Dasha could see Ludmila.

The girl sat at the desk writing diligently. Seeing Grandma Dasha in the doorway, she froze and looked at her questioningly.

— Ludmila, your daddy is home, — Natalya Kondratyevna said.

Ludmila slowly got up from behind the desk and headed for the door. Her face was expressionless. Not a single emotion showed on it,

not a single muscle twitched. Nobody and nothing mattered to her at that moment except for one thing: her daddy was home. Finally! It had been so long since he left! She had waited for him for so long!

Proudly holding her head, she went to the door unaware of her classmates and her teacher looking at her.

When she got out of the classroom, Ludmila started to ask Grandma Dasha questions.

— Grandma, what does he look like?

— Don't you remember your daddy? — Grandma Dasha asked. — He is the same as he was before, only very thin.

— Grandma, do you think he will recognize me?

— Sure, he will, — the woman said anxiously. — He will recognize you no matter what, you will see.

They were on the way to classroom "11-A" where Gennadiy studied.

Aunt Dasha knocked on the door as she stroked Ludmila's hair to calm her down.

The door opened and they saw Galina Klimovna, the teacher of Ukrainian language and literature teacher.

— What's going on, Dasha? — she asked.

— Gennadiy's daddy has come home. Please allow Gennadiy to go home.

Galina Klimovna hesitated, but then she turned to the class and said loudly,

— Gennadiy Leventhal, go outside!

Gennadiy didn't have to be told twice. He quickly ran out of the classroom and froze at the sight of his sister with Grandma Dasha.

— What's going on, grandma?

— Your daddy has come back. He is waiting for you at home.

Gennadiy turned pale. He had been waiting for him for so many years!

The children were almost running home. Grandma Dasha could barely keep up with them.

When they got home, Ludmila opened the door and both children ran into the kitchen screaming.

— Daddy! Daddy!

Their father was standing by the table hugging his wife.

In that small town, the news of Leventhal's return had spread rapidly. Somebody saw Leventhal get out of the truck and rushed to the tea-house to tell Olga about her husband's return. When Olga heard the news, she dropped everything and ran home.

When she entered the house she rushed to hug her husband weeping from happiness.

Alexander caressed Olga saying,

— Calm down, calm down. Everything is behind us. We will have a new life now. You will see. It will be even better.

That was when Ludmila and Gennadiy entered.

— Look, our kids are here. — With these words, Alexander tenderly moved Olga aside. Reaching out he went towards his children, who he had been constantly thinking about all those years. He had remembered them as young children, the way they were when he left. Now his son was over eighteen years old, and his daughter was over fifteen.

— Children, how big you have grown! My God, I left when you were so young and now I see grown up young people.

The children ran to hug him. Gennadiy was as tall as his daddy.

— Gennadiy, my dear son, you are so grown up!

Then he turned to Ludmila.

— My baby girl, you are not a baby any more. You are a beautiful young girl now. Let me look at you.

He took Ludmila's face into his hands and looked into her eyes.

— Your eyes are exactly the same as Grandma Hanna's. They are the same color and of the same depth. My darling, how you have grown up and how beautiful you are!

Alexander was crying. His children had grown up without their father's guidance. The best years of life were taken from him. And then he heard a question.

— Daddy, where is your beautiful black hair? Is it going to grow back?

It was Ludmila asking.

— Yes, dear, it will. It will be even better. Do you know why?

— Why?

— Because it was shaved for eight years. And now it will grow back faster and more beautiful, — Alexander joked.

The whole family sat at the table, and Aunt Dasha began to pour soup and pass the bread. Suddenly the door opened and a close neighbor, Garbar, showed up. Right behind him was Nina Ivanovna Nechayeva with her husband. Nina held a big packet with food and a bottle of vodka. Aunt Dasha was glad to see Nina Ivanovna and her husband.

— Come in, come in, dear guests.

— I hope we are not intruding. After all, we have come uninvited, and that's the worst kind of guests there could be.

— Not at all, Nina Ivanovna! Please come in, — Alexander said happily. — Do sit down. How did you know I came back?

— It's no secret, Alexander Grigoryevich. The whole town of Dobromil is buzzing that Leventhal has returned from prison.

As soon as Nina Ivanovna finished speaking, there was another knock on the door. Aunt Dasha rushed to open it. There was a man standing in the doorway with his head low. He was fumbling with his hat. It was Matsey, who had committed perjury against Alexander.

The people present lost their tongues looking at the guest, and Matsey fidgeted silently, still fumbling with his hat. Finally, with difficulty, he managed to speak.

— Mr. Leventhal, I have come to ask you for forgiveness. Forgive me for putting you in prison. Do whatever you want to me, just forgive me.

His voice echoed in the silence. Nobody said anything in response. Suddenly Garbar jumped up and without saying a word grabbed Matsey by the chest and began to shake him.

Regaining his senses, Alexander ran to the door and grabbed Grabar by the arm.

— Don't guys. I don't need this, or I will be put in prison again, this time for disorderly conduct. And I don't want to go back there.

Garbar let Matsey go.

— You know very well, Matsey, — Alexander addressed him, — that nobody could truthfully testify against me. But you and Podolyak lied. Have you come to me today because your conscious tortures you? This is what I want you to know: you have taken my best years away from me. Not just from me, but also from my wife and children. I will not do anything to you, but I am not capable of forgiving you. Let God forgive you. I am not God. I am not as merciful as He is.

Alexander turned his back to the unwelcome guest and went into the house. Matsey went away like a beaten dog.

Six years later news went around Dobromil that Matsey had died from leukemia. For the remainder of his life, he had constantly talked about the wrong-doing he did to Leventhal. Several years later illness also struck the second perjurer, Podolyak. Doctors had to amputate both his legs.

On the day of Alexander's homecoming the doors to the Leventhals' house never closed. The house was full of friends. Everybody wanted to talk with the host.

The next day Alexander's old friend from before the war, Mark Abramovich Kuhenberg, came to visit.

When he came in Alexander hugged his friend tightly.

— Hello, Max.

— How are you, Sasha?

— Better that anybody else.

They hugged again.

— Would you like to move to Stryi where I live?

— Thanks, Max, but I don't want to complicate your life.

— What makes you think you will complicate my life? There was a time when you welcomed Klava and me and helped us after the war. Now it's my turn to help you.

— No, my friend. You know I was convicted.

— What are you talking about, Sasha? That's small potatoes! You are like a blood brother to me. All our kind died in the war. We must help each other. Remember, we are of the same blood. We are Jews and we shouldn't forget that.

— Max, I'll think it over and will let you know my decision, — Alexander replied after a short pause.

— Well, please consider it, friend. Here are 300 rubles. Let me know what you are going to do.

— OK. Thank you, Max. Thank you. I will pay you back.

— Please don't offend me, Sasha. I want to help you from the bottom of my heart. Money doesn't matter. You should understand that you survived and came home to your family, and not everybody was fortunate enough to do that. But the main thing is they haven't broken you.

— That's true, Max, — Alexander responded.

The friends parted.

Andrey Tokar, another of Alexander's good friends, came to visit him that night.

Alexander had known Andrey, who was famous all over Dobromil for his strength, since his childhood. Andrey's first words were,

— Sasha has come back! Many were executed but you made it! Well, tell me everything.

— I will tell you everything, but first I'd like to thank you for all the help you gave to my family during my absence.

During the long eight years Alexander spent in prison, Andrey Tokar had helped Olga and her children in many ways. He would give them flour or fire wood or coal. He bought boots for Gennadiy. He did whatever was needed. Olga wrote Alexander all about it.

— Thank you for everything, my friend.

— Don't mention it, Sasha. It was my duty to help them. You can't imagine how difficult it was for them to live without you — it's terrible to recall. On top of being the wife of a convict, she was a sheeny. If they could, they would have eaten your family alive. It's lucky you have come back.

— What are you going to do now? —Andrey asked after some silence.

— I don't know yet.

— I do. I know how knowledgeable you are about cattle. Let's go to Turki together. They hold a big market there. Remember how you bought and sold bull-calves? That's what we will do. We will go to Turki this Sunday. I will lend you money for a cow and you can pay me back later.

It was a great idea. No one else was as good at the cattle business as Alexander. Father Gersh had taught his son well. With his seasoned eye, Alexander could determine the weight of a cow and how much meat it would provide with one glance.

The friends decided to put this plan into action, but they were unaware that at that very moment, Alexander's fate was being discussed in the director's office of the Furniture and Integrated Woodworking Plant.

The plant's director had called his deputy.

— Have you heard that Leventhal has come back?

— Yes, I have.

— What do you think of him?

— Nothing, comrade director.

— Well, I think that we have got to hire him here immediately. The deputy director looked up in bewilderment.

— Yes, don't be surprised. We need him. We need his head. He is a very smart man and we need him. Send for him. We need to hire him immediately.

— Yes, but he was convicted — the deputy director protested.

— So what? We won't give him a position of responsibility. Everybody must work and we need him. We need his Jewish brains. Send for him right away. He is a smart and honest man. I have heard a lot about him.

On the third day of his return Alexander was in the office of the Woodworking Plant. The plant's director, Comrade Yachminskiy, hired him as a laborer. After a while he was promoted to an engineering position, but he actually worked as a purchasing agent. He was given the title of engineer because a purchasing agent had a position with material responsibility.

Soon the Dobromil Integrated Woodworking Plant was the highest rated facility of its kind. Furniture produced at that plant became famous not only in the Soviet Union, but everywhere it was exported.

Ten years later, "engineer" Alexander Grigoryevich Leventhal still functioned as the chief supply officer of the integrated plant.

A Big Decision

Time passed and life changed for the Leventhals. Aunt Dasha had died and Alexander's children had gotten married and started families of their own.

As his family grew, Alexander discovered that he loved to cook. He was unaware of it, but by watching mother Mindlya cook, he had learned how to make all the family recipes. Alexander's flexible work schedule often allowed him the chance to surprise his family with these various dishes. By the time the others came home from work, Alexander had prepared a very tasty meal.

Ludmila, who was now a nurse and married with three children, liked to cook, too. She enjoyed learning from her father, diligently memorizing the family recipes. Father and daughter never got bored with each other. They always had things to discuss. Ludmila loved it most of all when her father told her about the past. She could immediately visualize the scenes in her mind. Each episode appeared in front of her eyes as if she were a participant in the events.

One day Ludmila came home from work and approached her father. He was busy in the kitchen making an apple pie according to mother Mindlya's recipe.

Ludmila put her hand on her father's shoulder.

— Daddy, what do you think of the many Jews leaving for Israel?

Alexander looked at his daughter with surprise. He didn't respond.

— Daddy, I would like to apply to go there, but I am not sure I will be approved. Would you like to go to Israel with me?

Alexander looked at his daughter in silence, not understanding what was going on.

— Daddy, I want to leave this country, — Ludmila repeated.

— What are you talking about? — Alexander said finally. — They will never give us permission to leave. I was convicted. And your brother has been in the air force for ten years. Who will give you permission to leave? Don't do it, baby girl. You will get both yourself and your family in trouble.

— No, Daddy. I want to take a chance while the political climate is favorable. I want to leave.

— It's crazy. You will get everyone into trouble. Think about your children.

— I am thinking about them. That's why I want to leave. Do you remember taking me to the field to pick up flowers and showing me a star when it got dark? You said that Grandma Hanna and your mother had taught you to find your way with the help of that star. You told me that it is the Star of David, which shines to show all the Jews the right way. Now it is shining for me and calling me. If I don't leave now, it will be too late.

Alexander didn't answer. He just silently looked at his daughter.

— Daddy, I will try to get permission to leave the country myself, — Ludmila said after some silence. — The only thing you need to do is give me permission... to say that you don't object to me leaving.

Ludmila Leventhal, 1967
Photo from the author's archive

Alexander sat on a chair. Thoughts were tumbling in his mind. He had just paid the State to get his house back. He had just gotten back on his feet after his release from prison. Things were going well. He tried so hard to give his children what he hadn't been able to give them while he was behind bars. All he wanted was to live surrounded by his children and five grandchildren; to provide them with comfort, prosperity and enjoy their happiness. In prison, he had dreamed of living quietly and peacefully with his family! His dream had finally come true. And now what? If they were denied permission to leave, which was very likely, everything would be turned upside down again.

Ludmila's husband, a school principal, would be fired. The whole family would be under Soviet repression as enemies and traitors to their country. They would all be in danger. But Ludmila was persistent. She wanted to try to leave the Soviet Union no matter what.

The situation bothered Alexander a lot. Germans had destroyed his home in Kvasenina. Russians had destroyed his home in Dobromil. And now, after all those hardships and all the time he spent in prison camps, when everything had just been restored, his daughter wanted to destroy it all again. What should he do?

Ludmila's youth was calling her, but he was so tired. He had gone through so much. Would he be capable of gathering his strength again? His daughter would not be able to leave without his help. He would have to break everything up again. He would have to fight with the authorities once again, putting everything they had at stake.

It was a sleepless night. Alexander was deep in thought remembering everything that had occurred in his life. Ludmila had reminded him about the Star of David. Grandma Hanna had told him that the star keeps Jews safe and shows them the way home. But he also knew something else: during the war the Star of David led everybody who lived according to its laws to death.

Not long ago a friend had sent him a letter from Israel. He wrote in it that mixed families like Alexander's, in which one of the spouses was not a Jew, better not go to Israel. Children not born from a Jewish mother were not considered Jewish. In Ukraine, Russia and throughout Europe, the children of these mixed families were considered Jews and humiliated as unworthy to live on Earth. In Israel these children were not considered to be Jews and were humiliated there, too. What should they do?

His thoughts took him back to his childhood. "That place is best of all where we haven't been at all." Alexander's father, Gersh, frequently repeated. Thinking of that led Alexander to recall the fate of his namesake, Dmitr Leventhal. Dmitr, who was called Yudka at the time, was his mother's only son. In October of 1942, all the Jews from the village were forced to go to Dobromil. Yudka's mother foresaw that they would all be killed and on the way to Dobromil she began to ask her son to escape to the forest. But the son loved his mother very much and did not want to leave, wishing to share her destiny. The woman begged him to save himself, but he wouldn't listen to her.

All of a sudden the policemen began to select and pull aside young and strong young men.

The mother whispered to Yudka,

— If you go with these guys, you will be dead. Run to the forest, my son.

Yudka continued to hesitate, but his mother insisted.

— You will be taken from me. We won't be together anyway. Run before it's too late.

Yudka made up his mind. He promised his mother he would find her if they survived, and she promised she would look for him in their native village.

Yudka rolled inconspicuously into a ditch and with nobody seeing him, hid in the underbrush. When the column of people disappeared into the distance, the young man carefully got out of his hide out and ran into the forest.

After 24 hours, Yudka was getting hungry and cold. He decided to go to his native village to search for food. But who could he turn to for help? Everybody treated Jews badly.

Yudka had a Ukrainian friend, Mikhailo Edynak. He had been a good friend before the war but what was his attitude now? The young man decided to risk it. Late at night he sneaked up to Mikhailo's house and knocked on the window.

Mikhailo heard the knock and looked out of the window.

Yudka came out of his hiding place.

Upon seeing his friend, Mikhailo ran out of the house.

— Where did you come from, Yudka? — he asked anxiously.

— Help me. Give me a slice of bread. I have escaped from the group.

— Come into the house quickly, so nobody sees you.

Yudka quickly sneaked into the house, but Mikhailo stood outside for a while to make sure that nobody had seen Yudka.

Mikhailo decided to hide Yudka in the stable. He was to hide in the hay and wait.

Mikhailo's sister, Ganka, brought him food. Her black curls excited the young guy. One night the boy and girl sat on the barn's threshold looking at the starry sky. Yudka was stroking Ganka's hair. Suddenly they heard steps. Yudka immediately dove into the hay and Ganka remained sitting on the barn's threshold.

Soon everything got quiet and Ganka went to the house.

At dawn a policeman came to the house. Searching in the barn he went up the ladder where the hay was kept. He began to poke the hay with a bayonet, and soon hit something solid. It was a big army buckle on Yudka's belt.

When the policeman saw Yudka he began to smile.

— Aha, sheeny! I've got you! Get up out of the hay.

Yudka got out, raised his arms and stood in front of the policeman.

The policeman ordered him to go down the ladder.

Yudka obediently approached the ladder, but seeing there was no one below hit the policeman on the face with all his strength. The officer fell and Yudka jumped down and ran into the forest like the wind.

In the forest Yudka found a big hollow space in a tree and hid there. But hunger and cold forced him to look for people. One day he noticed a neighbor in the woods gathering brushwood. He called her by name. The woman was scared at first, but when she recognized Yudka, she approached him. The young man asked for some food. She gave him all she had with her.

From that time on she came to the forest every other day to bring him food. This went on until Soviet troops liberated Arlamov, Yudka's village.

Ganka, Mikhailo and their whole family were also able to return home. They had been forced into hiding from the police for helping a Jew.

Yudka went to the Edynaks' house and proposed to Ganka. In 1946 Ganka gave birth to a son, Yaroslav, and in 1949 to a daughter,

Tonya. But things in Arlamov did not improve. Running away from possible massacre in Arlamov, Yudka and his family crossed the border into Poland which was not yet guarded well. They settled in Dobromil not far from the railway station. Ganka christened their children in the Dobromil church and gave them the last name of Edynak. Yudka was also christened and given a new name — Dmitr. That's how Yudka became Dmitr Leventhal, and all his children were registered under their mother's last name.

When Dmitr visited Alexander, he explained that his desire to protect his children from everything bad, from anti-Semitism, had made him risk crossing the border.

Yukda-Dmitr had recently passed away. Alexander remember the funeral and how big it was. Six men carried the coffin on their shoulders for over a mile to the cemetery, even though a hearse was available. By that act, the residents of Dobromil and the workers at the furniture plant where Yudka-Dmitr had worked, showed their respect to this courageous man. The monument on Yudka-Dmitri's grave is inscribed with a Christian cross and a Star of David.

It was Dmitr's courageous story that convinced Alexander that they should try to leave. Yes, life was good at the moment, but who could guarantee that something wouldn't happen again? Politics is so unpredictable.

He had often dreamed of going abroad. He had even tried to join Moisha in Poland, but got denied for unknown reasons. He guessed that the KGB had convinced his wife Olga to sign papers, and that's why Alexander was not allowed to leave.

Just like Dmitr, he wanted happiness for his children. If they wanted to leave, he had to help them. If they received a denial... he didn't want to think about it.

In the morning, Alexander made another attempt to talk to his daughter, but Ludmila was insistent.

— Daddy, we have been enemies of the people for as long as I can remember. I have seen a lot and I am not afraid of them. What else can scare me? We have been offended so many times in our childhood, but look — it has only made us stronger. I am ready for anything. I don't want to miss this chance.

Alexander finally agreed.

The Leventhals applied to leave the country, but as Alexander foresaw, their request was denied. The tough fight with the Soviet authorities lasted for two years; two tough years of denials, surveillance, and interviews with high level agencies. But nothing stopped Ludmila.

Who knows how it all would have ended if it hadn't been for people like Lina Semenovna and Leonid Romanovich Vaninov, who could be called heroes of those times. They selflessly and nobly assisted refuseniks in getting exit visas. They, with many other people that Alexander and Ludmila will never know, helped the Leventhal family leave the Soviet Union. By repeating the heroism of Shindler and Valenbeg, these people saved many refuseniks and their families.

On the day Alexander went to say good bye to the people at the Integrated Woodworking Plant, everybody was very upset. Tur, the plant's director at that time, was trying to convince his purchasing agent to stay, but Alexander only smiled. Then the director asked him,

— Alexander Grigoryevich, give me a Jew like you.

Alexander looked at Tur sadly.

— Where will I get you one? Who is alive? They are all lying in the ground. They were shot at Lihtman's sawmill; or buried in the salt mines; or shot walking down the street or eaten alive by dogs. They were killed for being Jews.

The plant's director hung his head.

— Yes, Alexander Grigoryevich, your family is the last Jewish family left in Dobromil. And now you will be gone, too. Have a safe trip. And good luck to you.

On November 14, 1979, Alexander and his family left the Soviet Union.

AFTERWARD

אבל oisha Leventhal and his dear friend Peter Petrov became soldiers in the Russian Army and entered Berlin next to one another. They, with their friend Yarmak, were wounded in battle but they all flatly refused to be hospitalized. When Germany capitulated, they were discharged and sent home. The two friends returned to their native Kvasenina as heroes of the Great Patriotic War with medals "For taking Berlin" and "For Bravery" on their chests.

Peter Petrovich Petrov married a girl from his village and they had two children.

Yarmak married a Russian girl named Tatiana. Soon after the birth of their third son they moved to Israel. There, during the Seven Day War, shoulder to shoulder with his sons, he again stood with a machine gun on his chest as a soldier of the Israel Army. He wrote in a letter to Peter: "The war will never be over for us. We will always have to fight for our children's right to live."

Moisha married a Ukrainian beauty, Yana, and moved to Poland, his historical motherland, in 1957. He waited for his brother to move there, but Alexander could not get permission to leave the Soviet Union. One day the Polish Communist Party leader, Gamulka, made an anti-Semite statement on TV. This statement was the precursor of coming changes for the worse. Scared for the lives of his children, Moisha left for the United States.

On January 20, 1980, Michael Grigoryevich Leventhal (Moisha) met his brother Alexander (Shmul) and his family at the JFK airport in New York. The two families still live near one another in Boston, Massachusetts.

Many years later in America, while telling his children and grandchildren about his life, Alexander would say,

— I don't get it, what did they want? Where did they get this inhuman hatred towards the Jewish people? They had everything. They had things that we didn't even dream of. What did they want from us Jews?

ABOUT THE AUTHOR

Ludmila Leventhal works in the medical profession and contributes significantly to the success of her family's business. This is her first book, a true story motivated by her father's amazing life during World War II. Her passion for sharing her family's fascinating history has inspired Ludmila to continue writing. Books about her life in the Ukraine as a young girl and her family's successful attempt to leave the Soviet Union are in development.

Ludmila lives in the Boston area with her family. She cherishes time spent with her family, especially her three grandchildren and her beloved father.